ROBERT HELLER is one of cou̶ː̶ː̶ː̶ː̶
management. He was the fou̶n̶ː̶ː̶
Today and took it rapidly to the ̶ː̶ː̶ː̶ː̶ː̶ː̶ː̶ː̶ leading
management magazine. He is the author of many acclaimed
books, including *The Naked Manager, The Supermanagers, The
Age of the Common Millionaire, The Super Chiefs, The Fate of
IBM, The Way to Win* (with Will Carling), *In Search of
European Excellence* and *Goldfinger*. With Edward de Bono,
he launched *Letter to Thinking Managers*, which won sub-
scribers worldwide. He advises leading companies on strategy
and is a frequent speaker to management groups all over
the world. He lives in north London.

PAUL SPENLEY is the Founder and Managing Director of
the Leading Change Partnership which offers a unique
methodology for leading and implementing change, providing service, support, training and development with an
unrivalled track record of success in companies.

For more information, visit www.ridingtherevolution.com

ROBERT HELLER AND
PAUL SPENLEY

RIDING THE REVOLUTION

How Businesses Can and Must Transform
Themselves to Win the E-Wars

HarperCollinsBusiness
An Imprint of HarperCollins*Publishers*

HarperCollinsBusiness
An Imprint of HarperCollins*Publishers*
77–85 Fulham Palace Road,
Hammersmith, London W6 8JB

www.**fire**and**water**.com

This paperback edition 2001
1 3 5 7 9 8 6 4 2

First published in Great Britain by
HarperCollinsBusiness 2000

Copyright © Robert Heller and Paul Spenley 2000

The Authors assert the moral right to
be identified as the authors of this work

ISBN 0 00 653166 0

Set in Meridien by
Rowland Phototypesetting Ltd,
Bury St Edmonds, Suffolk

Printed in England by Clays Ltd, St Ives plc

Contents

Acknowledgments

This book sprang out of our work with BT, many of whose executives have stimulated our ideas, encouraged our efforts and helped us to test our theories in practice. To all of them, we owe a great debt of gratitude – especially to Chris Downing who, as business development manager for Internet and Multimedia Services, has been our principal colleague in the *Riding the Revolution* venture. His energy and knowledge have been invaluable.

In the world of cyberspace, where contributions to the Revolution multiply daily and come from all corners of industry and the globe, debts to others abound. The book could not have been written without drawing on the writing of others. They include the excellent reporting staff of *Business Week*, *Fortune*, the *Wall Street Journal* and the *Financial Times*: they spotted what was happening before most business leaders, and have been wonderfully quick to understand and report the developments, large and small, that are reshaping the world. We are greatly in their debt.

The contribution of consultancies to the understanding of events and trends in cyberspace has been outstanding. We have drawn on highly informative work by Arthur Andersen, Ernst & Young, Forrester, A. T. Kearney and PriceWaterhouse Coopers. We are especially grateful to the IT Management Programme: Robert Heller's work on their Management Briefings provided important knowledge on customer relations management and IT benefits in the new e-world. The Web itself has, naturally, been a valuable source, especially *CIO WebBusiness*.

One impressive by-product of the Age of the Internet is the flow of brilliant books on every aspect of its impact on management and commerce. The authors who have influenced and informed our thinking are acknowledged in the bibliography. But we would like to mention and thank especially Michael de Kare-Silver of CSC Kalchas, a mangement consultant who in two separate books, *Strategy in Crisis* and *E-Shock*, has produced extraordinary insights into both corporate strategy and e-commerce. Seminar addresses by speakers such as Gary Hamel and Manfred Perlitz have also been inspiring.

All these authors, like ourselves, have been impressed by the practical achievements of managers in the thick of the revolution. We have learnt much from the Riding the Revolution sessions with BT customers, and the Winning Market Acceptance programme for BT commercial staff from many parts of the corporation. Our Visionaries Panel, consisting of top managers from leading-edge companies, has given precious support: people like Ivor Tiefenbrun, Adrian Mears, Mike Peacock, Phil Jackson, Steve Merry, John Catling, Tony Belisario and Peter Mowforth have kept our sights high – but our feet on the ground.

That is also true of the companies with whom we have worked since the Killer Apps workshops and Implementation Teams already mentioned got under way. Their enthusiasm for the new world has been contagious and has reinforced our belief that companies facing the revolution have nothing to fear but (as so often) fear itself.

We have had the inestimable benefit of excellent support from many co-workers, including Pathika Martin, Catherine Hill, Jackie Steel, Anne Helene and Angela Spenley. Our warmest thanks go to them, and to Lucinda McNeile of HarperCollins Business, without whom nothing would have been possible.

Foreword by Sir Peter Bonfield, Chief Executive, BT

The revolution described in this book – in information, management and global markets – probably affects BT far more than most companies. Our basic task is to provide customers with the best and most appropriate means to communicate data wherever and however they choose. The rapid evolution of technology and the massive expansion of demand make this task on its own very demanding. But the Internet has added a vitally signifcant new dimension to BT and its customers.

In this book, Robert Heller and Paul Spenley show how the new technology of cyberspace offers unprecedented opportunities at all levels of business – opportunities to cut costs, improve information, accelerate performance, broaden markets, create new enterprises, and outflank the competition. The threat of being outflanked, in turn, can only be countered by moving rapidly into the new world of the 'Killer App' – developing new applications that radically transform the capability and competitive power of a business.

Not surprisingly, BT itself is in the forefront of these vital changes. For example, our pioneering intranet, is one of the most intensively used and most effective in existence. BT is also a major force in providing Internet connections and we have a growing, strong position as a catalyst of change, helping customers to adapt the new technology to their business purposes. The workshops and application teams run by the *Riding the Revolution* partners, together with BT's Internet and Multimedia Services team, offer practical and fast-acting responses to customer needs.

Data services have become increasingly important as our customers join the Information Revolution and BT is committed to extending and developing its strong position in new technologies. Yet the 'revolution' is still in its early days. E-commerce, despite staggering growth rates, still represents a tiny minority of retail sales; and even in the far larger business-to-business market (where growth rates are just as extraordinary) conventional trade remains dominant. However, as this book makes clear, this is a traditional stage, in both retail and business-to-business transactions. The speed, convenience and low cost of Internet traffic are transforming commerce of all kinds as we move into the new Millennium.

The market is moving at a tremendous pace. Very soon, access to the Internet will not be achieved predominantly through personal computers, but through a variety of 'appliances' – from set-top boxes, games consoles and 'personal digital assistants' (PDAs) to fixed and mobile telephones. The authors emphasise that 'the race is to the swift' it will be a case of 'first come first served' – and the last served, as latecomers, will be forced out of the race. That is why BT has been encouraging its corporate customers to take the initiative while they still have time.

Closer and more innovative partnerships between supplier and customer must be the way forward in applying the new information and communication technologies. These are subject to continuous, rapid change that companies dare not ignore. They need continuous and instant help to negotiate the 'triple revolution'. Providing that help is vital to BT's plan to become the most successful ICT group in the global marketplace. This book explains, both broadly and in detail, why it is true that 'the Internet changes everything'. It is certainly changing BT.

Robert Heller and Paul Spenley show why, how and where the changes are coming, thick and fast, and what BT's customers must do both to seize the opportunites and to counter these threats. What BT must do is equally clear. We are absolutely committed to providing innovative solutions to satisfy the requirements of our customers.

BOOK ONE

Riding the Revolution

1

Management's New Challenges

The millennium marks a watershed. After 2000, companies will not survive long unless they join a threefold revolution – in management itself, information technology, and global markets. The three feed off each other. The radical changes in management have become inseparable from those in technology. Without either the global revolution could never have developed such power.

The technology of information and communications did not create the Triple Revolution, but is the great enabler. Technology is expediting the onrush of organisations into brilliant new modes of management: not only global, but interactive, innovative, collaborative, anti-hierarchical, user-friendly. But the technology and its suppliers are themselves changing at critical speed, which puts further intense pressure on managements. They cannot stand still: they have to ride the revolution.

It did not spring full-born out of cyberspace. The late-twentieth-century revolution in management was accelerating well before the Internet rewrote the business books: the first website opened as late as 1993. The revolution is being driven by irresistible forces: fragmentation of markets, anarchic technologies, more demanding customers, intensified competition and general over-capacity have all helped to undermine the old principles of business economics.

Old-style physical strengths have been superseded by intangibles. As the battle switched to the arena of ideas, the IT revolution both sponsored and responded to management's unstoppable advance into the era of 'globalisation and know-ledge'. Both depend heavily on the information powers of hardware and software and the connective abilities of telecom-munications – as the *Harvard Business Review* acknowledged in a landmark celebration of its seventy-fifth birthday. Nothing in the first seventy years had hinted at the seismic upheaval of the five ending in 1997.

The special edition included a chart of the long progress since 1922 from 'scientific management' (whose chief hardware was the stop-watch) to the Age of Information. As the chart maps the approach of the millennium, the Internet, intranets and extranets combine as a great arrow, swooping upwards. Whether the purpose is measuring results, adding value, running sales and marketing, or managing people, the leadership of organisa-tions now hinges on present and future digital breakthroughs.

The New Corporate Armoury

The new corporate armoury includes integrated database systems, 'virtuality' (in which company, customer and supplier are wired together), mass customisation, and flexible organisa-tional forms. These developments, along with many others, are changing the nature of management. A networked company is a different kind of company, but most managers do not yet appreciate the difference.

Even the special edition of the *Harvard Business Review* shows a strange lag in perception. It lists scores of its 'influential' articles and 'classics'. Most have no direct, and little indirect, connection with IT. The exceptions include, in the early mainframe era, 'managing to manage the computer', an understandable concern in 1966. In 1974, the horizons had expanded: now readers were told about 'managing the four stages of EDP growth'.

This must have failed. For in 1979, the 'crisis in data-processing' needed to be tackled. Five years later, the frontiers of the Brave New World were at last crossed. The problems of managing the machines receded into the past as managers were told that IT 'changes the way you compete'. So it does. Then why have so few 'influential' classics covered IT's revolutionary impact since 1984? Has even Harvard run behind the pace of the revolution, and the realities of what we call 'Silicon Management'?

Merely to stay in business, IT companies, in Silicon Valley and elsewhere, have been forced to take the lead in developing brand-new managerial concepts. As *Business Week* enthused: 'With their flatter, more democratic organisations, giant talent pools, enormous web of interlocking relationships among companies, super speed and can-do culture – especially the can-do culture', the young electronic leaders 'are changing the rules of management'. But the magazine is right to add that, outside microelectronics, the business world has been slow to follow these exciting paths.

True, management strata are fewer, product life-cycles shorter, dress and manners more casual. But that hardly adds up to a revolution. Read that anniversary issue of the *Harvard Business Review* and you sense that these tentative steps will have to be overtaken by giant strides – and quite soon. Thus, for all the headlong advance in IT, as Peter Drucker points out, 'approximately 90 per cent or more of the information any organisation collects is about inside events'. If you think that can create victory, think again. Mark the words of Paul Saffo:

Increasingly, a winning strategy will require information about events and conditions *outside* the institution: non-customers, technologies other than those currently used by the company and its present competitors, markets not currently served, and so on. That information may already exist: harvesting the data and, still more, making sense of the crop has been the essence of the alleged 'information overload'.

The problem is not just the mass of information, but its management. The argument goes back all the way to 1966; only now the issue isn't managing costly hardware and expensive software, but managing incredibly cheap information to achieve enriching results – or to avoid impoverishment. Only consider the sad story of *Encyclopaedia Britannica*, whose sales halved in half a dozen years in front of the onslaught of CD-ROMs selling at a thirtieth of the price.

How can you compete with a product that costs only $1.50 to make when yours requires $200–300? You can't. That information was available to Britannica; so was the fact that its direct sales force, now superfluous, was the company's major cost; so was the knowledge that people bought Britannica to do right by their children – an aim nowadays achieved by buying a PC that comes complete with a reasonably adequate bundled encyclopaedia. The facts were not properly managed, and business disaster followed.

The state of the information revolution mirrors that in management itself. What needs to be done, and what works elsewhere, is evident. The problem is sluggish response, which is an ugly feature of hierarchy: information can only move in steps up and down hierarchical pyramids: each step imposes delay and effort. Authors Philip B. Evans and Thomas S. Wurster, both of Boston Consulting Group, argue instead for 'hyperarchy' – and they offer a prime example: the World Wide Web.

Within a totally flat structure, all information on the Web is available to everybody who has access. Also hyperarchical is 'the pattern of amorphous and permeable corporate boundaries characteristic of the companies in Silicon Valley' – the pattern described above.

More conservative models offer no real alternative to the Brave New Web World, even in the medium term. Not only can $200 not compete with $1.50: old 'legacy systems' in management are as disadvantaged as they are in IT. The options are expiring fast. Quite soon, the choice will lie between the new model or nothing.

The Revolutionary Winners

Consider who wins from successful revolutions. The answer is always the same: those who lead the revolution and win power. The losers are those who stick with the status quo and get dethroned. Their followers also suffer as the revolution rumbles on. But the revolution now hitting business all over the world is not rumbling on. It is racing ahead. There is no way in which businesses that fall behind the revolutionary pace can offset their lag.

The public sector is affected, too, because of new insistence that non-profit organisations should be run as effectively as commercial operations, and on the same principles. Just like the profit-makers, 'non-profits' are affected by the same Triple Revolution – in information, management and globalism. These revolutions interact in the same way that Moore's Law (chip density and computing power double at constant cost every eighteen months) dovetails with the lesser-known Metcalfe's Law.

This holds that networks (of phones, computers, humans or anything else) 'dramatically increase in value with each additional node or user'. Either law by itself would have profound effects. Feeding off each other, they generate exponential increases in the power of electronics to transform businesses. The rise of the American digital economy, with heroes and hero companies like Bill Gates and Microsoft, Andy Grove and Intel, Steve Case and America Online, has been a consequence of awesome extent.

The heroes' 'Silicon Management' has become an object of admiration and worship. Where once books flooded forth explaining the marvels of Japanese industry, a spate of titles devoted to the Valley's magicians and magical ways has begun to flow, with titles like *Relentless Growth*, *Innovation Explosion* and *Giant Killers*. The latter, by Geoffrey James, has a revealing sub-title: '34 Cutting Edge Management Strategies from the World's Leading High-tech Companies'.

Mark the plethora of strategies. There is no single Silicon Valley formula that can be bottled and safely drunk. Grove manages Intel differently from Gates at Microsoft, just as Michael Dell and the recently deposed Eckhard Pfeiffer were well apart at Dell and Compaq. There are common features, but they flow inevitably from common pressures of rampant competition and ferocious technological pace.

The free-and-easy, quick-on-the-draw dynamism of the software and hardware leaders must be imitated by more staid industries as global competition really bites. The Valley's explosive philosophies are changing the hardware and software of management. Just as the Japanese brushed aside Western competition in industries ranging from copiers to cars, motorbikes to cameras, supertankers to transistors, so new Western entrepreneurs are undermining even the giants of the new technology – like Motorola and Hewlett-Packard.

Motorola reacted enthusiastically to the Japanese incursions, adopting Total Quality Management (TQM) to savage costs and transform efficiency. Former chairman Robert Galvin became America's leading TQM practitioner. But the company's severe troubles as the old millennium ended demonstrate that, in the new age, TQM is not nearly enough. Once supposedly as swift as any top gun in Silicon Valley, Motorola was late and uncompetitive in digital phones. Its core mobile business was sabotaged – by itself.

Silicon Valley gunslingers are just as keen on efficiency and cost reduction: but they combine their gains on these scores with sustained drive for the largest possible market penetration, founded on high levels of investment, innovation and downright ingenuity. Forget the conventional Western approach to long-term strategic planning, with its three to five-year cycles. That's among the pillars torn down by Silicon Management.

A fascinating study of electronics leaders by Andersen Consulting found that they plan only eighteen to twenty-four months ahead. Top management lays down an overall 'vision' that establishes corporate objectives. Within that framework, individual business units are delegated the task of devising and executing the strategies demanded by the market. Nobody expects the forecasts to be accurate. Everybody expects flat-out, effective correction of errors resulting from the inaccuracy.

There is a word for this revolutionary strategic approach, but it isn't English. *Meikiki*, which means 'foresight with discernment', is how the Japanese describe a process that they fully understand and apply. Significantly, five other central concepts that Andersen found in California are equally familiar in the Japanese philosophy and practice that long ago launched the Management Revolution:

1 Continually change the basis of competition.
2 Seek multiple sources of competitive advantage.
3 Organise to achieve new levels of agility.
4 Enter into sophisticated collaboration with suppliers and customers.
5 Focus on core capabilities to execute strategy successfully.

Western firms still bear many bruises from Japanese moves to change the basis of competition (as with small copiers). That concept is backed by the search for multiple sources of competitive advantage, which is basic to Japanese management. So is organising to achieve new levels of agility. Toyota, for example, revamped its development system so effectively that in 1996–7 new and reworked models totalled eighteen, some getting into production a mere (and stunning) fourteen months after design approval.

This is partly accomplished by taking sophisticated collaboration with suppliers and customers to new heights. The last concept that Andersen observed in Silicon Valley – focusing on core capabilities to execute strategy successfully – is another Japanese foundation. It explains why Hitachi, Matsushita, Sony, Toshiba and NEC are still leading powers in the global electronics landscape, despite the Intel-led resurgence of American semiconductors.

The like prowess of Toyota in automobiles drew the admiring comment from a Japanese professor that 'Toyota's real strength resides in its ability to learn ... The company's practices are constantly changing, even though its basic principles remain unchanged.' The state-of-the-art in American management theory promotes the 'learning company', basic and undying values, and change management. Here, too, Silicon Management's hot-shots, wittingly or unwittingly, are riding in Japanese models.

The moral is that the Management Revolution is powering ahead in ways long known but long neglected by Western companies outside the Valley. The causes are not technical inadequacies and lack of resources, but inferior strategy and people management. By and large Western management is still extremely top-heavy and top-down (though that's changing, slowly) and still wedded to conservative thinking. Companies have consequently wasted the fat fees paid, and still being paid, to consultants who promise to eliminate waste, promote change, install teamwork, generate innovation, and so on.

Western consultants have also long been preaching the virtues of what the Japanese and the Silicon Managers practise: collaborative, collegiate, people-based management that extends beyond the borders of the corporation and aims at long-term pay-offs. The long-term lesson has apparently sunk in. In 1998 the *Financial Times* was pleased to discover (destroying a persistent myth) that only 7 per cent of Britain's 100 biggest companies felt hampered in 'taking the correct long-term strategy' by the attitudes of institutional investors. But how many of those companies were actually pursuing long-term strategies, let alone correct ones?

The Success Formula

The challenge facing managements is severe, but self-adjusting. If they whole-heartedly adopt the new technologies of information and communication, they will immediately and powerfully enhance their ability to exploit the buried treasure in their organisations: people, knowledge banks, ideas, global market potential. The key technologies are mostly available off the shelf at off-the-shelf prices. They work brilliantly as they enable applications that win high reward from simple concepts. These 'killer apps' fundamentally alter processes and radically raise competitive superiority. The success formula, too, is simple:

1 Link the computers and the systems.
2 Accept that you won't manage the organisation as it has always been run.
3 Act accordingly.
4 Manage the transition to achieve precisely what you, the users, want.
5 Accept that changes in circumstances and technology will demand continuous change in the systems.

The obstacles are psychological. People prefer to run organisations as they always have done. They put off action, even on issues where they know what is needed. They still let the information and communications technologists tell them what to buy, instead of demanding what they, the management, require. They still want to pay single bills to several suppliers, rather than commit themselves to never-ending expenditure and single partners who can apply the technology to their needs. All that confines them to a dead past, a dying present and no future.

The five-point formula, in contrast, opens the door to the 'killer opportunity', the remaking of the organisation to enter and exploit the new age. It is a killer in two senses. Positively, you can achieve a killing advantage over the opposition. Negatively, you can be killed, and probably will be, if you fail the test of the times. The winning alternative is unmissable. Ride the Revolution!

2

Everybody's Business

'All companies are in the IT business today. The difference lies
in how well or badly they use the technology.' This statement
by Percy Barnevik, then the chief executive of ABB, Europe's
most admired company, should be a tailpiece to every vision
and mission statement. It was made before cyberspace changed
everything, but the enormous pace of Internet growth (over
fivefold between January 1990 and end-1998) has given Barnevik's text still greater urgency.

The Internet and all it stands for imposes a new imperative
on speed of thought and action. All managements now face an
intensified, common challenge, easily stated, less easily understood. The business conditions they have known and mostly
loved have become as obsolete as the one-track assembly line,
the radio valve or the old-style pre-container docks. Management priorities too have changed.

Strategic thinking has grown big as 'business process re-
engineering' (BPR) has faded and operational effectiveness (the
target of re-engineering) has been demoted. But what is strategy
for? And what is information technology's place in achieving
those ends? Managers are much more receptive today to the
concept of IT as a strategic tool. The concept, though, is like the
computer itself: only as good as its application. Even in the US,
as recently as 1996, a startling 85 per cent of large companies
did not use state-of-the-art IT. Two years later, 95 per cent of
directors at their British equivalents admitted to being less than
well-informed about the Internet.

Yet the newest and not-so-new tools open up rich and exciting horizons. For instance, any sensible customer or product strategy depends on accurate knowledge of costs, realised prices and price comparisons. In most companies, the data is available some-where or other in some form or other. But few organisations can bring all the items together rapidly in order to make the key decisions: which customers to drop, which to cosset, which contracts to renegotiate, which products to phase out, which to push, etc.

Applied right across the market, and right across the product lines, information collected and distributed via a 'data ware-house' can help to transform the entire business. It will, for sure, lead to lower costs. But these savings aren't a strategic end in themselves: warehousing provides the springboard for the most valuable form of strategy, which aims at achieving organic growth. That objective has risen in importance as the long-term value of cost-cutting alone has been tried and found wanting.

The conclusion – that you can't grow by shrinking – is straight, unadorned common sense which needs no jargon. One viable approach is to shy away from the word 'strategy' (and never mind, either, 'vision' or 'mission'); but to relentlessly pursue the lowest cost position in your industry – using technology to the full – so that you can pick off and exploit the most attractive sectors of the market, outgrowing competitors in sales and profits alike. That's *upsizing*, which is a strategy truly worth hav-ing: downsizing isn't.

The winning formula (in the marketplace and in the market for business ideas) is to expand the customer base and raise revenue per customer while lowering the cost of capital and other inputs. The first half of the equation counts for most, by far. In the words of a professor at Harvard, Jeffrey Rayport: 'The companies that are leading have cost-compression on autopilot. The real potential is to deepen and augment customer relation-ships.' That poses a real challenge to IT directors: because they may get left behind in the strategic rush.

Rayport was quoted in a *Business Week* article which concluded that, among the minority of new technology leaders, 'the chief financial officer, rather than the chief information officer, has

typically emerged as the central player'. Thus at Johnson &
Johnson, the top finance man was the force behind a data warehouse named Darwin, 'a sophisticated system that enables managers in some 50 countries . . . to slice, dice and analyse masses
of information . . . on everything from accounts receivable to
inventories'. The health products company has also consolidated
all its payroll functions into a single site, saving nearly four-fifths
of the administrative costs.

Making such economies, as noted, is the easier bit – in decision
if not in execution. Here, the IT directors are on comfortable
ground, although the ground would be much cosier if they,
rather than their internal customers, took the initiative in
demanding and achieving major economies through these
sweeping reforms. Far greater effort will be required for IT directors to seize the strategic chances which lie in the fact, to quote
Business Week, that IT 'is fostering a sea-change in the way companies assess their growth prospects'.

Exploiting the Sea-change

To exploit the sea-change, IT directors have to swallow any
pride and possessiveness and become allies of other strategically
placed managers, including the financial supremos. One of the
greatest obstacles to strategic breakthroughs is the 'Not Invented
Here' factor: for instance, some IT directors, deeply infected with
NIH, will resist outsourcing to the death, seeing it as a threat to
their own organisations, even if the consequences retard the
progress of the company as a whole.

In the worst-case (and not uncommon) scenario, this could
result in adopting a new IT strategy, but seeing it fail. Obstinacy
will open the door for other managers to take charge, not only
of the largest strategic opportunities, but of specific IT developments. Non-IT managers are going to demand information as a
tool for creating and sustaining powerful, winning strategies.
Boards won't want to know much about the technicalities of
massively parallel servers, RBDMS, data extraction & transformation tools, metadata tools, OLAP, data access & query tools,

data mining, etc.; but they will want the full strategic benefits of this warehousing technology.

The revolutionary potential of new technology faces every business with the same challenge that Japanese methods once posed to Western factories. At the same time, the imperatives of business have changed in a way that is inimical to traditional organisation. The two forces are working hand in hand. As the telephone did, the new hardware and software make it possible, and in most respects essential, to change to new methods of working.

Before the telephone, communication either took place through exchanges of paper or face to face. The bullpen office (with hundreds of people packed into an open space) evolved partly for reasons of discipline, partly because more bodies could be put into smaller areas. More important, the passage of paper and the spoken word is obviously eased by the absence of barriers and the proximity of desks, just as City and Wall Street traders, in the ultra-modern, high-tech bullpens, can yell at each other across the crowded room.

For those with work of higher degree, cacophony and lack of privacy were both demeaning and counter-productive. Like the Victorian father with his study, the seniors had both dignity and high-level work to protect. So barriers (doors, walls, separate floors, even separate buildings) were erected to separate the barons from continuous direct contact with the commoners. Face-to-face discussion was still inevitable, even vital; but the walls served to ration and limit the meetings, for which special rooms were supplied (right up to the holy of holies, the usually empty, expensive boardroom).

Thus the historic office developed, and thus it has largely remained. But now electronics offers the means for instantaneous communication and information anywhere in the company or anywhere in the world. This has happened at exactly the time when group working has of necessity replaced individual decision-making. Not only did the old-fashioned cellular office evolve for the one-man mode. It also powerfully reinforced the individual method of office work by isolating the office worker – and the higher the position, the greater the isolation.

Isolation is yielding everywhere to collaboration. Managers who don't recognise the potential of such developments will be like the failed companies of a frequently painful past: locked into ways of thought and action that will never cope with a fast-changing outside world. The pace of technological advance is so frenetic that the full extent of the revolution can't be predicted. But hardware or software already exists, or lies round a near corner, that will perform any task currently done by and for management much faster, more conveniently, more accurately; and many tasks which now can't be done at all will become routine.

The New Business Technology

The revolution is of a wholly different order of magnitude from the slow changes of the earlier twentieth century. The business technology of the past saw five major and crucial developments: the telephone and its printed allies, the telex and the ticker tape; the typewriter; the copier; the adding machine and its replacement, the electronic calculator; and the computer.

The first three represented new and vastly improved methods of conducting business as before. The post and the personal meeting were no longer the sole means of communication. Laborious and slow longhand was replaced by the sometimes amazingly fast typist. Her skills, in turn, were supplemented by the far greater speeds of the xerographic copier.

Like the phone, the typewriter and the copier, the computer, in its first use as a glorified adding machine, produced an enormous enhancement of existing processes. The new electronic technology, however, makes new processes not only possible, but inevitable. The most exciting aspect of the revolution is the impact that new technology will have on the process of management itself, as witnessed by the unglamorous example of payment systems.

Using electronic data interchange (EDI), firms have for years been able to give and take orders, and supply and pay for the goods, without any paper changing hands, without any direct human intervention, and with automatic book-keeping for the transactions. This humdrum change is a whole new world, and like the inhabitants of Europe when the Americas opened up, nobody living and working in a business will be untouched by a revolution that still goes sweeping on.

By 1992, a quarter of all payments in the US were electronic. By 2004, with IP (Internet Protocol) technology taking over, the proportion is expected to be 58 per cent. No wonder an American magazine writer declared that 'over time a proportion of practically every transaction will touch the Internet'. Clearly, such technological change is imposing new realities at an accelerating speed that has no precedent. The pace varies from industry to industry. But all industries, just as Percy Barnevik said, are affected by IT, where a century's normal change seems to have been crammed into a couple of decades.

In their working lifetimes, managers have seen fabulous transition. They began in the relatively settled world of stand-alone mainframes and dumb terminals, served by custom-made software of limited scope. They have migrated to a world where complex choices are required among a virtually unlimited variety of processors, programs, applications, systems, desktops and laptops. The choices, moreover, must be made in the full knowledge that they may well be obsolescent (though still highly effective)·at the moment of implementation.

Legacy Thinking

Since IT is so pervasive, in services and manufacturing alike, change is being forced on corporations whether they like it or not. As hardware and software suppliers know, change is rarely welcomed by most managers – including those directly responsible for IT. Not only must so-called 'legacy systems' (those in which millions of dollars or pounds have been invested) be taken into account, but there is also legacy thinking. The state-of-the-art appears to legacy thinkers not as an opportunity but as a threat.

Legacy thinking opens up a dangerous gap between what IT

systems can deliver, and what many users actually receive. A similar gulf yawns between the business strategies proposed by managements and the actual operational results. By closing the IT gap, however, the second one, too, can be decisively bridged. This is not a matter of exhortation and indoctrination. Implementation is the key.

Senior managers too often seek to alter thinking, when the real object should be to change behaviour. This in turn is conditioned by circumstances outside the control of the people whom management supposedly wants to enlighten and empower. If they are the prisoners of obsolescent or obsolete information and communications technology, nothing they can do personally will overcome their disadvantages. You cannot, to give an example, readily integrate job opportunities and learning needs with available training if nobody, including the human resources people, has access to the Internet.

This may be the direct fault of the IT department. But the indirect blame lies higher up. The most influential area of behaviour is that of top management itself. If the chief executive and his entourage fight shy of training, IT, teamwork and shared decision-making, they can forget about riding the revolution – it won't happen. You need, not just top commitment, but top participation if the push for change is to advance beyond being a 'programme', with a beginning and an end, to become a way of corporate life. Many chief executives will accept this – 'though more in concept than in practice'.

That's the correct judgement of a leading consultancy, the IT Management Programme. Managing director Peter Sole stresses that the evolution of business from relative stability to continuous change and discontinuity 'requires a change in strategic focus and leadership style. It also implies using IT in different ways and a different role for the information systems department.' As his 'board briefing' notes, 'IS [Information Systems] is the one department experienced in living with continuous change – both enduring it and applying it.'

This argues for making IT the spearhead of revolution, whatever strategy a management adopts. The briefing sets out four possible strategic contexts:

- Production (stable products, stable processes).
- Customisation (dynamic products, stable but flexible processes).
- Improvement (stable products, dynamic processes).
- Innovation (dynamic products, dynamic processes).

Very few firms can afford the old luxury of production: more and more are being dragged towards its opposite, the fourth category, innovation. Information needs here revolve round the question, What's possible? The answers envisage a corporation which uses knowledge as a basis for new concepts and ideas; employs unstructured, intuitive data; boldly embraces assumptions and beliefs; seeks pattern recognition; and relies on systems and data integration. This is light years away from the transactional data, reports and archiving that typified the production strategy. But it's also, of course, very far from the general reality.

The right IS manager for the customisation strategy, though, is beginning to emerge: a manager of infrastructure, a broker of information and IT skills, who is closely integrated with the business. Those last five words hold the key to the whole process of revolution. It rests on integrating all processes and all the owners of processes. IT earns part of its sovereign importance by providing the means of integration.

Networks, group-ware, websites, extranets and intranets will promote radical change, anyway. But the object of the exercise is to drive the revolution in the direction in which the whole corporation wishes to go. That demands treating the corporation truly as a whole. Top managements mostly recognise that demand. But the move from concept to practice, from lip-service to service, can't come a moment too soon.

3

The Global Dimension

Once, only great corporations were multinational. Now companies become great and global simultaneously. Even start-ups have rapidly achieved worldwide penetration of hugely promising markets. The role models date back a long time. For instance, Compaq Computer recognised from its start in 1983 that personal computing was an international, not a domestic industry. Compaq's rise was sensational, from a world record first year of $111 million to $2 billion in five years: but in the age of the Internet even that pace seems strictly routine.

The clusters of American superstars revolve around start-ups like Netscape, whose inspired breakthrough with browsers set the Internet booming; or Cisco, which grew from 200 people in 1989 to 11,000 in 1998, partly on the back of its Internet routers. The markets such companies created were automatically global, because cyberspace knows no boundaries. Companies large and small, moreover, have equal access to the new, revolutionary global networks and telecoms products. So smallness is no liability. Rather, size may be a serious disadvantage.

The new channels of communication and commerce bypass the established, terrestrial networks. Huge volumes of traffic move through these familiar networks, and vast revenues are generated. But the revolutionary newcomer has no need of the old means of distribution, nor of the massive overheads which accompany them. Nor does it need the fixed assets – regional and national HQs, warehouses and distribution networks – that multinationals acquired as they crossed frontiers and tapped new geographical markets.

Most multinationals were (and are) nothing more than great national companies with overseas subsidiaries. But the revolution in communications technology has turned the truly global company from grand idea to attainable reality. The global means, including the World Wide Web, intranets and extranets, have received a crescendo of publicity. It is not misleading. These wonders make possible mighty and necessary improvements to the way in which companies are managed.

Globalism intensifies problems of complexity and spans of control. You can see the new dimension at Stuttgart, where Daimler-Benz in 1998 began creating a new global company after buying Chrysler. The 'war-room' (according to the *Wall Street Journal*) 'hums with state-of-the-art communications technology'. The sharp end of this technology includes six banked computer screens, a big-screen TV that converts into a giant terminal, video-conference kit, and clocks showing the time in Detroit, New York, Johannesburg, Tokyo, Bangkok and Sydney.

A few doors away is the 'integration room' that enables managers in Stuttgart to work in concert with their Chrysler colleagues in Auburn Hills, Michigan. Writing on a giant whiteboard is translated on to a screen in the US. There a companion integration room handles the American end. Frequent teleconferencing is accompanied by heavy input of data to the combined 'infobase'. Using Lotus Notes, both sides keep track of no less than 989 priority integration projects which are monitored by traffic lights: 'Green means everything's on schedule. Yellow signifies hangups. Red screams trouble.'

This abolition of geography by telecoms is proceeding so rapidly that most businesses have yet to begin catching up. One entrepreneur, however, got lucky. Alan Willett of Willett International had expanded all over the globe, selling in seventy-five countries and opening subsidiaries in a third of them. He was about to establish a regional office to co-ordinate the furthest flung satellites, in Asia Pacific, when he made a sudden, marvellous discovery: teleconferencing.

He promptly scrapped plans for a regional HQ, saving much money, killing the imminent extra layer of potential bureaucracy, and maintaining his personal contact with the managers running the Asian companies. The teleconferences work fine, and his organisation has stayed flat and fast. Since delayering and speed of reaction are two of the prime virtues in today's management, other companies must surely reach the same conclusion: manage with the full, flexible aid of information technology, not along tramlines laid down by organisation charts.

The impact of communications on management is nothing new. Peter Drucker has celebrated the remarkable effectiveness of the men who ruled India. Because messages took so long to reach distant officials, and the replies so long to come back, their superiors had to agree objectives and action plans at the start. Perforce, they let their subordinates get on with the job and judged them by their success against the plans. That elegant simplicity vanished in the era of worldwide telephony and jet travel: superiors and bureaucrats could interfere to their hearts' content, and the discontent of everybody else.

The Indian Principle

Just as electronic shopping turns the wheel back to pre-war home delivery, so electronic management is returning in part to the Indian principle. The boss, like our entrepreneur, delegates full responsibility to people who have contracted to perform agreed tasks. But modern bosses, like him, have an advantage. While they can directly contact managers at will, they don't have to. Thanks again to IT, they can check on performance day to day (hour to hour, if they're wholly neurotic) without bothering anybody with questions. The answers are instantly available via the system.

In theory, senior management's ability to 'dig down' the database to check on sales in Droitwich, Osaka and Cape Town, or to verify profit margins in Bangkok, Wichita and Lima, makes possible more Draconian control than the most dedicated bureaucrats ever envisaged. But long ago the telephone was expected to have the same effect, reducing middle managers to mere tools of the top. Instead, as Shoshana Zuboff pointed out in *The Age of the Smart Machine*, the phone liberated subordinates. At a safe distance, they were readier to answer back, argue, put their own points of view.

You need to generate a similar effect from modern systems in order to optimise use of the managers in place. Simply adding more managers is no answer to the challenges facing the executive armies which are already fighting the global wars. Exploiting the opportunities of global markets, all the way from sourcing R&D to improving the response to customer enquiries and complaints, places great demands on managers whose thinking has previously been conditioned by domestic markets.

This is still the case with most British companies. Their managers speak of Europe as if it were another, foreign part of the globe, and not their new domestic market, to which Britain belongs as much as Germany and France. Americans, too, are far more insular than the stupendous spread of their global businesses suggests. But the enormous improvements in communications technology are increasing familiarity with overseas markets and making the difficult tasks far easier.

Take the quest for customer focus, a stretching enough target even within national markets, sought like the Holy Grail, and with as scant success. The task of satisfying customers spread around Europe, let alone the globe, is trickier still. How do you achieve the same excellent perceived service in Hanover and Hounslow? How do you obtain instantaneous, meaningful feedback from customers in Rio and Ontario? How do you ensure vital simultaneous availability of a new product in forty-four different markets?

This is no theoretical matter. As the life-cycle of personal computers has shortened dramatically, to a mere six months in many cases, the requirement for rapid global distribution has intensified. This new imperative gives the manufacturer no more than a couple of weeks to get products into the world markets in suitable quantity. What's true of PCs today is applying to more and more industries. Gone are the days when major overseas markets could be told to wait. Gone are the days, too, when head offices could design products without attention to overseas affiliates, which had a zero chance of influencing what they had to sell.

Companies can now gather vastly more and more precise customer information from around the world, and far more quickly. Yet researchers for the IT Management Programme were astonished to find major firms absurdly lacking in this respect, even in their local markets. They could analyse sales and financial performance by market and product readily enough, but couldn't repeat the exercise by customer. Some 'do not know how many customers they have, let alone calculate the value of individual customers'.

Global managers gather and communicate this information in order to separate the sheep from the goats, the profitable customers and markets (to be loved and cherished and made more profitable still) from the unprofitable. The latter can be dropped, or (preferably) made profitable, very possibly by use of IT-based techniques for cutting the worldwide cost of sales and service. An obvious instance is the use of one-site global call centres (which can be combined with faxes and e-mails on a single website for integrated handling of complaints and queries).

Segmented Opportunities

There are also invaluable techniques (again, mostly IT-based) for identifying and serving segmented markets. If managements aren't using these methods, unrepeatable opportunities are being lost. Tiny segments are now large enough to feed global businesses. One Huddersfield company, Camborne Fabrics, sells only fabrics for office furniture, but worldwide. Its systems allowed Camborne to boast of a 97 per cent level of next-day delivery to any market: it responded by investing in still better systems to exploit the profit potential of satisfying the under-served 3 per cent.

How you use such systems is decisive in the worldwide wars. This is, however, a time of painful transition. Generally, data is now garnered and communicated faster, more accurately and in more convenient form – yet information overload and control failures abound. Electronic meetings have burgeoned rapidly, too. But none of this has lessened the insatiable pressures for face-to-face, round-the-world contact. Similarly, few innovations have caught on so rapidly as fax, mobile phones, e-mail and the Web, yet without easing those same pressures.

The technology has enlarged companies' ability to reach their managers on the run, in hotel rooms, airports, and their homes, on trains and on holiday. The result? One survey found that half the questioned managers couldn't escape from their work even when vacationing, even when sick. The fax and the mobile phone have made interruptions easier: the portable computer, with its links (now enhanced by the Web and intranets) to corporate data and colleagues, has made the office global as well as the business.

Tomorrow's global managers will spend even less time in their offices, and even more living out of briefcases which contain the means of communication – with the laptop revolution now enhanced by the Internet. The age of PDAs (personal digital assistants) has dawned too. To all intents and purposes, twenty-first-century executives will be in constant touch with their work. They are at personal risk from the increases in stress that are being reported as managers find it harder, even impossible, to 'get away from it all'. With distance management, there's no 'away'.

The pressures are not inevitable. The time-saving, speed-enhancing lifestyle for which hard-pressed global executives yearn is within reach. The wondrous technology isn't really to blame for excessive workloads. If IT is used more effectively, the quality of managerial life improves in practice as well as in theory. The key is familiar to experts in boosting productivity through information systems, factory automation or any other application of state-of-the-art technology.

Before buying any costly hardware or software, the truly expert expert studies the processes and applies something which isn't state-of-the-art at all: common sense. By eliminating whole processes and process stages, streamlining flows, relating means to redefined ends, and so on, huge improvements are won intellectually before a single technological penny is invested. The transition to truly global management rests on improving the processes by which the parts form a worldwide whole.

This is not just a matter of taking out intermediary regional managements. The existence of the latter may often be unjustified. But companies have to avoid the downsizing trap. Taking out whole layers of management, or the many managers who only act as relays in the processes, will save payroll costs. But if processes are unchanged, the remaining managers will slump under a heavier workload. The whole global system will begin to malfunction and lose its capacity to grow profits.

The Consultant Manager

Building the business and its management round its properly identified customers, wherever they are in the world, is entirely feasible. But that only happens where the new electronic powers of gathering information, communicating, organising and meeting have been directed to proper ends. There is no point in going global only to find that unexpected costs of serving customers in far-flung and unfamiliar markets devour any prospect of profits for years to come.

The new management processes, employing the new tools for managing at a distance, strengthen the trend for managers to become more and more like consultants. The latter have long been successfully peripatetic, depending on IT to keep in touch with their offices and files. Now corporate managers work increasingly outside the conventional structure of offices and departments, often operating in multi-disciplinary, cross-functional teams whose location round the globe is determined by their purposes.

These global changes are so far-reaching in their potential that even far-sighted thinkers, let alone practical managers, have yet to come to full terms with their times. Even the distinguished contributors to a 1997 collection of essays entitled *Rethinking the Future*, assembled by Rowan Gibson, barely mention the telecoms revolution, managing at a distance, or the Internet itself.

That's not surprising, in view of one passage from contributor Warren Bennis:

> I have a board in my leadership institute, made up of very terrific leaders, and they all have e-mail. But when I asked how many of them use it, only half of the hands went up, and some of those went up rather lamely. Rather haltingly.

Yet what's so new? Managers like Microsoft's Bill Gates have been using e-mail as a distance management tool for years. Long ago I came across an electronics entrepreneur whose highly successful business interests were in England: he ran them electronically from the Caribbean. Five years before the first website appeared in 1993, Francis Kinsman wrote that 'many managers in the next century will be faced with the facts of ferociously competitive international telecommuting'. So they will, once their companies get round (as they must) to grabbing their new global and technological opportunities.

When they do, ferocity will probably be less evident than liberation. Much managerial frustration stems from inability to contact the right person at the right time, or to get the right information in the right place, or to be certain that the right actions are being taken with the right results. Today, managers can achieve over earth's greatest distances what, in the past, they couldn't achieve under their own noses.

BOOK TWO

The Management of Change

4

Transforming the Pyramid

Managers have become increasingly concerned with 'change management'. Like it or not, this has moved from a desirable skill to an indispensable process. Few companies, though, have yet rebuilt the corporate structure and processes (especially those of communication and information) to take full advantage of the brilliant, abundant opportunities that external change creates. This will not be achieved without a non-technological revolution in the treatment of 'human resources'.

In Bill Clinton's first campaign for the Presidency, the slogan 'It's the economy, stupid' became famous. There's a new equivalent for management: substitute 'people' for 'economy' – and you don't have to be very clever to see why. Take the idea that other staff are customers who depend on management for excellent service. Think for a minute, and its truth is obvious. Yet it leads to the antithesis of the command-and-control methods by which most organisations are still run.

'Increase power by dispersing it'; 'encourage creative dissent'; 'build autonomous teams'. These are among the watchwords of the alternative management which has been led by the gee-whiz companies of micro-electronics. The quotes come from Geoffrey James's *Giant Killers*, a book that explores the world dominated by Microsoft, Compaq, Dell and a multitude of others. James heavily endorses the argument that in this phenomenal industry necessity has been the mother of inventing new ways of running organisations – methods that are based pre-eminently on people.

He argues, for example, that the old concept of the corporation as a machine has lost all validity; that now it is a community, in which managers seek to communicate directly with people, create opportunities for social interaction, and 'make work fun'. You treat employees as equals rather than as children. That means hiring those who are self-motivated, ending the 'fancy perks' that separate the boss class from the workers, and encouraging informal ways of working. The climate of fear, along with the whips and chains that fostered it, goes out of the window. Instead, you operate by trust.

The formula not only sounds attractive, but is supported resoundingly by fabulous business results. All management writers know, however, that cause and effect may not apply. If you have a near-monopoly position, like Microsoft in PC operating systems or Intel in microprocessors, the profits flood in because of your market strength and the high price that the traffic will bear. Success may reflect brilliant management: or it may conceal gross errors in both decisions and execution (that has certainly been true at both Microsoft and Intel).

So is there good reason for thinking that the 'giant killer' lessons are universal? In fact, the trends are plainly heading the same way in businesses big and small. Even inside the established hierarchies, people-based management is making headway. More and more companies, for example, are forming alliances with suppliers, customers and competitors. The traditional control mechanisms won't work with people who are not actually your employees. But the old controls work no better with those who are: that is, not if you wish to encourage self-motivated people, discourage bureaucracy, and turn decision-making into a collaborative process reaching deep into the organisation.

At General Electric in the US, chairman Jack Welch declared war against what he called 'Type IV' managers – even those delivering excellent short-term results – who resist the new people-based values. The Type IVs get results 'without regard to values, and in fact often diminish them by grinding people down, squeezing them, stifling them. Some of these learned to change, most couldn't.' Welch's reaction was to begin dismissing Type IVs. Using the autocratic power of dismissal to inculcate democracy is more than a mite paradoxical, but Welch is adamant that 'it had to be done if we wanted GE people to be open, to speak up, to share'.

He also wanted them to 'act boldly' outside 'traditional lines of authority' and 'functional boxes' in this new 'learning, sharing environment'. Welch wasn't writing in some progressive management journal, but in the GE annual report for 1995. His argument is that short-term thinking damages the long-term interests of a company, not only by the actions it encourages, but because it undermines people-based management. People who are expected to respond only to orders will eventually act accordingly – like human machines.

The Super-Manager's Story

You can see the results in one fascinating case history. The super-manager in charge of the company concerned 'developed and led a culture in which managers were often tested to destruction, where there were always complaints and criticisms, virtually never compliments, praise or thanks'. One manager, who 'could see I was going to get crushed', left after five years of 'tremendous learning experience' because he wanted to avoid the fate mentioned above: 'You become a loyal servant – you've had all the initiative bashed out of you.'

In this company, bullying manners allegedly became routine, while the senior people at head office became courtiers working 'for place and position'. It was also a blame culture, in which the boss 'assumed that if a business is going well, that is because of the manager, and similarly a bad business is the fault of the manager'. This could lead to false judgements of people's abilities and to arbitrary dismissal. Not surprisingly, the style 'bred excessive caution and defensiveness' in many managers.

There's a tragic waste in this account. The company was positioned by its technology, businesses and traditions to take advantage of some of the great opportunities for growth seized by the 'giant killers'. Its leader didn't actually slaughter projects designed to grab those chances, because his management theory,

while based on fierce challenge to managers, stopped well short
of telling them 'what they should or should not do'. But people
are naturally disinclined to put their heads in the lion's mouth
by backing projects that might fail.

'If you don't try and fail, you can't be criticised for the failure,'
said one observer. The tragedy is that the man at the top would
actually have been in favour of new initiatives, 'but he doesn't
properly understand that he runs a system that frustrates it'.
That's the case for people-based management in a nutshell. In
any organisation, the leader needs to develop a system that
encourages and facilitates the behaviour that will best and most
rapidly achieve the ambitions of the entire organisation and the
people it employs.

The company in the sad case just described was the General
Electric Company, no relation to Welch's GE except in name,
where the top man until his eventual retirement in 1997 was
Lord Weinstock. His methods served shareholders well. The
quotes are from a biography (*Weinstock*) in which two financial
journalists, Alex Brummer and Roger Cowe, note that in thirty-
three years sales rose from £147 million, with profits of £6 million, to £11 billion, with profits of almost £1 billion. Moreover,
Weinstock left the company sitting on £1.4 billion of cash.

As the authors point out, though, the key advances were
made in Weinstock's first decade. He worked wonders through
imposing rigorous controls and placing strong emphasis on the
individual manager's responsibility for the financial results of
clearly defined businesses. It was a fine recipe. Since 1973, however, the world has greatly changed. GEC was poised to profit
enormously from rich growth markets like mobile telephony,
semiconductors, medical equipment and consumer electronics,
even software. Instead, defence became dominant, to be suc-
ceeded by belated, multi-million investment in high technology.

The whole story is a parable for the new management age. A
firm of head-hunters, Theaker Monro and Newman (TMN),
commissions an annual survey among higher paid executives
that charts the changing attitudes over recent years. The emphasis has shifted markedly from downsizing to organic growth.
Companies want managers who are skilled in running projects

and leading change. They require marketing skills so that customer focus can be intensified. They need to break into new industries, to match new competitors in old markets, to cross-fertilise between businesses.

For all this to happen, management has to become multi-disciplinary, cross-functional and interdepartmental, while vertical chains of command are supplemented or superseded by horizontal relationships. The pressure for technological and other change has been intensified as competition becomes more and more global. Not surprisingly, the firms interviewed for the TMN survey found that the supply of management skills wasn't matching the crying and growing need: two-thirds reported current skills shortages.

The Training Gap

Firms make shortages worse by inadequate and inappropriate training. Only 28 per cent of the TMN sample were equipping their managers to cope with change, while less than 5 per cent were training people to make the most of IT – totally ignoring Percy Barnevik's pregnant comment, quoted earlier, that 'All companies are in the IT business today. The difference lies in how well or badly they use the technology.'

Barnevik and his company, ABB, are among the examples which Brummer and Cowe hold up as shining contrast to Weinstock and GEC. The similarities between these two conglomerates of independent businesses, with their flat structures and strict financial controls, are marked. The key difference lies in their people management. The inspirational Barnevik is contrasted with the 'distant, anonymous' Weinstock. The latter served his shareholders well, as noted, but the issue is whether he served his managers, and thus their people, as effectively as they deserved.

Companies which want to ride the revolution have to pass this questionnaire, which tests how well a management is serving its people. Does the company have:

1 The right culture to reach its goals?
2 The required knowledge, skills and abilities?
3 The appropriate measures, rewards and incentives?
4 The right organisational structure, communications systems
   and policies?
5 The ability to improve work processes, to change and to learn?
6 The leadership required to meet its goals?

The six questions are derived from the *Harvard Business Review*, in
which Dave Ulrich argues that the human resources function
must take the lead in meeting the challenges of globalisation,
achieving profitability through a mixture of growth, information
technology, knowledge management and 'change, change and
more change'. These areas are pre-eminent in the strategies of the
'giant killers', but there's another. Ulrich notes that 'the primary
responsibility for transforming the role of HR belongs to the CEO
and to every line manager who must achieve business goals'.

But this doesn't go far enough: every manager, not only CEOs
or line managers, must be a people manager first and foremost.
You wouldn't get that impression from another article in the
same issue of the *Harvard Business Review* in which Robert Simons
and Antonio Davila explore the interesting notion of 'Return on
Management' (ROM). This means the amount of productive
organisational energy released in relation to the management
time and energy invested – though just how do you measure
either managerial or organisational energy? Leaving that difficult matter aside, the two authors ask five questions:

1 Does your organisation know what opportunities are out of
   bounds?
2 Are your company's critical performance measures driven by
   a healthy fear of failure?
3 Can managers recall their key diagnostic measures?
4 Is your organisation safe from drowning in a sea of paperwork
   and processes?
5 Does everyone watch what the boss watches?

The article produces anecdotal studies of companies like
Motorola and Pepsi-Cola as examples of high ROM. Note,

however, that people figure little in the five questions, all of which could have been answered with a resounding yes in Weinstock's GEC. The ROM concept focuses on control: people-based management is founded on freedom. No opportunities are out of bounds, nobody fears failure, measurement is less important than achievement, and 'everybody turns when father turns' is anathema.

Management Gridlock

The only point on which people-based managers agree with the ROM thesis is the healthy disrespect for paperwork and for non-productive processes. But that is surely found in any serious attempt to manage effectively. In *Giant Killers*, Geoffrey James gives a convincing picture of what happens when management is defined as control. You get gridlock: 'The attempt to control creates resistance and spawns other attempts to control, causing decision-making to grind to a halt.' He quotes from a Xerox escapee:

> Everything from the press release to the product description to the information sheet had to be reviewed and approved by multiple vice presidents and announcement committees. We spent almost six months trudging through the paper-work.

You don't have to look much further for an explanation of Xerox's failure to exploit the greatest invention it ever had, the personal computer. The culture of control, inward-looking and obsessive, blotted out the vision that might have created the world's most successful industrial enterprise. It's bizarre, too, that a company which lives on automated document handling hadn't used IT to reduce its press release trudge from six months to six days – if not six hours.

It isn't only gridlock that grips the organisation. As James says, there's also the 'yes-man syndrome', when 'people agree with their managers even when there are better ideas and better ways to approach a situation'; and (see GEC) there's the 'limited power' syndrome, according to which 'control that is limited at the top limits the exercise of power to the executives, slowing corporate growth'.

The issue of power is behind the difficulty in moving to people-based management. The more absolute the power, the less the possessor has to care about his or her behaviour or what happens to others. But a manager's conduct directly affects the performance of those others, and their performance depends on how much or how little they can influence their own work and its outcomes. The issue of outcomes is fundamental, but it may appear to have no direct link with the issue of power.

In an anti-absolutist book entitled *The Power Principle*, Blaine Lee thus lists six types of behaviour that will change managers from GE's Type IVs to the adventurous types who enable the giant killers to kill. You've crossed the divide if you can answer yes to these questions. Can you:

1 Learn about alternatives?
2 Get help from others?
3 Develop a desire for something different?
4 Recognise opportunities to choose?
5 Make the decision to change?
6 Take a leap of faith?

The difficulty with these questions is that they are 'soft' in a world where hard results are decisive. How can you translate people-based management into hard practice? First, give recruitment and training top priority, including training in the use of IT. Second, take every opportunity to place people in multi-disciplinary, cross-functional, interdepartmental teams. And finally, copy Percy Barnevik at ABB, and make special efforts to achieve cross-fertilisation between businesses and (if it's a factor, as it may well be) across frontiers.

Deconstruct the pyramid. Eliminate layers of management, not to eliminate people but to speed decisions and implementation. All this is needed to meet the demands not just of fast-changing markets and technologies, but of changing people. The nature and nurture of today's generation of managers differs in many respects from previous times. People are taking responsibility earlier, and these relative youngsters are more outspoken, more open to new ideas, more articulate, and more likely to move to other employers if the opportunities or the environment look better.

As the electronic giant killers have shown, with such people you can have your cake and eat it. You can apply soft principles with hard methods to create a people-based business that is both enjoyable and vastly rewarding. For once, the technology does not operate against the people. It is on their side.

5

Planning Strategic Action

You don't change for its own sake. You change to realise the strategic vision. What must the firm excel at? What does that mean for processes, people and customers? Who does what in management, answering to which goals, actions and measures? Who does the planning and controls the implementation? Most important of all, perhaps, when do you decide that change must be radical rather than incremental, revolutionary rather than evolutionary?

The answer to all these questions used to be easy. Leave it to the senior management, usually the topmost manager or managers of all. The truly modern answer is to refer the questions to teams which contribute to the answers and supply the implementation to fit. In itself, this represents a tremendous reform which demands and generates genuine, rapid change throughout the organisation – including its information technology.

Few of today's management truisms are more widely promulgated or believed than the dictum that IT strategy must be aligned to corporate strategy for either to be successful. Yet repetition of this seemingly obvious truth betrays the equally obvious fact that only a minority of managements have made this preaching the basis of their practice.

That's despite the force of another truism: that the first company in an industry or sector to make effective strategic use of IT steals a long and possibly permanent march over its competitors. What is the problem? The usual answer is to blame the unfamiliarity of most managers with the technology; the inbred, uncommercial nature of some technologists; and a pace of change so hectic that today's state-of-the-art is tomorrow's dinosaur.

Moreover, yesterday's dinosaurs, in the shape of expensive legacy systems and their associated software, are a major deterrent to innovative investment. Throwing out the past to substitute the future is not only expensive, maybe hideously so, but possibly impractical: the company, after all, has to go on running. This and the other excuses listed above are real enough obstacles. But they are not the ultimate reason why managements resist the truism.

To align IT strategy with corporate strategy, you need to possess a corporate strategy in the first place. The existence of powerful IT tools, like customer databases, may influence the choice of strategy. But management still has to formulate overall objectives, to define the ends for which IT will help to provide the means. And the number of companies with clearly envisaged, robust strategies is astonishingly small, even at the top end of the corporate spectrum.

Take the extraordinary case of Unilever, which came to the conclusion that its 57 varieties of business were far too many, so that half of these operations were 'low priority' (i.e., disposable). In a group packed with brainpower, all those businesses, and the brands that proliferated within them, must surely have been added only after careful thought and for what seemed like sound strategic reasons. Often, however, the reasons weren't truly strategic, and the additions didn't fit into any master strategy – because there wasn't one.

According to an eyebrow-raising survey by Renaissance Solutions, this is by no means unusual. It found that 90 per cent of its respondents 'believe that clear, action-oriented understanding of their strategies could significantly influence their success'. And so say all of us. But less than 60 per cent of these directors and senior managers 'believe they have a clear understanding of what their company's strategy is'. In these circumstances, it's no surprise that under 30 per cent 'believe that their organisations' strategies are effectively implemented'.

Renaissance did find that 'a large majority of companies now have some form of clearly stated strategic intent'. A strategic

intent, however, is not the same as a strategy, and a 'clear statement' is not the same as a plan, or, for that matter, the same
as a clear understanding, let alone an effective implementation.
The survey notes that these companies, despite their good
intents, were 'failing to direct their activities to achieve these
strategic goals effectively'. In large measure, this is because the
goals are vague and not translated into specific tasks for managers or workforce.

Deeper in the Dark

The workforce, anyway, is deeper in the dark. The survey
observes that 'fewer than one in ten of the entire workforce'
have any clear notion of whatever strategic thinking goes on up
above. If that includes the labourers in the IT vineyard, talking
about alignment of strategies is peculiarly pointless. In general,
integration simply isn't on the menu: 'Only a third of companies
integrate their budgeting and strategic planning activities – for
most companies, these activities are driven by distinct organisational units and different management processes.'

The picture is depressingly familiar. The operational takes pre-
cedence over the strategic, even though strategy is supposed to
establish the framework for operations. But IT offers an escape
from this everyday trap. Renaissance notes that 'companies do
not collect the right information to monitor progress toward
their strategic goals'. They make do with standard operating
and financial results – they don't 'focus on co-ordinated and
appropriate measures of performance that go beyond' these traditional measures.

Achieving such a focus emerges as one of four simple steps
that will cure the depressing paralysis confirmed by the survey.
The prize that IT directors can dangle before their boards is far
better and better co-ordinated information about performance,
within the company and in the marketplace. These facts are
the ammunition for strategy, which must begin by establishing
where you are now, and end by showing that the goals involved
in moving to a better position have been achieved.

That's another of the four steps: 'Transform strategy formulation into a continuous process that adapts to performance feedback on the achievement of strategic goals.' The remaining two steps are turning visions into robust programmes and developing strong ownership. The more effectively the IT function supplies strategic information, the more likely its ultimate masters are to satisfy the four criteria, and to deal with three major strategic issues.

The first is timing. How do you know when the moment for strategic renewal is ripe? The second is start-up. Who initiates change, and how? The third is extent. Do you turn the whole organisation upside down, go in for gradual change here and there, or settle for something in-between? The uncompromising answer is that you dare not settle for remaking one aspect of an organisation, even such crucial aspects as its IT or its product line. It is a question of all or, very possibly, nothing.

The truth applies to all sizes of company. The analogy is with a share portfolio. You hold ten stocks in equal proportions. One of them doubles, while five rise by 10 per cent and the other four fall by 5 per cent. You feel great until you value the entire portfolio. It has risen by only 13 per cent. The very hard lesson is that it's no use tackling just one or two aspects of a company, however brilliantly; you have to do everything – and, so far as possible, at once – from shopfloor relationships to high-level strategy.

Without strategy renewal cannot occur. That makes the rarity of renewal far from remarkable, if you believe consultant Michael de Kare-Silver of the CSC Kalchas group. His book, *Strategy in Crisis*, endorses the Renaissance findings. Kalchas interviewed 100 chief executives of the top 100 groups based in the UK and US to find their priority agenda. The average response put 'future strategy' below technology, information management, new products and the regulatory environment. The latter came above everything else in the list of priorities.

That result is very peculiar. First, regulators are outside the CEO's control. Second, what about that cliché of information strategy that it can only be successfully formed in tandem with overall corporate strategy. How can the former possibly outrank the latter in priority? Third, innovation can only take place intelligently within a strategic framework. Fourth, technology also only makes sense as a servant to strategy. These CEOs seem to be putting the cart before the horse. Small wonder that the top 100 UK companies averaged only 2.6 per cent real growth in the five years to 1996.

De Kare-Silver suggests that a vicious circle explains 'the lost art of strategy-making'. Because it's low on the agenda, corporate planning is relegated in importance, so that the necessary skills and understanding dwindle. This means that still less value is attached to paybacks on planned strategy. The outward-facing, uncontrollable future thus loses out to inward-facing, controllable present activities like re-engineering. As the short term dominates at the expense of the long, the voices for strategic change become still less audible, and the lost art loses out still more.

The Strategic Renewal

A renewed focus on strategy-making can set up a benevolent circle. But Silver argues that none of the well-known strategic frameworks will do the trick, whether it's the Boston matrix, PIMS (Profit Impact of Market Strategy), Michael Porter's 'five forces' and 'three generic strategies', core competencies, 'parenting' or the 'three value disciplines'. In his view, none of these provides a satisfactory answer to seven critical tests of strategic robustness:

1 Does the strategy reflect the business realities of the new century?
2 Does it begin with the customer?
3 Is it rooted in and imbued with market understanding?
4 Is it practical (not theoretical)?
5 Is it specific (not superficial)?
6 Does it encourage a longer-term view?
7 Is it measurable?

To those seven we would add a most important eighth criterion. Does the strategy embrace the present and future potential of information, and especially Internet technology? This is an indispensable ingredient in implementing the seven other criteria. Today's IT brings a unique dimension, creating an entirely new system of doing business, and uniting a company, its suppliers and customers in a new and vibrant marketplace.

New is the key word. Sheer old age explains why some of the strategic approaches examined by Silver have faded. The Boston matrix is especially hoary. It divided operations into stars (for backing), cows (for milking), question marks (for possible stardom) and dogs (for killing) according to their market share and market growth. As Silver points out, this approach says nothing whatsoever about strategy. It's a guide to investment, not to creating a better business. And it is fallible even as an investment guide, because of self-fulfilling prophecy: dogs and cows get treated like dogs or cows, and that's the end of that and them.

Silver gives his highest rating to the 'three value disciplines' promoted by Michael Treacy and Fred Wiersema. Their theory attributes market leadership to a choice between operational excellence, product leadership and customer intimacy. But they offend against the principle that you have to do everything. Operational excellence which results in products that don't lead the market or please the customer is useless. Since none of the three can stand on its own, the model falls down.

But all seven strategic models share the same fundamental weakness – that at best they treat IT as no more than ancillary. Yet embracing the new technology and using it to revolutionise the business model are every bit as important as the key factors in 'commitment' which Silver describes:

- Developing an understanding of and immersion in the market with customers.
- Establishing a long-term horizon and determination to win out, overcoming the inevitable uncertainties of any millenial market.

Silver observes that these two elements 'go hand in hand; identifying future goals and opportunities must be born out of totally rigorous, deep-rooted market immersion'. His example is Microsoft, which was heading into possible oblivion with a strategy that ignored the Internet. Bill Gates turned the company on a dime, switching R&D spending dramatically, forming key alliances, buying Net start-ups and striving to drive Netscape out of the browser market (with tactics to which US anti-trust regulators and the courts took great exception).

Microsoft has always been fond of that form of commitment which, in the words of Brian Arthur, a Stanford professor, 'discourages competitors from taking on a potentially dominant rival'. One traditional weapon to this end is price. British Airways, for example, was accused of 'predatory pricing' when its tactics helped to drive Laker Airways out of business. In Silver's lexicon, though, pricing strategy is not just about 'low price'. In some cases, price-competitiveness may well be fundamental. In other cases, there are other key ingredients: value for money, quality and service.

That observation leads straight back to the all-or-nothing principle: all forms of potential advantage 'need to work harmoniously together to provide and sustain . . . lasting and successful market position.' That position is also dependent on what Silver calls 'emotion'. A power brand harnesses people's powerful feelings – whether they are buying shirts or Intel microprocessors.

The Test of Performance

Intel's devices have usually passed Silver's test of performance, whose core is 'about the basic functionality and reliability of a product – does it do the job it's supposed to do well and better than its rivals?' This is far easier said than done in most industries these days. All products aspire towards the same standards, those that don't reach the top tend to drop off the tree. By approaching the market in innovative ways – the 'changing the rules' approach recommended in Chapter 19 – leading companies can keep ahead of the game. But performance by itself is not enough.

The crucial extra ingredient is service. Silver calls for 'going beyond customers' expectations and creating levels of service that had not been imagined', through what he calls 'Hustle', defined as being:

- Comprehensive ('whatever I want').
- Available ('wherever, whenever I want it').
- Personalised ('tailored just for me').
- Symbiotic (provided in a context of an enduring, mutually beneficial relationship).

As Book Six shows, these aims are all more easily achieved by the use of IT – indeed, their realisation is often only possible because of IT. People who see IP technology as the platform for growth are indispensable members of what Warren Bennis, writing with Patricia Ward Biederman, calls a 'Great Group'. Their book, *Organising Genius*, argues that Great Groups have replaced great men as the driving forces for organisational breakthroughs. The authors' recipe is:

1 Gather the ablest people you can find to lead the revolution.
2 Place them under a highly effective leader.
3 Continue to recruit talent as a key activity.
4 Form and share a powerful vision and mission.
5 Set up a separate revolutionary HQ.
6 Focus revolution on a chosen opponent: 'The Enemy'.
7 Pick the right person for every job.
8 Leave creative people free to create.
9 Insist on delivery against objectives.

Intel's domination of microcircuitry exemplifies all nine steps. It tackles recruitment so seriously that half a dozen people may interview a single candidate intensively. One interviewer even refused to take a call from Robert Noyce, the chairman of the board, because 'I have a candidate'. As Silver's Market Commitment Model recognises, strategy revolves around people and their enlistment in the cause.

People-based strategy uses IT as platform and cement for the nine-step regime. The steps create exactly what Riding the Revolution requires: a group of dedicated, optimistic people who believe that they can accomplish anything; who won't rest on their achievements; and who see strategy, animated by its powers of information and communication, as a living, breathing force.

6

Structures of Success

The set-up is critical to success. This doesn't mean just the structure of the organisation itself, but also that of the whole business system within which it operates. Structural change, mismanaged, causes havoc at worst. In most cases, it only sets the stage for the next upheaval. With the help of Internet and related technologies, though, an organised process of change can transform any organisation – much faster than managers expect, much faster than many prefer – and go on doing so.

Managers understandably prefer continuity to discontinuity, evolution to revolution. But as the year 2000 approached, that preference became increasingly irrelevant. In discontinuous times, efforts to evolve at your own pace are doomed. Your internal thought and action must keep up with the pace of external change, or you will be unable to cope with external pressures that, equally, demand a revolutionary approach to structure – the construction of a new business model.

This consideration is so compelling that several speakers at a 1998 IBC seminar on 'Strategy as Revolution', commented that the title should have been transposed: 'Revolution as Strategy'. The argument is that if strategy is not revolutionary, it is not strategic. Yet the harsh fact remains that the great majority of companies are not revolutionary, in strategy or structure. They are not truly aligned to the fast-changing world outside. Revolutionary thought may be winning the battle for minds, but action still lags many miles behind thought.

For example, take the most common structural initiative:

downsizing. Even City financiers now accept that cutting numbers and eliminating assets, either by closing plants or sell-ing businesses, is not a new business model. What Gary Hamel calls 'denominator management', cutting costs, is out of intellec-tual fashion. 'Nominator management', improving the top line by raising revenues, is seen, even in the City and on Wall Street, as the key to optimising 'shareholder value'.

So much for words. As for structural deeds, Philips at the time of that conference was closing one-third of its factories worldwide, Siemens announced its retreat from businesses with a turnover of $10 billion (the same size as Gillette), Boeing was laying off 20,000 workers, Zeneca and Astra would eliminate 5,000 jobs by merging . . . and so on, and on. The last two, note, are engaged in the trendiest sector (life sciences) of the highly favoured pharmaceutical industry. Astra's management, more-over, had decried the mega-merger wave in its industry in most scornful terms – until the moment came when its own organic growth prospects seemed insufficiently rosy.

You can improve the bottom line by cutting expenditure, increasing sales, or (preferably) doing both. However, the first is much the easiest. That's because the other two probably can-not be achieved without transforming the whole structure of the company and its management. That is a tremendous test of both will and skill. The struggles at giants like Royal Dutch-Shell, Siemens and Philips show how fruitless it is to attempt radical changes in behaviour unless you first tear down a conservative framework.

You can see that framework physically simply by visiting the Shell head office in the Hague, where directors and their flunkies occupy whole floors apiece. Significantly, some top executives in Silicon Valley, even a mega-rich mogul like Andrew Grove of Intel, have been abandoning their private offices for desks on the executive floor. The dignity and privileges of the summit are among the first targets of revolutionaries in politics. They should be equally prominent targets in management transfor-mation.

Confirmation of this truth came in the pre-millennial turmoil over the top post at Marks & Spencer, the retail group once thought by many to be Britain's best managed company. Commentators remarked, almost unanimously, that the chairman, Sir Richard Greenbury, who stepped down as chief executive in the turmoil, was too powerful. The case also illustrates how the concentration of power and privilege at the top goes hand in hand with conservatism in strategy. Not long before, Greenbury had told a public audience that he would believe in electronic commerce when he saw it.

The Electronic Threat

He didn't have to look very far. As Michael de Kare-Silver points out in *E-Shock*, already some 15–20 per cent of consumers say they would prefer to buy electronically rather than visit shops. He quotes the managing director of a $2 billion-plus retail group: 'Even a 10 per cent loss in consumers visiting our stores would be a worry. For many of our outlets, that would push us below breakeven.' The author's consultancy, CSC Kalchas, reckons from its own research that 'average retailer margins will be eliminated by a 15–20 per cent reduction in consumer traffic through their stores'.

Against this dynamic background, M&S was still conducting a leisurely eighteen-month strategy review when Greenbury stepped down as chief executive in 1998. In eighteen months, usage of the World Wide Web, doubling every 100 days, multiplies over thirty times. The only policy that can work in such circumstances is transformation – and fast transformation, at that. A former chairman of ICI once said confidently that 'you can't turn around a large company like this every eighteen months'. He would not have recognised today's landscape in which, according to Alan Stevens, managing director of EDS in the UK, the time between corporate restructurings has generally halved – to eighteen months.

ICI itself has disposed of its best business, Zeneca, and shifted its entire focus from commodity chemicals to specialties, and has still failed to crack its strategic growth problems. As Stevens went on to observe, you can't grow dynamically with the wrong structural system. Just as information technology has progressed from high centralisation (the mainframe) to distributed processing (the mini-computer) to total decentralisation (the PC and the Internet), so freeing up corporate structures along the same route offers the same benefits in speed, responsiveness and flexibility.

In this process, the first eighteen weeks are much more important than the first eighteen months. A third of a year is quite long enough to prove that anything which requires changing will be changed, that no cows are sacred any more, and that the new technology will be embraced until it permeates every process in the business – from people management to customer satisfaction (two sides of the same coin), from 'knowledge management' to achieving radical and continuous change.

The precondition of successful transformation is to close the gap between management's perception of present reality and the truth. Large and rich companies spend heavily on advertising and new products, which convinces them, but nobody else, that they have established meaningful distinctions between themselves and their competitors. The reality is that the market often can't tell any of them apart.

Gary Hamel, co-author of *Competing for the Future*, has a convincing explanation. Companies in the same industry tend to follow the same road. They even benchmark against competitors to ensure that they are doing the same things at least as well, preferably better. But no lasting advantage can be gained from marching in step. By far the most successful financial services firm today is Charles Schwab, which turned the investment industry upside-down by being wholly different. Schwab didn't emulate the established industry: it forced its rivals to follow its lead – but too late to prevent Schwab's upsurge.

In contrast, every car company in both East and West, to greater or lesser extent, has followed the strategic lead of Toyota, basing their programmes on reducing costs by improving productivity. Despite that, their operating margins have fallen, clustering around a low 3–4 per cent. Across whole swathes of the industry, there is no real differentiation in either product line, quality or methods. Innovation has largely been confined to doing the same thing better. In consequence, the performance of Ford only looks really good in comparison to the industry laggard, the giant and perennially troubled General Motors.

Here, too, attempts at transformation have been hamstrung by the survival and resistance of the old structural order. GM's market value has been running at half the dollar volume of its sales. In contrast, Microsoft and Intel, the microelectronic champions, have been selling at extravagant multiples of their revenues (29 and 7.5 times respectively). Both, of course, dominate fast-growing markets, where succulent profit margins are available and are even getting larger. But both companies, being agents of revolution as well as its beneficiaries, have shown the ability to engage in the new necessity: continuous transformation.

Two Years From Failure

Bill Gates of Microsoft has expressed the driving force well: 'We're always two years away from failure.' The drawback for large established companies, like Shell, GM, Siemens and Philips, is that, no matter how strong the evidence of market failure, they refuse to believe in anything but their own permanence. They think themselves among those organizations which are '*Built to Last*', to quote the title of a book by James Collins and Jerry Porras. Hamel points out, however, that several of the book's heroes have not lasted, in the sense that their shares have heavily underperformed the stock market: companies of high repute like 3M, Ford, Sony, Motorola and Hewlett-Packard.

The last three until quite recently were management superstars, and still are, in the minds of most people. As noted earlier, Motorola has been greatly tarnished by its failure in the digital phone market, and Sony's reputation has suffered along with those of other stars of Japan's dead miracle. But HP seemed particularly strong, as a company highly decentralised, yet strongly directed from the centre, which had exploited established positions, as in printers, with unrelenting drive; and which had even emerged as a powerful contender in the cut-throat battle in PCs.

But that last success was relatively profitless. Because HP's business model needed restructuring, it missed the big, rich plays in its industry – software, microprocessors, the Internet – and such opportunities, once missed, are gone for ever. Hamel tells how he was present at the launch of IBM's laptop PC. He observed to an IBM man that the product was more than somewhat late: five years behind Toshiba, in a market that was already worth $6 billion. The IBM man gave a lordly answer: 'We'll catch them.' To date that has not happened, and certainly never will. These days, missing an initial opportunity may mean permanent disadvantage and major loss.

Think of the billions in sales and profits that IBM lost through its tardiness. As Hamel remarks, any IBM executive who had misspent a mere million would have been in deep trouble. But corporate structures are not geared to sins of omission. Though somebody should, nobody counts the losses from what might have been, and wasn't. For that reason, it's easier for executives to reject great ideas than to turn them into reality. Forcing through a project exposes you to the risks of failure, which are measurable. Opposing innovation exposes the company to the risks of obsolescence. They may be far graver, but will not be laid at the door of any individual.

By the same token, downsizing produces rewards that are measurable and relatively rapid. But the sums usually bandied about, involving billions of costs 'saved', are fraudulent. They take no account of extra costs incurred, through redundancies, plant closures, etc. Nor do they allow for the weakening of the firm's true asset base. In 1996, for instance, AT&T announced that it would reduce its workforce by 40,000 people. One consultant worked out that this write-off of 'human capital' was equivalent, at between $4 billion and $8 billion, to 'wiping out more than a third of the company's stock of property, plant and equipment'.

Five Revolutionary Morals

The quote comes from Thomas Stewart's *Intellectual Capital*, a fascinating study of the discontinuous present, in which intangible assets, which may have no place in the balance sheet, prove to be the overwhelmingly dominant source of wealth. The aforementioned Charles Schwab has grown to 5.5 million customers on the strength of ideas. Back in 1975, Schwab was like every other small brokerage house. But then the eponymous Charles decided to become a discount broker. The key was the regulatory outlawing of fixed commissions.

Revolutionary Moral 1: Look out for major shifts in the conditions governing your marketplace, and transform the business model to fit.

Schwab soon found that simply undercutting the full-service brokers was too easily imitated. So Schwab differentiated further. He invested in new technology (including telesales) and advertising to increase the value offered to investors. He moved to put their interests first (for instance, by placing salesmen on salary instead of commission), and advertised heavily. By 1988 he had a market share of 40 per cent in discount broking, with revenues of $392 million.

Revolutionary Moral 2: Build your business model to be better, different and more dynamic.

As Adrian Slywotsky and David Morrison report in *The Profit Zone*, Schwab next turned his attention to independent financial advisers. They could stay happily independent, but Schwab would look after all their back office requirements. By end-1991 even happier IFAs had helped Schwab's equity to rise to $1.2 billion of market value.

Revolutionary Moral 3: Look for allies to help you outgrow your rivals in a restructured business system.

But why were the advisers doing so much business? Because they focused on helping customers, who were not well served by the big mutual funds. Schwab decided to become 'customer-centric', too. It pioneered acting as 'one source', through which customers could buy many mutual funds with no front-end load and no transaction fees. This third transformation took Schwab to $1.07 billion of revenue by 1994, with $19.7 billion in fund assets.

Revolutionary Moral 4: Let the customers and their needs determine your business model.

Schwab had already added online trading to a brilliantly efficient telephone service. But it saw the Internet as both promise and threat. To quote *Fortune*, 'all that their research told them was that lowering prices to compete on the Web would cost them as much as $125 million in forgone revenues'. But that price was worth paying for what Schwab's co-CEO, David Pottruck, called 'the transforming event . . . the ability to deliver personalised information to the customer in real time, at virtually no cost'. Schwab now has 2 million active Web investors, who account for a third of $433 billion in customer assets.

Revolutionary Moral 5: To buy the future, be prepared to cannibalise the present.

Moral 5 isn't a new concept. It has always made sense to scrap or sell a perfectly good machine if a new model offers much better performance. The same is true of business systems. Change the model to boost performance. Revolutionaries like Schwab and Pottruck look at current riches as a source for future growth, and at current strengths as platforms for change. For others, that is easier said than done.

Consultants A. T. Kearney looked at the non-financial companies in the FT-SE 100 share index between 1984, when it was launched, and end-1997. Total sales, corrected for inflation, were £260 billion in 1984, and only £2 billion higher at end-1997. Thanks to cost cuts, earnings before interest and tax had risen by 76 per cent, and return on invested capital had practically doubled. But the researchers found no correlation whatsoever between individual profit performances and total returns to shareholders over the period. Why not?

The answer is that downsizing is one-off, and subject to sharply diminishing returns. Whatever Siemens gains from, say, $10 billion of sell-offs will be offset in time by loss of the growth potential of the sold capital, human and otherwise. Moreover, the downsizing knee-jerk draws attention away from two crucial issues:

- How and why did we get into this mess?
- How and where can we find the transformations that will regrow the company?

The answers to the first question begin and usually finish at the top. The answers to the second lie in structural revolution in information, management and global strategies. And that demands finding, promoting and retaining real revolutionaries.

BOOK THREE

The Information Explosion

7

Controlling the Flow

If information was 1 in 1978, according to one estimate, it was 600 by 1986 and 1000 in 1993: on that basis 2000 by 2000 is certain. The accuracy of these figures is not the issue. Everyone is painfully conscious of a flood of information, in which it is only too easy for managers to drown. To us, the speaking symbol of this threat is the printer spewing data in the corridor of a US car company and feeding it straight into a shredder.

That was the easiest way for the division's executives to handle unwanted information which head office insisted on sending. They are by no means alone in their feelings of helplessness before the unwanted, unsought tide. Nearly half of 1,300 managers surveyed in the US, UK, Australia, Singapore and Hong Kong felt themselves unable to handle the masses of data that descended upon them.

The survey, conducted by Benchmark Research for Reuters Business Information, reported several other alarming facts. It found that 31 per cent of managers received unsolicited information; 38 per cent wasted substantial time trying to find the information they actually did want; 47 per cent said that gathering information took their attention off their main responsibilities: half of them took work home or stayed late at the office to make up for the time lost in the information jungle. As many as 61 per cent admitted that information overload had affected their personal relationships. Yet these alarming statistics, as reported in *Next* by Ira Matathia and Marian Salzman, do not cover the most important question by far. Were these managers getting the information they actually needed? It is worth sorting through a great deal of mud to find nuggets of pure gold.

Indeed, managers who only recently seemed to be stuck (if not drowning) in the mud can now move powerfully forward by controlling the flow and storage of data to meet their prime objectives. The storage alone has become a massively growing industry. According to International Data Corporation, in the four years to 1998 the demand from corporations for data storage grew at over 80 per cent annually. That rate is even accelerating: IDC thinks that it will double annually into the future.

By 2001 the market could easily be worth $35 billion. Fortunately for the customers, the price per bit of information stored is falling – though not as fast as the storage need is rising. Dataquest figures put the price decline at 35 per cent per annum. Despite this fall in prices, the dominant position of a Massachusetts storage company, EMC, has given it a soaring share price (210 per cent in 1998 alone) to match its booming sales, which have passed $4 billion. The capabilities of storage units like EMC's, which combine hardware and software, make them essential peripherals to any corporate system.

There are plenty of other storage devices: disk drives, tape libraries that back up stored data, even technology that allows users on a network to get straight into the storage without going through a server (the company making this wonder got valued by the stock market at a mind-boggling $3.3 billion, or fifteen times its sales). Without adequate storage, easily accessible, the Information Revolution cannot proceed. That is the base requirement on which other vital solutions can be imposed.

What are these solutions? A number of needs are highlighted by Sara Kiesler in an important article in the *Harvard Business Review*. Here are some of them:

- How do you prevent the generation and exchange of more and more information that is less and less useful?
- Who decides what information gets collected and distributed to whom?
- What criteria should govern the selection of distributed information?

- How do you maintain the correct balance between internal and external information?
- Who has access to what corporate data?
- Who controls the use of the network – and why?
- How can you ensure that electronic messages are not only sent, not only received, but acted on?
- If the answers involve several people, how are their decisions and actions to be co-ordinated?
- Is it OK to circulate messages devoid of business content that nevertheless bring people together in an 'electronic community'?
- How far can you use the network, instead of face-to-face discussion, in making important decisions?

None of the questions is easy to answer, and it's tempting to fall back on trust. Once you have computers on the desktops, as you must have, for information access alone, then networking, IP technology and other facilities are manifestly both logical and economic. Once you are connected, the ten tough questions will, somehow or other, answer themselves. Kiesler sums up this loose, if comforting conclusion in these words:

> In the computerised organisation, most people will have information that always existed and some people will have new information. Computer networks will change existing groups and will create new, electronic groups. People will relate to one another in different ways, and the dynamics of decision-making may change.

Her plea for a 'light-handed policing policy' suggests letting nature take its course as far as possible. Undue constraints will only limit the potential of systems which, in any case, will make up some, maybe many, of their rules as they go along.

Delegating and Sharing

But the fundamental issue behind all ten questions is delegation, or sharing. Delegators are sharers. They give some of their authority, their work, to somebody else, without altogether relinquishing property rights. They can, for example, grab back the delegated work. They may be held responsible for its quality and achievement, anyway, by those above. Traditionally, proliferation of information has been curbed (but also often created) by top-down methods. Paperwork bonfires are always initiated from above, often in face of extreme opposition lower down.

That's because the files and the reports symbolise the delegated powers. Remove them, and, regardless of their importance (or unimportance), the possessor feels weakened, emasculated. The idea of management work cascading down from the top is intrinsic to the whole concept of hierarchy. But the management of computer systems raises more immediate issues. They are not problems with which senior management has been much concerned in the past. Like the organisation and control of the despatch system, those of the information system really have been delegated.

The role and importance of the chief delegate, the manager of information systems, or some similar title, inevitably rose in stature as information moved to centre stage. But now the drama is unfolding in a different way. 'Decentralised computing is sweeping business like a wave rolling onto a beach,' wrote John J. Donovan in the *Harvard Business Review* as long ago as 1988. Economic considerations were among the factors that made the advance unstoppable. At that year's relative prices, the average cost per mip (millions of instructions per second) on a mainframe came down by 98 per cent on a PC.

The organisational potential of the new, amazingly cheaper technology only intensifies the pressures for change: Donovan, an associate professor at MIT's Sloan School of Management, identified centripetal forces within organisations themselves. 'Employees want to operate their own systems, in their own way, and when it's convenient for them.' This fundamentally healthy desire has permanently changed management.

The migration of computing power from corporate headquarters to divisions, plants and desktops has not only reduced costs and enhanced competitiveness, but also offers to renew organisational creativity. These three aims are the agents of the Triple Revolution. The answers to the ten questions posed in this chapter will have to come from the bottom up, almost by definition. But this process must be disciplined. The disciplinarian is the network, without which, to quote Donovan again, you would 'wind up with hundreds of isolated applications . . . unable to share data'.

You certainly don't want that. Equally, you don't want, in suppressing too much non-conformity, to crush the very vitality and personal system ownership that are the essence of the revolution. This poses a major threat to the information systems manager, known in the US as the chief information officer. Unless these people convert themselves from overlords of vast hardware and software investments and budgets, and concentrate instead on networks, the Net and getting practical business results, their companies cannot ride the revolution.

The culture shock for IT professionals mimics that of the whole bureaucratic, hierarchical organisation framework. Like other senior managers, the top IT executive has to make surrender after surrender. Authority over hardware and software purchases is the first thing to go, but its loss is only part of a much wider surrender, sacrificing order for chaos. When anybody and everybody can buy programs and machines within their own budgets (or possibly download the programs free) anarchy has replaced the old absolute control.

The Big Brother Mode

In his article for the *Harvard Business Review*, Donovan described the 'Big Brother' mode: 'Large mainframes available only to data-processing professionals run programs designed and written by centralised software teams . . . this set of policies is an organisational and technological dinosaur.' This is an exact description of the corporations the IT brontosaurus was designed to serve. This beast has evolved. But the next stage, with the hardware distributed, the users setting priorities, and the central experts doing all the technical work, is simply not responsive enough.

Try to maintain absolute control as the organisation moves

towards controlled chaos and you get nowhere. Probably the most natural course for companies that haven't fully understood the new imperatives is the 'watchdog' stance. You let people get on with their own computing, but keep ultimate control in the centre by establishing an overriding authority. You supervise standard operating systems and programming language, and the operation of 'frequent and rigorous audits'.

But, according to Donovan, this generates 'the most severe built-in tensions' of any model he had studied 'and is therefore the least stable'. You can certainly see why. Only an organisation belonging to the clan of 'large inflexible bureaucracies with clear lines of authority and hierarchy' could even attempt to live within this system. It has no place in a world which is moving from bureaucracy to entrepreneurial college, from inflexibility to suppleness, from clear lines of authority to a criss-cross grid of relationships, from vertical hierarchy to the horizontal authority of expertise.

The problem of exercising control over everyday computing is best resolved by abandoning the attempt. Control rests with use: users have responsibility for what they use. But IT professionals are still left with some significant difficulties. The revolution requires perfect connection all the way up from hand-held devices to the mainframe (if any). Each machine must have perfect individual, physical connectivity. Throughout the network all systems must connect perfectly. And there must be perfect connection between all applications running on any of these systems.

It used to be nigh impossible to construct the perfect set-up, where every piece of hardware and software fitted perfectly together, with the same operating systems, data storage and exchange, and mainframe-to-mini-to-workstation-to-laptop connections. Nearly all companies had their work cut out to turn the Tower of Babel into an intelligible, universal language. IP technology, though, brings the near impossible into day-to-day reality. True compatibility has arrived.

The evolution of open, multi-vendor standards opened the door, and the World Wide Web threw it wide. You can get a best-of-breed solution from a single overall supplier that combines the best of each piece of hardware and software, irrespective of its manufacturer. In this climate, how it's done is less important than getting it done. The IT professionals have to ensure the robustness of the infrastructure to minimise interruptions and downtime and maximise speed. The users, though, will take all that for granted. The utility of communications will be like the supply of electricity, water or gas: on tap, all the time.

The technical details – the modems, multiplexers, local and wide area networks, browsers, routers, servers and so on – are of no interest to users. They want a consistent, easy-to-use interface between the network's components; they want to safeguard its secrets; they want to use new applications anywhere on the system: they want anything that's part of the system to work with anything else. Above all, they want to exchange information freely with all other users.

Relationship Marketing

They want all this for important purposes, like 'relationship marketing'. The idea is to build a total relationship with individual customers, even within a huge client base, like that of a bank. The commercial prizes in establishing such a relationship are great. But bankers, to take that example, have been stymied by their inability to analyse, evaluate and change the client's whole financial portfolio. That demands mobilising information from the systems – usually several, separate and complex – that control respectively the customer's mortgage, fixed interest investments, current accounts and loans.

The technology already exists to run the relationship in this way, generating large revenues for the bank in the process, and welding the customer seamlessly to the supplier. Relationship marketing is communication. The thrust of the revolution is for communication to take over as the central function of the electronic network. Sheer processing performance, the god in the temple for most of the computer age, has been toppled from its pedestal. Managing the intercommunications has taken over as the means of control and direction, while managing the hardware and software united by the network will rest with the user.

Relationship marketers will be no more aware of the electronic conduits that assemble their customer's data than passengers are of the air traffic network that guides their plane safely to its destination. They will care only about getting there. And they will arrive, together with all other marketers who see that the customer, and not the product or service, is the true asset of the business.

The responsibility for getting the information, however, belongs to the line manager. Understanding complex, and even simple, issues requires reliable, timely information. That in turn demands that users be proactive – people who manage information rather than being managed by it. The essential equipment of modern managers includes knowing what information they need, how they want it, where they want it, and when.

The essential, matching task of the information manager is to meet these internal 'customers' more than halfway, in the interests of an overriding purpose. In an age of complex competition, the system must provide knowledge easily, and make the hard task of turning it into action easier as well. Without doubt, the new technology fits that bill: the difficulty arises only from management's uncertainty in face of its powers. Abolish those negative emotions, and the positive benefits of the Revolution will flow through thick and fast.

8

Networking the System

It's not what you know, but how you use the knowledge that makes the vital difference. And that depends crucially on two-way, open exchange. Intranets and extranets are the latest means of bringing together all parties to the business system – including the key outsiders and every last employee.

As early as June 1995 *Business Week* ran a special report on the 'Networked Corporation', and 'making it work for you', with the powerful advice that this is 'a necessity'. It reported that from 'making widgets to posting Internet ads, businesses are going online, or trying to'. This might have been published in 1999. Four years on, most businesses still could not answer Yes to two simple questions:

- Does your legal department let you accept a contract that has been sent by e-mail?
- Can your employees fill out their expense forms on PCs, then get them approved and filed electronically?

These may seem minor details, but No answers are symptoms of a much wider malaise. For such companies will surely not be able to answer Yes to far more critical questions:

- Does information flow freely throughout your organisation to wherever it's needed, rather than up and down the hierarchy?
- Can customers dial into your computers to check the status

of orders instead of trying to find somebody in your sales department by phone?

• Is the company saving money by electronically linking with suppliers in a just-in-time inventory network?

The managers of 1995 had an excuse for non-compliance. They were told that linking up was 'hard to do'. The magazine supplied a beautifully drawn 'anatomy of a network', which showed on one side a Wide Area Network (WAN), connecting through groupware to factories, warehouses and mobile workers; on the other side an Integrated Services Digital Network (ISDN), giving access to a World Wide Web server, and a Network server. There sat a central phone office 'where switching equipment completes local calls and passes long-distance calls to the fibre-optic lines of long-distance carriers'.

In the centre of the anatomy sat the Local Area Network (LAN), which linked all the computers in a building via groupware, connected the computers with the external phone network and the internal private branch exchange (PBX), and gave access to e-mail and voice mail systems. You can understand how dismayed the manager of 1995 must have been, surveying this complexity and lacking several of the mapped elements, to be told that networking was a necessity but at the same time that it was hard to do.

Today more of the elements are in place. The network architecture has been simplified, and in the age of the Internet installing the right technology with the right applications is no longer difficult, but routine. That only strengthens the 1995 warning that getting wired to speed up internal processes and reach out to others electronically is an imperative. In *Business Week*, George Shaheen explained why:

> The ability to do more and more commerce over a network is at the forefront of everybody's thinking. What's going to happen – because we want it to – is that the network is going to take time, distance and space out of the equation.

These statements have become truisms. So what explains the continuing lag? Look back at those five questions, and you can't

imagine any manager who wouldn't want his or her organisation to answer yes. The difficulty is not new. Each advance in
communications technology has profoundly affected the way in
which managers manage. Today's extraordinary array of communication tools is like Pandora's box. Open it, and the world
will never be the same.

The 1995 *Business Week* issue spelt out one especially awkward
aspect of change. Management had to take another great step
forward on the long journey from 'order and obey' to 'advice
and consent'. Christine Arntz correctly perceived that getting
the most out of the network meant giving up control:

> A key difference between companies that make the net
> work for them and those that don't is their approach to
> information . . . until a company is willing to share infor-
> mation with workers at the sales counter or the shop floor,
> the most sophisticated network technology won't help the
> bottom line.

Making the Network Work

Making the network work is not optional. Mobile phones,
e-mail, voice mail, the World Wide Web, video-conferencing,
call centres, portable computing, etc. are becoming as commonplace and essential as the obsolescent fax machine. The impact
on management is already clear. Group working, supplier partnerships, horizontal or flat organisation structures, em-
powerment and the other guru-blessed elements of the new
order have all been facilitated and encouraged by the telecom-
munications boom, which, in some respects, is still in its infancy.

The examples are mind-blowing by the conventions of quite
recent times. A successful American challenger to a Japanese
world-leader in high technology operates from a base in the
Philippines over a network of PCs and telecommunications. A
fast-growing computer services company is based in London,
but hooked up to its low-cost programmers in India and Ireland.

A plastics business and its largest customer marry their computer systems to share invaluable information in real time.

A European multinational locates all its accounting services at one location, but its customers dial a local number in their own country and speak to somebody in their own language. For another multinational, not of British origin, customer service enquiries worldwide are handled from a single site in Scotland. Task forces composed of several nationalities and functions in several locations share files and discussions over the network, but never meet face to face. A Mid-West manufacturer finds out through his computer network exactly why his sales have slipped in Germany without speaking to a soul.

But speaking to people, and listening to their responses, is the essence of communicating. There are worrying signs that the amazing increase in the technological efficiency and sheer breadth of communications may not lead to better understanding. Most major firms these days boast a 'vision' and a corporate strategic plan designed to turn that dream into reality. But few firms, hand on heart, can boast that the strategy has been effectively communicated throughout the business. Without real understanding and co-operation throughout the firm, how can the strategy be carried through to success?

It can't. Managers are very familiar with the concept of the 'strategic gap', the distance between where the business wants to be, and where it is now. But there's another strategic gap in many cases: between the ambitions of top management and the understanding of those plans among the vital parties – customers, suppliers and employees. The last and most important category doesn't only mean the shop floor or the counter staff: managers are just as likely to share alarming ignorance about the policies which they are expected to implement – that is, to judge by a major Ernst & Young survey.

It found that in most organisations suppliers had no understanding of the strategic plan; customers had only a little understanding; while among middle managers, knowledge was only partial. Yet, as the examples given above show, the means exist as never before to communicate with all these groups through a combination of voice, text and images – which, as every public speaker should know, is vastly more effective than using any of the three elements on its own.

Use those means, and deeply satisfying results will flow. Raise the strategic understanding of middle managers from partial to full, by better communication, and, according to Ernst & Young, a significant rise in productivity, quality and profitability will follow. The investigators were so impressed by this improvement in the three – the Holy Trinity of modern management – that they declared the communications exercise to be 'a strategy for competitive advantage'. If middle managers are fully informed, of course, they can lead other employees out of what must be even deeper darkness.

Such ignorance is inexcusable. The technology has made possible a quantum leap ahead of noticeboards and printed media. Halifax, the personal financial services giant, is one of many companies that have introduced 'business television'. Organised like a broadcast news programme, employees in the branches watch it as part of the staff meeting. Companies can put out messages from top management, to explain breaking news (good or bad), and – if the company is far-flung geographically – to reach around the world via satellite. Interaction between speakers and audiences is technically feasible, which makes the medium more powerful still.

Powerful is the key word. One of the more entertaining episodes in IBM's generally gloomy decade of travail, the Eighties, came when the former chief executive, John Akers, delivered a diatribe to a group of senior people attacking their flaccid management at a time when the company was in crisis. A member of the audience was so deeply impressed by the message that he sent his notes to the staff by e-mail, forgetting that the system was open. Within minutes, Akers's rage had sped around the world and into the headlines.

This was involuntary embarrassing use of communications technology. But what if Akers had wanted to electrify the company deliberately by awakening everybody to the urgency of its situation? And wouldn't that have been wise? Just as the telephone widened communication, so do the new media. They make it much harder to keep unnecessary secrets or to withhold information – the time-honoured way by which managers of the old school preserve their power. The new communications and the new school of management thus work hand in hand to the benefit of customers, suppliers, employees at all levels – and investors.

The Connected Home

The network phenomenon is not confined to offices and factories. By 2002 there may well be 24 million homes in the US alone that have more than one computer. Just as in the business world of 1995, home networking has been held back by complex hardware and software. But the geeks are hard at work on simplification. Matsushita has invested in Epigram, a California start-up that aims to link computers, printers and high-speed Internet connections without the need for new wires – all to propagate an industry in 'home networking'.

Small wonder that Microsoft and 3Com are joining forces to tackle this market, which may be worth \$1 billion by 2002, and in which at least four other major players are actively interested. When a technology moves into the domestic market, you can be sure of two things. First, the applications are relatively simple, multiple and multiplying fast. Second, the costs are tumbling down. Back in 1989, the cost of a network of twenty workstations using PCs was \$95,000, already a fantastic bargain in those days. Today the price is \$20,000 and falling.

The benefits of networking are thus available to the small business as much as the great. You have six banking offices, and want to bring in new customers by charging on a sliding scale that gives increasing discounts for large clients. The network will link the cashiers, do the sums, and transform the results. Do you want to eliminate paperwork entirely? The network will save you jobs and money by doing precisely that – and improving processes as it does so. Once again, the questions demand only one answer – Yes:

- Do you want to make it easier for your people to communicate by computer?

- Do you want to save time (or increase effective employee hours, at no greater employment cost) by reducing the number of meetings and making it possible for several of your staff to work simultaneously on the same problem?
- Do you want generally to increase the information available inside the organisation, while at the same time making it more digestible, and increasing the company's reaction speed and competitive prowess?
- Do you want a better return on your IT investment by expanding the combined powers of your computers to grapple with new tasks?
- Do you want to reduce software costs by stopping people from buying copies of the same programs?

Even though any sentient manager will answer Yes, a surprisingly large number of companies have taken little if any action to achieve these five easily won benefits. They are the opposite of what was expected by the computer prophets. They believed that the computer would reverse decentralisation as top managers, aided by IT, took back the functions that middle managers and unit heads had usurped. In fact, the dream expressed in a *Harvard Business Review* article in 1988 has come true. The old choice between centralisation and decentralisation has become obsolete: 'Today there is a third option: technology-driven control systems that support the flexibility and responsiveness of a decentralised organisation as well as the integration and control of a centralised organisation.'

The Infinitely Eatable Cake

In other words, this is one of the rare occasions in management where you can have your cake and eat it and where trade-offs are not required. But the infinitely eatable cake exists throughout the networked world. The *HBR* authors speculated that companies would have the benefits of small and large scale simultaneously; that even large organisations would be able to adopt more flexible and dynamic structures; that the distinctions between centralised and decentralised control would blur. The writers scored three bull's-eyes – a rare event in forecasting.

It is becoming less rare in IT. In *Culture Shock*, published in 1990, Robert Heller predicted that three highly desirable miracles would be commonplace by 2018: managers would have at their disposal tiny but very powerful computers that could process at great speed all the information that they are ever likely to require; to all practical intents and purposes, storage capacity would be infinite; and 'computerised communications networks' would 'handle computer output, text, images and speech over any number of channels and outlets'.

In the event managers had this forecast armoury of 2018 at their fingertips nearly two decades ahead of schedule. That's why they can genuinely hope to have the best of all possible worlds, whatever the size of their company. The Information Revolution means that the small competitor can now match the giant in the strength of its decision support and communications systems. There is no excuse for anybody to shun the power of the networks. Rather, the imperative to use them becomes greater day by day.

Ten years ago, managements in large organisations could still rely on their immensely strong positions in terms of size and customer franchise. They didn't need to behave like small entrepreneurial companies, because they had no small entrepreneurial competitors. They did have a clear need to exploit the often buried talents of the able people inside the organisation. Their sluggishness in adopting networked management has made this need even more urgent. The Internet, with its globally networked reach and entrepreneurial challengers, means that nobody can escape that imperative.

9

Killing with the App

Every industry in the world is running the gauntlet of the same all-embracing, potentially murderous 'killer app'. Everywhere, the application of new digital technology threatens to create hugely disruptive, hugely profitable competitors, capable of undermining the industrial establishment. In this kill or be killed world. The disrupted companies will be the victims as the two fundamental laws of the digital revolution, described in our opening chapter, work in tandem. To repeat, Moore's Law states that every eighteen months computer power doubles while cost stays constant; and Metcalfe's Law that networks dramatically increase in value with each additional node or user.

In their book *Unleashing the Killer App*, Larry Downes and Chunka Mui give a revelatory account of how those two laws interact to downsize even the mightiest industrial groups, replace incremental change with exponential, and impose a whole new set of managerial imperatives.

Today, argue Downes and Mui, the killers 'reshape the landscape': for instance, by cannibalising their own markets with abandon to create new ones, treating each customer as a market segment of one, and creating 'communities of value' (Internet clubs, say). They build new connections with customers and suppliers, and they 'redefine the interior'. That means reshaping businesses, a process in which assets become liabilities (like all those High Street banks), and old value chains are destroyed by new linkages.

To kill rather than be killed, companies must learn new ways to manage innovation ('as a portfolio of options', the authors suggest). They should also 'hire the children'. This is a young person's and a young company's world: so older people and older companies need to learn new tricks very fast. They must introduce their own 'killer apps', and the bigger the better. The successful killers will be the first and fastest at creating 'digital strategies for market dominance'.

The killer app in this broad sense is putting increasing pressure on management. The applications of new technologies – primarily those involved with the Internet – are expanding at amazing speed and working to change the way in which businesses communicate, the way they are managed, the way they win competitive advantage and the way in which they do business; all this in an age in which companies large and small are going triumphantly global. That globalism, too, hinges to a great degree on the killer app.

Within this wider picture, though, a myriad of gains can be made, not by revolutionising the entire organisation, but by making swift use of readily available technology. These may not be killer apps in the full Downes/Mui sense, but they can kill off problems that have bedevilled companies for years. Adopt these new methods before the competition does, and you may have a competitive advantage all the more potent for being invisible, and therefore inimitable.

The Halifax Building Society, as it then was, had trouble with files – millions of them, which even outnumbered its 20 million customers. Sometimes files got lost, items went missing, the branch couldn't get access because they were at the business centre (or vice versa), they couldn't be correlated because of differing systems, and so on. An intranet, installed by BT in a matter of months, replaced indiscipline with order. Now electronic files, updated and intact, can be tapped anywhere in the company by anybody with a terminal.

That may seem a simple matter. But the work that we have done with companies as consultants always begins by revealing knotty, costly problems, like those at the Halifax, that can be resolved with relative simplicity by applying basically off-the-shelf technology. The top five areas of attention could hardly be described as career-builders for the IT specialists:

- Sales support (shared intranet pages).
- Human resources (shared documentation).
- Current financial data (brochure-ware and live feeds).
- Real time supply chain (back-reach to suppliers).
- Product development (shared e-mail, pages and forums).

Examples of solutions achieved during our work with BT customers put flesh on these bones. They range from making use of e-mail attachments to customer-shared Web pages for feedback, engineering changes, and development; from shared knowledge of possible future products to taking customers orders through a 'virtual warehouse'; from key customer e-mail capability to the 'virtual stationery cupboard', which means that you no longer need to keep a supply of printed forms.

The Killer Application Workshop

We have developed the Killer Applications Workshop (KAW), a half-day event in which a team of BT people and their clients identify critical killer apps. Next the Killer Applications Implementation Team (KAIT), tapping many disciplines and different levels of employee, takes a killer app identified at the workshop and uses a focused process and specific tools to ensure the essential involvement and commitment of the users. The seven-stage approach joins supplier and customer as partners and relates needs to fulfilment:

1 Identify the need.
2 Analyse the problem.
3 Identify the solution.
4 Plan and implement the app.
5 Confirm that the app works.
6 Incorporate the app in the system.
7 Select the next need.

An example from real life is the company growing crops in

Africa which needed to send regular reports back to London. The reports were sent by fax and required laborious entries by hand. The need was to find a faster, cheaper, more accessible method. The idea of using e-mail had not occurred to anybody, including the IT specialists. The app was quickly implemented, and the company was £120,000 a year better off as a result.

The idea of a killer app is not new. The term has been applied to computer software programs since the 1980s. Payroll, billing and accounting systems, BACS (the banks' clearing system), word-processing, e-mail, electronic data exchange (EDI) and many more have, over time, established themselves as key, computer-based, fundamentals of business. The killer apps are continuing to be as simple as the functions described above. However, a key change from the past is the cheapness and speed at which the new killer apps are delivered to the marketplace.

In the past it took many years for systems to become an inexpensive fact of business life. Take word-processing, for example. The first systems cost about the same as a year's salary for the average secretary. Unless your business had a real need to duplicate documents (like lawyers and mailing houses), the cost could not be justified. Today it seems impossible to imagine an office of any size without a word-processor. What happened? The cost dropped to a twentieth of the annual salary of the secretary, systems became more flexible and user-friendly, and word-processing, anyway, came loaded on the PC.

In turn, word-processing became one of the stepping-stones to the next software technology on the market: e-mail. New killer apps now cost a few dollars or even nothing at all. E-mail can be set up free, thousands of Web pages are published free on the World Wide Web, the necessary software is borrowed for a month free (downloaded from the Net directly to your PC), and then costs a mere $40–100 to buy. Business economics are being transformed by technological revolution, yet most of business has not recognised that fundamental fact.

In reviews and presentations with BT client companies, working with BT's Chris Downing, we spotted an array of potential killer applications in companies and organisations of all types:

- In a major European airline with 1,000 suppliers (and some 100,000 individuals) in its supply chain, only 5 per cent of its communication involved electronic means. E-mail alone would achieve major operational savings and gains at no installation cost.
- A company which won 93 per cent of its sales from eight multinationals found it an easy decision to establish an e-mail facility with key customer staff members, and to share Web pages of production schedules and new product information. The company remains the only supplier with this competitive edge.
- A Local Education Authority adopted a 'virtual stationery cupboard' for its schools. The e-mail system that BT had already supplied had Web page publishing facilities. The LEA had only to transfer forms via the PC for storage on the system's Web pages. Result: no more storage (or shortage) of forms.

Each of the above possibilities was known to the IT specialists. But they were working to another agenda, one that would use their technical expertise. Much of their time was spent keeping existing systems running, supporting users and correcting current problems. Also, they had become used to rebutting over-imaginative claims about the potential of the Internet. Between 1996 and 1998, intranets were touted as offering 1,500 per cent return on investment and six-week to fourteen-week paybacks. Business managers were understandably sceptical about the huge claims, and confused by the vast array of available technology.

Winning Business Benefit

In the fast-moving markets of the Internet, where what once took years happens in months, and opportunities surface in bewildering variety, intimidated managers have left the IP decisions to the IT specialists. The latter have understandably focused on the best, most advanced technologies. But technology in itself has always been a slow route to market acceptance.

Identifying a substantial, quickly won business benefit convinces management, speeds implementation, and wins competitive edge for the early adopters.

The US is perceived to be, and in some cases is, a year to eighteen months ahead of Europe. The American market offers many lessons. The huge successes, like Amazon.com (the first Internet book store) or CD Now (the first CD retailer on the Internet), or IT direct sellers Dell and Cisco, remain in the minority. But their example is encouraging a shift from technology to business-led implementations, a shift that is also appearing in the UK:

- Harley-Davidson wanted to eliminate unacceptable delays of up to eight weeks on warranties. The company implemented HDNet to automate fax and phone-based processes. E-mail for dealers was launched through the simple application of a CD-ROM, a video, and a user manual. Huge benefits were gained in the first phases at very low costs, perhaps less than 10 per cent of an equivalent IT version. Base technology: Internet e-mail.
- Saturn Cars (part of General Motors) generates 70 per cent of new customers through the Internet. A simple Web page, which asks potential customers to type in their details, creates an e-mail link back to the corporate mini-computer, which alerts the local dealer by e-mail. Base technology: a few Web pages and an e-mail link back to Saturn.
- Life sciences company Genzyme used a student on summer vacation to develop a private intranet, built with basic tools, to meet the needs of 3,500 employees in 30 branches worldwide. The system contained a wealth of previously unavailable industry news, research and regulatory information. Base technology: intranet implementation package and e-mail.
- IntelSat is a multinational 'co-operative' that runs twenty satellites offering bandwidth for telephony, data and television around the world. The board used to meet in Washington every six months and then produce a full sixteen-page report in four languages. IP technology made this report available without the costly need for hard-copy versions. Then band-

widths and schedules available for transmission from the twenty satellites were put on the Web, updated as and when needed. Base technologies: Web publishing, intranet package and e-mail.

All the above, to use a phrase much beloved by management guru Tom Peters, is 'simple stuff'. Another catchphrase is 'five-minute implementation'. You may not be able to develop the world's most sophisticated Internet site in five minutes, but then maybe you don't need it. But you may well need Web technologies to give customers and functional managers a user-friendly, simple access route to complex core mainframe databases and applications. The Internet becomes a kind of glue that sticks together separate systems and provides an easy-to-use front-end for established information systems. And these new applications, remember, are either free or need only a small fraction of the established costs.

Dumbing Down the Technology

The developing change is the dumbing-down of the technology and the new emphasis on business-driven, real and measurable competitive edge or excellence in customer service. By making this the new focus and keeping the technology away from the solution, business people can now feel confident about identifying opportunities based on computer applications they all understand – e-mail and Web pages. Keeping the systems simple enables fast implementation and the ability to change information, processes, structures and content format almost as fast as typing speed.

The systems can be used with customers, suppliers and internally with very short lead times. If change is needed (as it certainly will be), pages and processes can be modified in minutes. Our experience confirms that a deliberately limited approach (one killer app at a time) is enthusiastically accepted. Consultants' 'shopping lists' that identify some fifty or so applications somehow step beyond the human ability to manage. 'Simple stuff' is starting to rule in this marketplace, to the mighty relief of managers.

They must still watch out for economic icebergs. The switch from an inflationary climate to one of stable or declining prices is an example. In *Fortune* magazine, Ram Charan analysed the switch and found six examples of iceberg zones where tried and trusted strategies and tactics need urgent revision. These icebergs are pricing, market response, cost, resource allocation, flexibility and communication. Each of them provides an opening for a killer app where IP technology can play a pivotal role:

- *Shift the emphasis to service*: Establish interactive websites that handle service enquiries, speed response times and enable a customer dialogue.
- *Shuffle the product portfolio*: Get continuous reports on profitability and growth potential on the intranet to raise issues of removal and replacement in real time.
- *Reform the supplier relationship*: Drive down costs through higher purchasing volumes by cutting the number of suppliers drastically and taking them into partnership, with extranets as a key means.
- *Switch resources to the most profitable uses*: Have salespeople sell a whole range in one city (more effective than one person selling one line in several areas), backed up by Web access over a PC.
- *Break away from the annual planning cycle*: Hold strategic meetings whenever issues present themselves, rather than wait for the annual planning round, by setting up a 'virtual' war-room on the Net.
- *Network the whole business*: Whether the company is large or small, and whether you opt simply for universal e-mail and shared databases, or jump to an intranet, get everybody hooked up. Whatever the task, that will increase speed of execution.

Speed is of the essence. An article in the *Harvard Business Review*, 'Time Pacing – Competing in Markets that Won't Stand Still', advises adding speed and time measures to your existing performance metrics. Then, look at critical transitions (say, from old to new products). Can you simplify, shorten or even abolish elements? (Netscape no longer gives new products out to selected customers for pre-market testing, for instance.) Are your 'rhythms' synchronised with those of suppliers, customers, etc.?

Once you start organising the business round faster execution, without loss of quality, nothing can remain sacred. And that includes the IT systems. The object of the exercise is to find the killer apps and the killer opportunities that the apps unwrap. Your motto, in the words of the cop drama *Hill Street Blues*, is 'Let's do it to them before they do it to us.' Get your retaliation in first. Second is last.

BOOK FOUR

The Silicon Corporation

10

Following the Valley

The new kind of company not only runs to a pervasive, expanding extent on silicon chips: it mimics key aspects of the new Silicon Valley management style. The old-style hierarchy is dying or dead. This is not just because electronic communication dispenses with the need to employ many human relays for command and control – hierarchic systems are simply inimical to the needs of the new model company.

In the electronics industry, where progress has been demanded by the frenetic, hectic, heaving pace of change, the new model is running through the stages of the managerial revolution well ahead of all other sectors. But the underlying forces of change are the same everywhere. And the most forceful among those factors is unpredictability. Would you, for instance, have bet on any of the following events?

- Hewlett-Packard, worried by poor performance in electronics (especially in Internet-related technologies), decides to spin off its original instrumentation business.
- Sony announces that it will close eleven plants round the world in an attempt to cut costs and align the company more closely to the Information Revolution.
- Levi Strauss decides to cut half its US workforce because of a global fall in demand for its blue denim jeans.

Now that these events have taken place – and others no less dramatic happen every week – they make sense. With the founders no longer around to force through change, HP had lost touch with its entrepreneurial origins. Levi Strauss had become conservative and slow-moving in a clothing market where fashion was moving faster. Sony's core businesses needed to be reshaped and realigned towards IP technology and the other developments that threatened its product line with obsolescence.

The awful events are logical in hindsight. All three managements had allowed a dangerous gap to open between new realities and present performance. But foresight demands that, in a world of such shattering discontinuities, companies should not bet on a single outcome. Plan A must be backed up by Plan B – if not Plans C and D – to insure against unwelcome and potentially catastrophic events. But what about trends? Surely managers can be more certain about major developments, which must, to a significant extent, already be under way?

Don't you believe it. In 1997, asked by Andersen Consulting to predict the future of the network data structure in 2005, half of a distinguished bunch of electronic firms opted for intelligent terminals; the other half for relatively dumb terminals. In other words, nobody knew. How can you engage in intelligent, long-term strategic planning in these circumstances? You can't, and in the new model of management, you don't even try.

That's why Andersen's electronics leaders (see chapter 1) now plan eighteen to twenty-four months ahead (against the conventional three to five years) and regard forecasting errors as inevitable. Their strategy successfully hinges on strength of vision coupled with rapid adaptation and iconoclastic execution. For example, they are flouting the old conventional wisdom in three key areas: product development, customer relationship management and supply chain integration. The new approach involves:

- Taking more time over deciding to enter a new market: the best performers deliberated an average 5.7 months over both new products and new technology, while the low performers gave the decision process only three months.
- Recognising customer focus as the most important factor in seizing competitive advantage – though only 40 per cent made it an integral part of their strategy (at 20 per cent, low performers are markedly worse).

- Integrating the supply chain to achieve huge economies and increased speed: best performers re-engineer, make products only against orders, rely on supplier-owned and managed inventories, employ third party logistics, exploit the Internet and engage in heavy outsourcing, including manufacture.

Management by Chaos

It all sounds more orderly and well-planned than real life. In reality, the new kind of company tolerates a degree of chaos and inefficiency as part of the price of making breakthroughs and billions. Look at one such management-by-chaos company in detail – Intel, say – and you hardly know whether to rejoice over its brilliance or cry over its incompetence; though the former must far outweigh the latter.

This is the company that gave the world the memory chip, the dynamic random access memory chip (DRAM), the erasable, programmable read-only memory chip (EPROM), and the microprocessor. These innovations not only represent unbeatable management of technological creativity, but also a formidably impressive business performance. Intel has used every available means to dominate its markets: hence its near-monopoly in microprocessors, the most influential and indispensable devices ever made. Its hard-driving chief executive, Andy Grove, created that monopoly by ruthless methods like Operation Crush, which crunched the competition before the PC era, even though the Intel product was technically inferior.

So where has Intel failed? According to *Inside Intel*, by Tim Jackson, the company ignored the potential of the mighty microprocessor for years and woke up to the prospects only when two of its best engineers set up in competition. Worse still, Intel lost so much of the memory chip market to the Japanese that it could have gone under. Instead, the American company abandoned its original business, and poured resources into microprocessors to fabulous effect.

The management lesson from this episode is powerful. When

in trouble, ask yourself, 'What would I recommend if I were a stranger to this business, brought in to turn it round?' Grove and his chairman, Gordon Moore, did exactly that before deciding to exit from memory chips.

But other lessons are just as indicative of new model management. Early in the company's history, in 1968, a new recruit asked about the organisation chart. As Tim Jackson relates, co-founder Robert Noyce, an acknowledged genius of technology, smilingly picked up a piece of chalk and drew a small *x* on a blackboard. Around it, Noyce 'swept a circle, and along the circle he added six or seven more *x*s. Then he drew a spoke connecting each of the *x*s outside the circle to the *x* in the centre.' The *x* in the centre represented the new recruit. The other *x*s were Noyce, Moore and 'the other people you'll be dealing with. That's what our organisation chart looks like.'

The new model company cares nothing for hierarchies and strict reporting relationships, and everything for swift access, accessibility and flexibility. Instead of the pyramid, Noyce had drawn a doughnut. Whatever the cost in untidiness, the benefits of this model were shown by constant examples of turning failure into success. For instance, the microprocessor sprang from a design done for Busicom, a Japanese calculator company. When its top engineers arrived to inspect the device, there was nothing to see (producing yells of 'You bad! You promised! You said design done! No design!', etc.). The Intel engineers calmed the Japanese down and produced a working design in record time.

The Intel culture has consistently nurtured people capable of such extraordinary technical feats, often taken on their own initiative. The high standard of a continuing inflow of skilled recruits has enabled Intel to escape from initial failures like the Busicom job and turn them to advantage. The Japanese market worsened during the delay, and Noyce, faced with the demand for a price cut, artfully exchanged a $60,000 refund to Busicom for the right to sell the device to other customers – hence the bulk of today's $20.8 billion of sales and $5.2 billion in profits.

Typically, at first the Intel marketing people couldn't see any worthwhile market for the new product. This was a 'disruptive technology', in the phrase coined by Clayton M. Christensen in his book, *The Innovator's Dilemma: When New Technologies Cause Great Firms to Fail*. Had the mainframe makers looked at this market, given that only 20,000 computers were being sold in a year, they would have agreed with Intel's marketers. The first customers were screwballs, like a young Seattle freak called Bill Gates, who first used an Intel chip in an unsuccessful traffic-light system. Then the PC boom, unforeseen, changed everything.

Just as the microprocessor had sprung from failure, so did EPROM. The phenomenon involved was spotted in correcting a design fault, and the eventual product was expected to have only limited sales for engineering purposes. But customers' engineers started installing the costly device into high-tech equipment on a large scale: another profitable monopoly was born. The EPROM saga fits beautifully with the new model as described by the Andersen report.

The Internal Start-up

Inside a big, established company you manage as if you were a start-up brandishing a disruptive technology. You break up the company into autonomous business units (as do 50 per cent of the report's high performers, against only 29 per cent of the low). You don't ask those units to share resources, because, in the words of one executive, you don't want 'to stifle creativity. The more people you have to ask permission from, the longer it takes to get things done.'

This doesn't mean that the new model company is undisciplined. Grove at Intel encourages 'constructive confrontation'; but managers are trained in how to fight over issues in the open, with force and without animosity. There's also a tough budget process, whose detailed cost and revenue predictions are updated regularly, complete with explanations of the changes. 'Management by objectives' is another important principle at Intel. Everybody, including Grove, has medium-term aims, plus key results by which performance is judged.

Then there are the meetings, starting with one-on-ones,

in which every subordinate talks to a superior every week or fortnight, and key results and written performance reviews are discussed. Also, a process called 'ranking and rating' marks you as 'superior', or 'exceeds expectations', or 'meets expectations', or 'does not meet expectations' and ranks you against others doing similar jobs. Rewards, including stock options, are determined by 'ranking and rating'. Woe betide the 'does not meet's', by the way. They don't last long.

At the monthly management review, divisions run through a SWOT analysis (strengths, weaknesses, opportunities and threats) for the benefit of their peers. What Intel offers, therefore, is the musculature of a rather heavily managed, traditional company, with the brains and blood of a disruptive start-up. The tough discipline and the free-style creativity exist side by side. The new model company, in other words, is not so much paranoid (Grove's latest book is entitled *Only the Paranoid Survive*) as schizophrenic. Chaos and order, success and failure, are built into the formula.

Another split of the mind is between fierce competition and close collaboration. Here the difference in the Andersen survey between high performers and low is startling. The former have almost three times the number of alliances. Many of these alliances take the form of a partnership between customers and suppliers – the basis for the new supply chain economies. But 'complementors' (other companies which complement your own strengths) and outright competitors are also being enlisted by high performers. They take their time over picking their partners, too, half as much time again as the low people.

Collaborative Strategies

The leading collaborative strategies are joint developments of new products, marketing alliances and licensing agreements, any of which can bring deadly rivals together. Intel and Hewlett-Packard, for example, collaborated to produce a new wonder-chip for a joint assault on the high-end of the market for client-servers, etc. If this technological leap succeeds, the partners will have obeyed another of the new model precepts: keep the competition at a disadvantage.

Intel is a past master at this strategy. A striking example is its sudden plunge into the production of the motherboards into which its microprocessors were fitted. This not only won the company a greater share of added value, but also brought new processors to the market much faster than before. PC makers who wanted an early supply of a new chip (which meant all of them, since to lag is fatal) had little choice but to buy Intel motherboards. The company's output multiplied tenfold in two years, as all but 20 of Taiwan's 300 motherboard makers went to the wall.

In effect, every new generation of chip has forced the PC firms to dance to Intel's tune. As Andersen puts it, 'best performers look to change the basis of competition by creating a new *de facto* technology or by significantly differentiating their products'. This isn't the prerogative of high-tech firms alone. As with all the other features of the new model company, it applies to every business: for example, razors.

High-road Brands

Gillette rejoices in what a *Harvard Business Review* study calls a 'high-road brand', whose return on sales exceeds 20 per cent. Gillette's initial reaction against cheap disposable razors was to descend into their arena. It switched, however, to changing the basis of competition. By investing $200 million in the Sensor shaving system, it increased the desirability of its product, which established a 25 per cent price premium over the most expensive brand on the market. In 1998, Gillette repeated the winning gambit with the still higher technology of Mach 3. Wrong-footing the competition successfully always depends on innovation, either in technology or the use of market power or both.

The Americans are proving more adept at this strategy than the Europeans, for a simple reason: they use it more. Only some 25 per cent of the European respondents told Andersen that they changed the basis of competition. This compared with 90 per cent of the Americans. This gulf is plainly a handicap. Europe's correct response means looking at the industry and the business system with the eyes of a belligerent outsider. Which part of the system can you change to your advantage? Get the right answer and you may win a breakthrough.

The essence of the new model company is its drive for success. Everything is subordinated to outcomes, and the culture continually mutates to meet new circumstances. You have to question strategy and tactics all the time.

- Are we changing the basis of competition in our favour?
- Does our competitive advantage (if any) arise evenly from cost, technology and differentiation, and not just a single source?
- Are we planning for a disruptive, shorter-term future?
- Is the business organised into viable, agile units that run themselves?
- Does it form many effective partnerships?
- Is it focused on improving the supply chain, customer relationships and new product development?
- Can it find new customers for new products with new specifications, launched on hunch and faith outside the existing business?

These seven questions lead to another. Are we using the technology of information and communication in the best way to answer the seven questions in the affirmative? If not, the answers are highly unlikely to be correctly implemented. That eighth question is the ultimate test of the new model. More and more companies are learning how that test can be passed – not just once, but again and again.

11

Speedy, Sociable, Single-Minded and Shallow

No company has exploited the trends of the Triple Revolution more remarkably than Cisco, the leading supplier of routers and much other equipment for the Internet. It epitomises the new 4S corporate model pioneered in Silicon Valley – Speedy, Sociable, Single-Minded and Shallow. When it comes to *Speedy*, Cisco has achieved some astonishing reductions in processing times. Seven out of ten customer requests for technical support are now dealt with electronically. This has increased speed, eliminated 1,000 engineering jobs and enhanced customer satisfaction.

Speed has also been enhanced by being *Sociable*. That refers externally to relations with suppliers and partners. *Business Week* cites a case where working with partners cut down development time from four years to eighteen months. Sociable also applies internally – John Edwards, the chief of Cisco, breakfasts with every person in the company in their birth month. He's also very friendly with customers, with whom he spends half his time.

Like every other hi-tech electronics star, Cisco is truly *Single-Minded*. It concentrates on its Internet business and expands in concentric circles round that core. The company is divided into many units – many of them acquisitions – which of itself demands a *Shallow* structure. Vertical management is obsolete. Horizontal management has become obligatory for any company that wants to ride the revolution and to take advantage of what it has made possible:

The new technology will create the new office, a place

animated by 'electronic text' – a portable powerhouse
whose users can tap, amplify and use its information
resources, alone or with colleagues, anywhere in the world.

These words were written as long ago as 1989 when computer
networks were spreading fast, but before the Internet had made
its breathtaking commercial début. A year later, the future tense,
'will', was redundant: the number of host computers on the
Internet was 5 million. Six years later it was 25 million. By then
the first websites were only two years old: now nearly every
self-respecting company has one (although many are virtually
useless).

Companies which are completely site-less (and sightless)
remain numerous. In 1997, over half of all British companies
with turnovers exceeding £100 million had no intention of having a site. That, of course, is nonsense. They will all have sites
eventually, and one day those sites will be interactive. But the
interim state of denial threatens these companies with the very
real danger of being left behind, let alone failing to exploit a
crucial fact: that getting in early has powerful advantages.

The competitor who is first with the killer app will use his
mastery of information and communications technology to
change the basis of competition to his benefit. The most cited
example is Amazon.com. While still a mere start-up, what is
now the world's largest bookseller became worth more money
on the stock market than the two largest US conventional chains
put together. Amazon is perhaps not the most wonderful
example, however, because (though its cash flow is excellent)
it was still not profitable in 1999.

Conservatives were nevertheless wrong to use Amazon's
losses as an excuse to ignore e-commerce. Management once
had three options when confronted by change: not to change,
to change as and when forced, or to seek to take advantage of
change. In the age of the killer app, the first two options have
disappeared. Trying to stand still is bound to fail in a rapidly
changing environment, because the company's relative position
is changing – or rather, being changed by others, and not to its
advantage.

The 'wait and see' policy of following change used to be highly effective. You could let others pioneer new products, before unleashing the power of your production and distribution machine to overtake the pioneers. IBM waited fourteen years before tackling the mini-computer market pioneered by Digital Equipment, and four years before entering the personal computer lists against the Apple II. In both cases, enormously successful products resulted in the AS-400 and the PC family.

Brand strength, heavy muscle among large corporates, and a tightly controlled sales army carried IBM through. It didn't need to repeat the gamble of the 360 mainframe series, which revolutionised corporate computing at the price of terrible technological, personal and financial stresses within the company. So when its first portables flopped, IBM simply withdrew and left the market to Toshiba, Compaq etc. Five years on, with the market worth $6 billion, IBM re-joined battle – and lost.

Leaders Lead or Lose

The strategy of being a market leader who behaves like a follower is no longer viable. Leaders either lead, or lose. IBM's world market share of computing has fallen from over 80 per cent at its zenith to single figures. A 4I company – Inert, Introverted, Inattentive and Isolationist – has no hope against the 4S model. Leaders are learning that they have to react to attack, as opposed to the time-dishonoured technique of wishfully dismissing the new-fangled competition.

To return to bookselling, store-based competitors, including the former world leader, Barnes & Noble, started their own Web bookshops to compete with Amazon.com. The likelihood, however, is that those joining the bandwagon will find it desperately hard to catch up with the pioneer. Example after example shows that today the laggard never catches up. First come is first served, and goes on enjoying the largest and lushest meal.

So waiting for others to lead is a dangerous strategy, far riskier than seeking to lead yourself and piling in with might and main to reinforce success. Even the great Konosuke Matsushita was

compelled to recognise that he could no longer grow his electri-
cal and electronics empire in the old follow-my-leader way. As
he lamented shortly before his death, the pace of technological
change has accelerated too much for 'wait and see' to be tenable.
By the time your vision has cleared, you will have been con-
demned to following the leader – probably for ever.

The true leaders are joining the Triple Revolution with a will.
Many companies, including start-ups, are making excellent
money from the Web – especially in business-to-business selling.
Many more are saving money. The Forrester research company
found that a third of fifty companies that had installed an
extranet, linking them with the outside world, did so for the
sake of online ordering. After the extranets had been installed,
economic online ordering rose to 46 per cent; but two-thirds of
these companies, against only 20 per cent in the pre-planning
stage, were using their extranets to communicate marketing and
product information far more economically.

That brings up the second reason for starting as soon as possible. Once intranets, extranets and websites are installed, their
use and utility expand hugely. In the Forrester research, companies were also using extranets for inventory management,
collaborative R&D, training policies and standards, as well as
'e-mail and chat'. In every case, usage was far greater than
anticipated, sometimes enormously so: 30 per cent compared to
4 per cent for training is a convincing example.

'Billing and account history' hadn't been included by any
company at first. The item now ranked level in usage with online ordering. The sooner you install the system, the sooner the
benefits start to multiply. They are real benefits, too: 'We save
one million dollars in toll charges per year because our resellers
use the extranet,' commented one company in Forrester's survey. This computer supplier calculated that on purchasing alone
a hard-copy order costing $45 to process can be replaced by an
automatic extranet replenishment system for only $1.25.

The attraction of such potential gains has led to an amazing
boom in business-to-business e-commerce. In 1996 this trade
was worth $8 billion in the US; in 2000, it will be $64 billion,
and two years later $327 billion. Europe is riding fast in the

American wake: a trade totalling $1.2 billion in 1999 is expected to reach $64.4 billion in 2001.

Six New Mindsets

The cost savings and the commercial potential are only part of the contribution which the Information Revolution can make to the Management Revolution. In its study of Cisco, *Business Week* elegantly summarised where that revolution is heading. The new kind of organisation is one built on change, not stability; round networks, not hierarchy; interdependencies, not self-sufficiency; technological advantage, not fixed assets. This summary fits well with the 'six new mindsets' that Geoffrey James proposed in *Giant Killers*:

1 Business = Ecosystem. 'The business world is made up of symbiotic relationships formed to exploit market niches.'
2 Corporation = Community. 'A company is a collection of individuals with individual hopes and dreams that are connected to their organisation's higher purpose.'
3 Management = Service. 'A manager's job is to set a direction and to obtain the resources that employees need to get the job done.'
4 Employee = Peer. 'Every employee is hired – regardless of position – as if he or she were the most important person in the company.'
5 Motivation = Vision. 'People know where they're going and are amply rewarded when they get there, so the process of working is filled with energy, enthusiasm and humour.'
6 Change = Growth. 'Change is a desirable thing because it's part of adapting to new market conditions and growing into new levels of success.'

James derived these mindsets from his study of giant-killing electronics companies and the way they win business results. The methods include pushing decisions down to 'the lowest feasible level within the company; teams form their own rules and direction without interference from corporate headquarters'. You need the new mindsets to exploit the new technology, which in turn helps you to create the new mindsets. The chief means is the intranet which links all your people, wherever they are in the world or the company, and which can also be tied into the 'eco-system' of suppliers, customers and partners outside.

Major companies, after a hesitant start, are now installing intranets as fast as they can. Many are adopting a do-it-yourself approach, which is mostly a mistake. Buying solutions from outside suppliers is quicker, cheaper and generally better – if only because the outsider has amassed plentiful experience with other customers. Some IT specialists have been tempted to make the Internet their last frontier where they stage their final stand for control of the revolution. If you let them stand in the way of progress, you may well miss the full advantages of the new model company. *Business Week*'s formula for the latter, derived from Cisco and others, describes its imperatives succinctly:

1 Network, network, network.
2 Focus on the customer.
3 Buy smart [make clever acquisitions].
4 Team up for success.
5 Share the wealth.
6 Apply the personal touch.

Note, again, the close fit with James's giant-killing recipe. In the context of arming yourself for the Information Revolution, though, points 1 and 4 are vital. 'Technology allows links with customers, suppliers, business partners and employees. So take advantage of the speed and productivity it affords.' And teaming-up with IT suppliers meets this prescription: 'Create alliances with partners based on trust and the potential for achieving mutual short- and long-term wins.'

If their alliances are smart enough, companies can get the same advantages as those provided by smart acquisitions. For these, faster growth and higher market share are less important than capturing 'intellectual assets and next-generation products'. At Cisco, according to one executive, if corporate buys produce 'no results in three to six months, people begin to question the acquisition'. This quotation in itself sums up the new climate and speed (three to six months!) that the Triple Revolution is engendering. It faces every management in every kind of organisation with the same question: What am I going to do about it?

The Chairman's Nightmare

One of our clients is a great financial services company. Its non-executive chairman confessed to nightmares about spending a billion or so to replace a miscellany of 'legacy' systems, once leading-edge technology, but now, he feared, obsolescent. Investigation showed that his fears were fully justified. Users and suppliers were unanimous in condemning an IT set-up which was defended only by its guardians.

By good fortune not only had the IP solution just arrived, but the company also had a visionary on the board who understood the Information Revolution. His chief executive was thrilled by the swift solution of his immediate problems, and it was certain that in a year's time many other applications would be bearing a rich harvest.

So the answer to the question, 'What do I do?' is: the most you can, as fast as you can. Start by linking your computers and staff over the Net or other networks. Accept that you won't manage the organisation as in the past, but must move towards the future, new model company. Act accordingly. Talk achieves nothing. Be absolutely sure about your strategic and tactical objectives, and manage the transition yourself to achieve precisely what the users in the company (all of them) want from the Triple Revolution.

Finally, accept that the revolution will neither stop nor slow down. Changes in circumstances and technology will demand continuous change in the system. There's no final state-of-the-art solution. To an extent, this means signing a blank cheque when forming a partnership with your chosen IT and communications supplier. You will never know the size of the final bill, because there will never be one. But you will know the size of the benefits, as in these examples:

- An electronics company that built an R&D site linking its joint venture partners – one of whom won $100 million of new business because of the greater efficiencies achieved via the extranet.
- Two brothers who three years after starting a website to connect buyers and sellers of plastics materials and equipment, taking a 5 per cent cut against an industry norm of 50 per cent, had a booming business. Sales had soared to $7.5 million, up fourfold in a year.
- An aerospace company that gets 5,000 enquiries and 300 purchases daily over its extranet, which has reduced its workload by 25 per cent.
- A mortgage broker who deals direct with housebuyers and has processed up to $70 million of loans in a single month, with a 25 per cent monthly growth rate.

Waiting to be sure of measurable results, though, is too dangerous. As Forrester says, 'By the time the results are in, the game will be over.' What will separate winners from losers? The Forrester view is that 'ultimately it will be corporate culture'. Companies that are stuck in the old model, with its insistence on financial returns, 'will delay . . . while aggressive companies are investing' in the future. 'This time the bean-counters will lose.'

So they will. But bean-counters, too, have a place in the 4S formula. Their counting is as vital as ever when it comes to measurement and assessment. But they also have to adopt 4S principles, using the technology to produce financial reports in real time – *speedily*, attaching themselves to the line managers in supportive, *sociable* fashion; stepping out of the hierarchy and into the *shallow* team structures that implement the strategy; and helping greatly to maintain *single-minded* focus on results and concentric expansion. Developing a 4S bean-counter sums up the Triple Revolution and its inescapable meaning. Act now. Later is too late.

12

Disrupting the Present

In December 1998 *Fortune* magazine's cover gave corporate readers a stark choice: 'INTERNET OR BUST!' The article inside, by Gary Hamel and Jeff Sampler, was no less stark in its message: 'Somewhere out there is a bullet with your company's name on it. Somewhere out there is a competitor, unborn and unknown, that will render your business model obsolete.'

This book sounds the same warning throughout. It is neither hype nor hyperbole. The bullet has already struck home, with devastating effect for the wounded and wonderful results for the shooters. It's not a new piece of ammunition. Managements have always faced the same threat: disruption as some radical development changes their business so severely that great setbacks follow.

It happened to transatlantic liners when the jets took off, to integrated steel producers when mini-mills opened, to Detroit when small cars and then the Japanese appeared, to US department stores when discounters muscled in. The Internet is different, though. It does not offer a specific threat to a specific industry. Not only is it disrupting somebody somewhere right now: it could place anyone in the firing line, and probably in ways that the victims cannot currently conceive. As Hamel and Sampler say:

The Internet will change the relationship between consumers and producers in ways more profound than you can yet imagine. The Internet is not just another marketing

channel; it's not just another advertising medium. The
Internet is the foundation for a new industrial order.

The threat to established companies is most dramatic when technology takes a great leap forward. The dilemma is whether you
meet technological threats immediately, or wait and see. The
latter course almost invariably ends in waiting too long, until
the new competition is out of sight. With nearly all technologies
the former strategy, on the other hand, seems to make no sense.
Your customers don't want the new technology, and you can't
make it pay. In other words, established companies are forced
to fail. Customer demands and competitive pressures make them
invest heavily to sustain their existing strengths and, if possible,
to enhance that prowess.

Some challenged leaders will try (as many have tried) to
match the new threat when it becomes obvious. But, as stressed
in the previous chapter, being late is too late. Also, you face
grave problems in trying to ride two horses at once. The major
technology (which dominates the organisation) fatally cramps
the style of the innovators, who have rings run round them by
counterparts in wholly new, dedicated firms.

As the Information Revolution powers on, many companies
will lose leadership to its highly disruptive technology. But the
genuine obstacles that blocked and eventually destroyed many
firms overtaken by other disruptive technologies do not, in fact,
apply to the technology of information and communications.
Your customers won't reject your innovations. They will
applaud, rather than oppose your IP and other investments.

Companies armed with the new technology, moreover, are in
a far stronger position to counter disruptive threats by becoming
disruptive themselves. Lower costs of operation enable you to
go after different categories of customers, who are attracted by
lower prices and by different functionality. Like the disrupters,
you can afford to head off into tiny markets in the hope that
they will one day become large and highly profitable.

Yet many companies are reacting to the Internet just as the
14-inch hard disc drive industry did to the 8-inch drives introduced by newcomers like Shugart, Priam and Quantum. In *The*

Innovator's Dilemma, Clayton M. Christensen reports how the 14-inchers, even though all the technology was available to them, even though their resources were more than ample, by and large ignored the development, or vainly hoped that it would go away. Two-thirds of them never introduced an 8-inch model. Those that did were around two years late, i.e. much too late.

Value Networks

They were trapped by Christensen's Paradox: that large companies fail, in face of disruptive technologies, not because they are poorly managed, but because their management is excellent. It would have been mismanagement to pursue 8-inch drives which offered smaller margins and a far smaller market (if any), and which present customers didn't want. Christensen firmly establishes the concept of 'value networks', in which customers and supplier develop a shared interest in a given technology which suits both their purposes, including their profit objectives.

The mistake of ignoring the new emerging market in these cases is clear only with hindsight. But that is not true of the Internet. The folly of ignoring it screams from every business journal. As the *Financial Times* stressed in March 1999:

> In boardrooms across the globe, executives are having to get to grips with the Internet and the e-commerce revolution. Many face the unpalatable choice of cannibalising their existing businesses to compete in the Internet era, or watching others do it for them. Either way, it is IT systems that will make the difference.

That accurate diagnosis leaves no options. There isn't a choice, like that between going up-market or down. In the old business school model every manager was urged to head up-market, aiming for the top left-hand corner of the price/performance matrix, where you win the highest price for the highest quality. That strategy optimised the present, at the risk of undermining, even eliminating, the future. The risk has now become insupportable. Today the killer app in many sectors is lowest price for highest quality – and that will not be achieved by out-of-date business models.

Firms and individuals naturally play to their strengths – what they are good at, which has worked well in the past and still works well. The time comes, however, when these strengths are threatened by obsolescence, even though they are still paying off. That was IBM's recurrent nightmare. The company may have deserved its one-time sky-high management reputation, but it derived its vast profits and massive market strength from serving large corporate customers – and deep market changes undermined the model.

Although IBM eventually reacted very effectively to the rise of both the mini-computer and the PC, its natural bent was towards those same big customers. But the phenomenal growth in PC sales lay outside the large corporates, and IBM's market share in PCs, once 80 per cent, slumped to single figures. This didn't happen overnight. But it might just as well have done. By lagging behind the new technology, you miss a bus that may not stop for you the next time round.

Missing the bus isn't a failing peculiar to IBM. In disk drives, Seagate, the disruptive 5.25-inch leader, came late into 3.5-inch disks, and by 1991 hadn't sold a single product to what turned out to be their prime users, manufacturers of portable, laptop and notebook computers. The problem for everyone is that the biggest opportunity and the greatest threat may well lie outside the existing business and value network. You can't, however, just abandon the latter, because that network provides your current highly satisfactory profits.

The whole organisation and its management mindset are geared, quite rightly, to what *is*. How can the same organisation react effectively to what *isn't*, and may never be? Christensen's unequivocal answer is that it can't. The existing organisation will never succeed with a disruptive technology. He cites Woolworth in the US, which attempted to combat the price-cutting discount stores by opening its own Woolco outlets and simultaneously expanding the traditional variety stores.

The effort failed even more abysmally than IBM's move to absorb its phenomenally successful PC operation into the mainstream organisation. The Woolcos disappeared completely. While IBM lost massive amounts of market share, it remains the world's largest IT company (though far from that in stock market value). Yet originally the PC operation was a model response to the innovator's dilemma. It's a solution which IP technology both requires and facilitates.

The PC activity was sited well away from any other IBM centre, in Boca Raton, Florida, under independent management with a distinct mandate. It met excellently most of the following key prescriptions, which apply forcefully to making the best of the new technology of information and communications:

1 Match the size of the organisation to the size of the market.
2 Learn about the market and its customers as you go along.
3 Get in early, while the market has still to be proved.
4 Accept the inevitability of mistakes.
5 Recognise the weaknesses of disruptive technologies and their strengths.

This sounds like an argument for the 'skunk-works', an organisation given a specific task and located in a site which makes interference unlikely. Many a skunk-works failed, however, usually either because the sponsoring management didn't have real faith in the project, or because R&D wasn't linked to manufacture and marketing. The catastrophic failure of Xerox to exploit any of the brilliant, epoch-making PC discoveries at its Palo Alto Research Center (PARC) sprang from separation of the scientists and engineers from manufacturing and marketing.

Sponsoring the Spin-off

There's an apparent contradiction between what happened to PARC and the argument for siting new activities well away from existing ones. But the contradiction is only apparent, not real: the spun-off activity should be a fully integrated operation, and not (like PARC) a self-contained outfit with no commercial affiliations. No matter how brilliant, R&D without a sponsor will be wasted. Even with a sponsor, though, the independent operation may not produce the right disruptive technology or market it appropriately to the different categories of customers who become involved.

The disruptive innovators have to learn how to play not from strength but from weakness. Since they can't compete with the established business for the established customers, and initially have little or no idea of where their products will sell, they have to create new strength. They have to learn how to find new customers and open up new markets from which brilliant success can spring. That, however, doesn't make it any easier to encompass disruptive change when those markets, in turn, become established.

What happened to the 14-inch disk drive makers was repeated again and again (as with Seagate) every time a generation of new boy entrepreneurs reduced disk sizes. The predecessors, now rich old boys, proved incapable of resisting the competition, even though it used the identical approach that had made their own wealth (and killed their established competition). The main lesson is that in every business disruptive technologies or the equivalent lie in wait – developments which, like the World Wide Web, will one day enlarge and upset the market to your disadvantage.

In the early days the main strength of challengers lies in their highly adaptive approach. In these disruptive businesses, with their uncertain markets, there is no alternative to the points made earlier: learn as you go along, making false starts and mistakes, but reacting swiftly until you find the better path. For perfectly sound reasons big companies discipline this behaviour out of existence in their mainstream operations. This is fatal in the context of the Triple Revolution.

The death knell of the old order was sounded when, to gain its potent market position on the Internet, the start-up Netscape famously gave away its browsers. You simply have to forget old inhibitions. For instance, companies need to compete with themselves, which means not being afraid to cannibalise your existing products: if you don't eat your children, someone else will. Winners distinguish themselves from the losers by observing four strategic principles:

1 They concentrate on the winning hand.
2 They cover every bet.
3 They work with strong partners.
4 They think really big.

A wondrous example of big thinking is Finland's Nokia, whose cellular phone technology has taken it to a market value of $9 billion. Once the Finns had spotted their winning opportunity in the potential of the cellular market, they poured in resources to achieve world leadership. That demanded intense concentration. For the sake of cellular, Nokia abandoned paper, tyres, metals, other electronics, cables, TV-sets and PCs.

Such tight focus, however, is only part of the story. It won't save you from Christensen's Paradox. The failed market leaders trapped by the Paradox had enough focus to spot the opportunity. They not only developed the disruptive technologies themselves, but often took the development to the point of a business plan. But it never made economic sense to take the technology to market, not within the established organisation. It never will. So don't try.

Taking Partners

Independent start-ups are not the only answer. You can also take partners. The Silicon Valley giants have formed the good habit of investing in small start-ups that have promising ideas. Cisco Systems bought or invested in thirty-four of them in three years; Intel set aside $500 million for similar purposes. If the investment succeeds with a new technology, the investing company has entered at the ground floor; if the start-up succeeds financially, then the investor cashes in; and the odds are, of course, that technological and financial breakthroughs will go hand in hand.

If the 14-inch drive makers had invested in the 8-inch disrupters, or started up a disrupter themselves, the leaders wouldn't have lost out – provided, of course, that they had allowed the upstarts to follow their own logic. Hewlett-Packard did precisely that when setting free a new organisation to make ink-jet printers and challenge its own immensely profitable position in laser printers. The disruptive technology then worked to HP's overall advantage and followed the logic of Christensen's Paradox. Anything else invites eventual disruption by others – followed, if you're 14-inched, by destruction.

But IT managements have matured in a high-speed world in which, remember, months are as long as traditional years. They know the rapidity with which disruptive technologies appear, win markets and swell to major scale. That's why they invest in promising new disrupters, just in case. Managers and technologists have also learnt to work across disciplines and corporate borders (internal and external) to force innovations into marketable shape and on to market success.

These principles are highly transferable. Managers in every industry need to honour the basics. First, forget about corporate shibboleths and 'the way we do things round here'. Second, make the independence of autonomous operations real: provide all the resources they need, and enough rope to hang the competition. Third, focus sharply on new competitors, and stay with them every inch of the way.

You may go up some blind alleys. Not all threats materialise. Hovercraft didn't have significant impact on existing forms of transportation, nor rotary car engines on the old technology. But never bet on such helpful outcomes: digital watches crucified clockwork, and Web-based entrepreneurs will demolish earthbound competitors. The Boy Scout motto applies. Be prepared.

BOOK FIVE

The Partnership Principle

13

Winning by Co-opetition

'Alliances are where the real growth is.' This challenging assertion comes from Peter Drucker, but he does not have mergers and acquisitions in mind. Most of these are not genuine alliances and, says Drucker, don't in themselves win real growth. Rather, many are costly efforts to counter adverse commercial trends in the often disappointed hope that just bigger will somehow be better at winning competitive wars.

Competition is commonly thought of in such militant terms. The opposition is 'the enemy'. Your strategy is designed to 'blow him out of the water'. In theory, no holds are barred and no prisoners taken. But the theory is being outdated by practice, and by the business results which prompted Drucker's observation. Today collaboration between adversaries is expanding rapidly and widely, and the best collaborators are also the most intense and successful competitors.

Modern alliances are increasingly the golden means to the end of building, not simply a bigger business, but a greater and better one. Alliances come in all shapes and sizes, but share the same essential foundation: the belief that as active and sharing partners, both sides will achieve high ambitions that otherwise lie beyond reach. Most alliances involve joint ownership, usually 50–50. The important principle, however, is not the ownership, but the mutuality. And the vital means is communication, in which the Internet, especially in its extranet form, plays the crucial role.

Rich benefits from alliance can be won without any shared

ownership, but not without shared communication channels. Among today's most powerful trends is the supplier–customer partnership; suppliers get involved as intimately in, say, product design and production planning as the customer's own staff. Plastics moulders Nypro, for example, are so integral to Johnson & Johnson's soft contact lens business that even their computers are linked. In telecoms and IP technology, BT likewise seeks strong umbilical relationships with customers to whom it acts as main supplier.

As noted in chapter 10, Andersen Consulting's survey of high, middling and low-performing electronics companies found startling differences on this crucial issue. The high performers had almost three times as many alliances as the low and the medium. Many allies are suppliers, one-time adversaries converted into partners. High performers are also particularly keen on joining forces not only with direct competitors but with 'complementors'.

You are a complementor 'if customers value your product more when they have the other player's product than when they have your product alone'. The definition belongs to Barry J. Nalebuff and Adam M. Brandenburger, who coined the word 'co-opetition' to describe the new world of companies working in alliance. Co-opetitors abound in information and communications technology, because no company, however mighty, can supply from its own resources all the hardware, software, connections and distribution that customers require – and customer needs drive co-opetition.

All IT and telecoms suppliers are in multiple markets. In this highly segmented world, for example, Intel and Microsoft are inseparable complementors in the Wintel combination that dominates personal computers. In the even faster-booming market for chips and operating systems used in consumer electronics, however, Intel is competing against Microsoft. That's characteristic of today's pattern of alliances. It shifts constantly, following the shifts of markets and corporate strategies.

You therefore need flexible and careful management to make co-opetition work. The high performers in the Andersen study not only pick many more partners but take extra care over the picking. As noted earlier, the collaborations cover a wide range: the most common are joint developments of new products, marketing alliances and licensing agreements. Any of these can bring fierce competitors together, because otherwise the opportunities created by co-operation will be lost to both.

Seizing these chances is so imperative that one electronics executive, interviewed by Andersen said, 'I would give equal emphasis to competition and collaboration . . . it is as important for us to work with the competition as it is to beat our competition.' That's a practical expression of what Nalebuff and Brandenburger expound as 'game theory'. The theory holds (irrefutably) that the company and its competitors form part of the same 'business system': that system is their shared 'game'.

Optimising the Score

Decision-makers need to understand these games thoroughly. You have common interests with other players: for instance, getting the largest possible combined 'score'. The idea is to enlarge the pie, as well as your share of that pie. To enlarge share, sometimes you will exploit your strengths to prey on the weaknesses of rivals. At other times, however, their strengths and weaknesses complement yours. So you play on the same side in one sector and compete in others to optimise your overall score.

In the supplier–customer alliances mentioned above, the traditional adversaries stop battling over price, and play together to streamline the relationship, thus lowering costs and improving performance. The benefits flow to both. Such partnering between customers and suppliers is essential if you want to integrate the whole supply chain to achieve great economies and increase speed. The best performers in the Andersen survey act internally to re-engineer their processes – manufacturing only against orders, say. But they also rely externally on supplier-owned and supplier-managed inventories, and on third parties who handle their logistics and much else, even manufacture.

Those external relationships are key alliances. The spanking pace set by the fast-changing IT industries has been especially fast and furious. Few, if any companies have more business alliances than IBM, which began the 1990s with over 20,000 such relationships worldwide. It has created many more since, including important alliances in telecoms. But while the time pressures are particularly urgent in these sectors, many others share the same imperatives. GKN, for example, operates in low-tech alliance with its Australian complementor, Brambles, in a worldwide pallet business. Allied Domecq, in common with other wine and spirits giants, has many marketing partnerships worldwide. In a key industrial supply, Pilkington jointly owns float glass manufacture in Latin America with its deadly European rival, St Gobain. Several pharmaceutical giants have partnered relative minnows to enter promising but unfamiliar fields like biotechnology.

This last variety of alliance, which aims to produce new breakthroughs, is the most exciting. Even ultra-rich companies benefit from pooling development resources, rather than competing to outspend each other. Apart from sharing expenses, each complementor stands to benefit by removing the other from the competitive ranks in the market concerned.

Co-opetition has thus become both inevitable and attractive. But it doesn't always work. The tripartite PowerPC alliance of Apple, Motorola and IBM, which was intended to tackle Intel's microprocessor monopoly, proved disappointing because neither IBM nor Apple could develop enough sales volume. There are other risks: at its extreme, the business with a network of alliances becomes a company which depends wholly on outsiders, and therefore on the success with which these often tricky external relationships are managed.

They require a high degree of trust, and this can be misplaced. But if co-opetition sometimes fails, so does competition. The prime example is the price war, in which everybody loses. Properly managed, alliances create games in which everybody wins, including the customer. The process, though, changes management decisively. The ultimate stage in this crucial development is the 'virtual corporation', the title of the path-finding book by William H. Davidow and Michael S. Malone.

Even a global search will uncover few genuine examples of such an organisation, one which, in their words, is 'almost edgeless, the interface between company, supplier and customer permeable and continuously changing'. Though near edgeless examples are rare, the underlying trend in that direction is common. In most industries, companies are outsourcing more production and services, forming more and more alliances with suppliers and customers, squeezing out more cost and time from the combined business system.

Outsourcing, alliances and productivity are the daily bread of the competitive jostling in PCs, for example. Customers for information technology – which means virtually everybody – never know who they're dealing with these days. That's always been true, say, of PC components. Until Intel began its 'Intel Inside' advertising campaign, many users didn't know that its microprocessors were the core of their desktop or portable. Most still don't know who made the disk drive or the host of other devices assembled and boxed by the ostensible manufacturer. But increasingly the components themselves may have more than one parent.

The trend is accelerating. When IBM and Toshiba agreed to invest $1.2 billion in a plant, sited in Virginia, to make advanced 64-megabit memory chips, the two were already partners in a Japanese plant making liquid crystal display panels, and also with Siemens in a project making the great leap forward into 256-megabit memory chips. These deals, while huge, are only a small fraction of the alliances that enmesh the IT industry like a monstrous spider's web.

More and Bigger Alliances

The IT deals, in turn, are only part of the unstoppable trend in world business towards more and bigger alliances of all kinds. On the day that IBM and Toshiba unveiled their latest partnership,

Wendy's, the fast food chain, announced a $400 million merger with a Canadian coffee and doughnut chain, Hortons. The two have been allies for four years, coming together to build 'combo' units selling both hamburgers and doughnuts.

The reasons for the alliance are strikingly clear. The combos save about a quarter of the costs, and sell a fifth more than either a Wendy's or Hortons on its own. That's often the basis of an alliance: to reap the synergies of sharing capital and operating costs while tapping a bigger market than either partner could achieve independently. The word synergy was once fulsomely used to justify takeovers and fell into disrepute when their promised pay-offs didn't arrive. But in their quieter way, alliances seem to be delivering the goods.

That's after a discouraging start, when alliance results appeared to be no better than those of allegedly synergistic acquisitions. It isn't just that managements have become more adept at handling strategic alliances (though they plainly have). The improvement results, first, from necessity: and second, from intrinsic aspects of the alliance relationship. Necessity is the mother of more than invention. If a project is absolutely vital to your future, the incentive to make it work is absolutely compelling.

Even three-way partnerships can pay off where necessity rules. The PowerPC chip mentioned above has been widely hailed technically. Nobody noted the managerial achievement involved in bringing so complex a device into production and to market. But Motorola, Apple and IBM all had very powerful motives in their respective confrontations with Intel. Without an advanced microprocessor, Motorola would have been forced out of the market; Apple could never have competed with its MS/DOS rivals; and IBM would have been wholly at Intel's mercy.

As it happens, Apple has probably gained most from this three-way partnership and IBM least, because the latter found prohibitive the inherent disadvantages in offering two directly competing PC lines. That happens with alliances – they evolve over time as circumstances change, and may even develop (as with Hortons and Wendy's) into full-scale merger. So the partners have to be flexible for the alliance to work. Flexibility is one of the key characteristics that explain why so many alliances have resisted the inflexible forces that commonly mar straight amalgamations.

Focus and Direction

For an alliance to be effective, each side must have a clear benefit in view. This clarity of purpose is linked with two other essentials of good management and winning strategy: focus and direction. The alliance is focused on a clear objective, and execution is placed firmly in the hands of an operating management whose task is equally clear. Moreover, a firm line is drawn between the operators and their overlords. There's no confusion between the two roles, as there is inside nearly all companies.

In fact the good alliance closely resembles a first-class piece of project management – the mode which is taking over much work inside large organisations. With external alliances also growing fast, the whole pattern of strategic formation and execution is plainly changing towards genuine partnership. This changes the nature of the corporation – every corporation. Consider the examples mentioned earlier of four major companies in different businesses – GKN, Allied Domecq, SmithKline Beecham and Pilkington. Their alliances are so important that none of the four could now realise their ambitions without their many partners.

SmithKline Beecham's necessities included tapping into drug-related research fields, such as biotechnology, where it had no position itself. Allied Domecq's plans for developing as a global force in spirits depended on continued success with partners in markets like Japan. For Pilkington, alliance with a Japanese competitor was the key to expanding into automotive glass in the US and other markets. At GKN, alliances were the foundation for its attack on global markets for automotive drive-trains.

The most striking element in all these relationships is their durability and relative smoothness. They became taken for granted, but only because the respective partners had worked hard, and were still working, to ensure that the benefits were mutual and the management effective. Whether the lessons of allied success were being transferred into the internal management of the allies themselves is another matter. But that's the next logical step – and the next necessity.

Too many companies joke about the 'tubular bells' or 'silos' that characterise their organisations: separate compartments that never unite in the common cause of corporate success. Sheer difficulties in communication used to explain (though not justify) these harmful internal divisions. But intranets and e-mail sweep away the difficulties. Departments, divisions and separate businesses can keep one another fully informed at all times and in real time. Nothing less makes any sense.

If companies genuinely want to grow, especially globally, the alliance route is almost sure to be required both inside and outside. Externally, the approach is identical whether the partnership dynamic is all or any of the following: scale, pooling expertise, cracking new markets, cost reduction, minimising and optimising investment, competitive advantage, sharing technology.

In high-tech, especially in information and communications, alliances are indispensable, not least in developing and marketing the technology that binds customers with their allies and enables them to achieve genuine synergies. The old adage, 'If you can't beat 'em, join 'em', has a new and universal twist: 'Join 'em, and you can beat anybody.'

14

Picking Your Partners

The relationship between the supplier of information and communications technology and the user has become basic to success, and a prime example of how the two sides in a supply partnership benefit each other. To ride the revolution, companies need far more than telecom products from the supplier: they need to commit themselves permanently to the state-of-the-art.

Given that need, it makes no sense to proceed by one-off deals with one-off suppliers. The two sides need to become not only partners, but also learning partners, feeding off each other's experience and capabilities. From the supplier's viewpoint, it's even more than that; a collaborative relationship may be the only means of keeping the customer's business. As *Business Week* has said: 'The virtual distinction between the producers and their ultimate customers has collapsed, sometimes to near-zero. All of a sudden relationships among producers, wholesalers, distributors and retailers, once virtually sacrosanct, are up for grabs.'

This is for two reasons. First, the advent of 'infomediary' websites – databases which list all available suppliers and supplies – spells death for most traditional purchasing relationships (see chapter 24). It also threatens to make the goods and services involved into commodities. This was already happening to telecoms, anyway. The large 'telcos' have perforce become wholesalers of airtime whose customers are on-selling the service at profits – taken, of course, from the telco's hide.

Second, large corporations are using IP technology to pool orders across all business units. Like the infomediary sites, these internal operations will seek out the lowest bidder. That potentially reduces a vast range of suppliers to nothing but order-takers. The large users of telephone time have long wielded their bargaining power to win reduced rates. As that power expands across all kinds of businesses and across the globe, it will unquestionably add to the commodity pressures.

The sale of services that add undoubted value is the only available escape from the consequent price squeeze. Partnership, though, goes further along the value-adding route. It binds supplier and customer by involving both at all stages of the business cycle and in a continuous process of change, designed to bring down costs and increase speed of supply. IT and telecoms companies have the model of the automotive industry to follow: former component suppliers now design and build whole sub-assemblies. In the more advanced examples, the supplier actually fits the sub-assembly on the customer's site.

The novel nature of such relationships changes attitudes profoundly. The difference can be gauged from a real-life exchange at an industry symposium in 1998. The parties were a car manufacturer and a supplier of wing mirrors. The car firm's executives complained in strong terms about the excessive drag from the mirrors supplied for a recent model. The supplier counter-attacked in force. He berated the car manufacturer for persistent, obstinate refusal to provide details of its windscreen designs. The excessive drag was a predictable result of working in the dark.

The mirror men publicly compared the car manufacturer's failure to co-operate with the total collaboration enjoyed with Toyota. Delegates who were unfamiliar with the new supplier relationships were astonished at the mirror firm's bluntness. It seemed no way to keep a customer – unless, that is, the customer has nowhere else to go. In most markets today (especially in IT and telecoms) that may be perfectly true. A design-and-build supplier partnership shuts off the customer's escape route – at least until a new model demands a new contract. So you can afford to be outspoken rather than servile. In an effective partnership, neither course should be necessary. Yet most supply relationships are not between partners in any meaningful sense. They are still fundamentally adversarial, and still give rise to supplier complaints like: 'We could do so much more for them if they would only let us.'

Interlocking the Systems

Doing more follows automatically when the two sides go the final mile and actually interlock their systems, including all their information technology. The idea of sharing confidential information would once have been anathema, and in many companies still is. But how else can you operate just-in-time supply systems, or share equally the benefits of cost-reduction programmes? The supplier in effect becomes an extension of the customer's business. When IT and telecoms are vital to the latter, suppliers and customer can scarcely be disentangled.

As the previous chapter reported, the two sides may also be competitors. IBM, for instance, in early 1999 signed a $2 billion long-term contract to supply Dell Computer with PC components. The two companies are deadly rivals in the PC market, which IBM once created and dominated but where Dell has been setting the pace. In earlier times the rivalry would have made co-operation impossible. Today, it is hardly an exaggeration to say that companies are only as strong as their partners.

There is an analogy with PCs. These are 'Mickey Mouse' products, using identical components from identical suppliers, and differing only in external appearance and/or in detail. They operate on the same software, which means that the 'manufacturers' (really, no more than assemblers and marketers) have parallel relationships with Microsoft, which in turn has parallel relationships with both Intel and the latter's competitors in microprocessors.

Similar conditions exist in cyberspace. Cisco routers, for example, are common to most Internet suppliers. Interdependence between suppliers has become inescapable both in the manufacture and the operation of communication systems. As in so many aspects of management, though, the developments in microelectronics are reflected everywhere else. Probably supplier partnerships are not being formed so thick or so fast elsewhere, or being operated so intensively, but the trend is ineluctable.

More and more firms are seeking economies of scale not by taking all manufacture in-house (as IBM and Ford used to do), but by outsourcing to specialised, often near-monopoly suppliers of components and sub-assemblies, or even of whole products. Apple, for example, has decided to hand over assembly of its Macintosh PCs. The equivalent in applications is for companies to hand over the management of their entire communications and computer networks to an outsourcing supplier.

The world is being criss-crossed by such relationships, and the lattice gets more complicated. At every level the Internet is becoming the indispensable means by which partners conduct their relationships at all levels, providing information on the status of performance, orders and deliveries, say, or exchanging technical information, or just allowing chit-chat between colleagues in the different but allied companies.

The Web has become a focus for collaboration in its own right. Warner Brothers, for example, has a joint venture with FortuneCity, an 'online community' which houses fans of Warner's cartoon characters. The big attraction of such communities for a company is access to customers. Another form of Net collaboration links search companies with firms that operate in the area where the search is being made. Joint websites are certain to proliferate both in number and traffic.

A collaborative area offering still bigger pay-offs arises when two companies that might have competed pool their resources and venture forth together. Both benefit from sharing costs which they would otherwise have to duplicate. Both gain from the available economies of scale. All these considerable advantages, however, may be small compared to those of combining brainpower and know-how.

IT specialists naturally gravitate towards this option, which makes challenging use of their talents. Some information systems managers though, are motivated by less worthy motives – like wanting to preserve their power. These motives can even lead them to blacklist suppliers who talk direct to corporate management or who offer solutions unasked.

The Standard Solution

For all the advantages of partnership, there's nothing to stop companies from following the traditional route, choosing their suppliers independently and putting together the components to provide whatever serves their needs. But the traditional approach heads off in the wrong direction. The whole trend of the technology has been away from bespoke, proprietary solutions towards standard, open systems. Personal computing's take-off and boom resulted from the fortuitous establishment of an industry standard by IBM. Its use of Intel microprocessors and Microsoft operating systems, both made freely (if weirdly) available to IBM's competitors, opened the floodgates.

There is no turning back from standardisation. The user wants a seamless system that can be readily adapted and enlarged as new technologies and new corporate needs demand. Nor is that all. Alliances with single systems contractors help to find the optimum route through an increasingly crowded jungle.

The process of convergence is bringing more and more players into the information and communications game. Some are information providers, like Dow Jones, Reuters or Bloomberg. Others make hardware and/or software, like Microsoft, Cisco, Intel and IBM. Others supply communications by telephone, cable and satellite, ranging from 'telcos' like BT to cable groups like TCI.

All these powerful players are jockeying for position in a new world where the old divisions will cease to exist. Computer companies will also provide information and communications. Telcos will supply information and communications and systems that combine hardware and software. Managements thus need to resolve a confusing choice between rival claimants for their business.

This isn't a small matter like ordering a new private branch exchange (PBX). The whole future of the enterprise may depend on the technological option. Partnership becomes even more important when the technology and the options are evolving so fast. The wireless infrastructure, for example, will have to move data much faster. The last year of the old millennium saw the debut of the first 64-kilobit networks: that's over six times faster than most existing nets.

This speed-up brings into the frame a new wonder product: the combined cellphone, pager and personal digital assistant (PDA). So-called 'smart phones' are certain to become universal. This smartness will reside in connecting users to the Internet and to any other computers. This is one field where Microsoft will not have an unopposed home run. Motorola, Ericsson and Nokia (the three giants of mobile telephony) have formed a consortium with PDA supplier Psion that aims to steal the mobile software market from the Gates empire.

Whoever wins the battle, the user will have the planet in his or her palm. Computing and communication power will accompany people wherever they go. The machines will achieve miracles of miniaturisation to make tiny keyboards more easily workable by human fingers. As always, new companies have popped up to turn problems into solutions. Teg Connections of Seattle, for example, provides software that in effect makes a keypad into a keyboard.

These tiny devices are by no means the only examples of a crucially important trend. IP telephony – making phone calls over the Internet – will not be a supplement to the existing networks; it will replace them. By 2003, on one prediction, international calls over the Internet will have grown from 1 per cent of all traffic in 1997 to 25 per cent. Comparing IP with a conventional switched phone network produces cost discrepancies of the same general order as the one cent to one dollar disparity between Internet banking costs and branch costs.

In this new IP world, corporations will enjoy the benefits of Virtual Private Networks (VPN), which replace the costly leased lines that connect employees to networks, or customers to suppliers. Then there are IP faxes, costing maybe a fifteenth of the amount of conventional fax. Beyond the business market, moreover, lie the millions upon millions of consumers. As telcos squeeze more and more information into their lines, Internet speeds will rise dramatically. That can only expand the market for Internet purchasing and other services, further enhancing an already exhilarating growth rate.

Telecoms in Flux

Without collaborative working, users and suppliers of telecoms will both lose out. The supply industry is in violent flux as mobile networks expand globally, as telcos merge with each other and with computer networks, as broadcasting and telephony converge – and as new types of supplier emerge from the upheaval. According to *Global Turf Wars*, by Tim Hills and David Cleevely, business users will face a different world in which a very few global suppliers concentrate on the low-cost transmission of voice and (mostly) data.

Another small group will consist of global full-service providers. These companies will have made the transition from communications to information. Their profits will come from adding value to the networks by enabling the customers to accomplish all their business purposes. Whether their roots are in telephony or the Internet (or possibly other industries), these companies will depend on the strength of their alliances with customers – on their ability to exploit IP technology to the benefit of both sides.

As global leaders like BT position themselves for this future, they will have plenty of competition to keep them working hard. Hills and Cleevely foresee the emergence of many specialists who will aim to cream off key market areas, operating at lower costs than the global suppliers, but aiming for the top end of the available business. The telcos thus face the same challenge as their customers, as the new technology undermines the old business model.

Companies are left with a stark choice: either they let newcomers impose a new model, or they remodel themselves. As Heather Green put it in *Business Week*, 'Toss out the dusty old business plan, think weird, and try the unexpected.' An example of the unexpected is the arrival of the cheap or even giveaway PC. In March 1999, unveiling a $1 billion loss on IBM's PC business, CEO Lou Gerstner pronounced the end of the PC era. But even as he spoke, the revenues of eMachines, selling its PCs for under $500, were zooming upwards.

Fortune magazine speculated that Internet service providers (ISPs), who already paid eMachines $50–100 for the privilege of connecting its customers to the Net, would 'pay for the PC and just give it away'. The company's CEO, Stephen Dukker, told the magazine: 'I'd be very surprised if we don't see that' before the millennium. In fact, it was happening by February 1999. The following month a second provider was offering free PCs; then a third appeared.

The giveaway mobile telephone provides a rich and superbly successful precedent, and more ISPs are bound to contemplate such a model. For it will bring nearer the time when every individual, household and organisation is permanently online, and when the Internet is not part of a market, but to all intents and purposes *is* the market.

That must mean outsourcing on a scale enormously beyond anything seen so far. Businesses will use their suppliers of information and communications technology (ICT) to install their networks, enable their applications, manage their systems, handle the interconnections with the outside world, and organise their internal information flows. The more intimate and pervasive these relationships, the more effective they will be. The prizes at stake on both side will be enormous – and somebody is going to win them.

15

Visionaries, Pragmatists and Conservatives

Facing the future is the supreme challenge to today's managers. In financial services, for example, many contenders speak of building 'the bank of the future'. The speakers obviously know, or sense, that this non-existent bank will be radically different from what exists today. But very few banks have any precise idea about this 'future', even though the issue is clearly a matter of life or death. Today's retail banks will become 'the new dinosaurs', on one prediction. As in every industry, the survivors will be the visionaries who best read the future.

What if the future is misread? This greatly troubled a manager who heard our message about the necessity of 'Riding the Revolution'. As an engineer he had seen too many predictions of doom and gloom falsified to have much confidence in futurology. Our description of the catalytic, dynamic and dramatic impact of cyberspace on all businesses reminded him of predictions of bug-induced calamity in the year 2000. The ex-engineer expected that the outcome would, as usual, fall between the forecast extremes. He revealed himself to be a typical pragmatist: someone who waits for proof before committing himself to a view or an action. But in revolutionary times, the pragmatist is as much a liability as the conservative who wants only to preserve the status quo. It is certainly true that some very clever and informed people get the future completely wrong, with the emphasis on the 'completely'. For instance, no less a person than Bill Gates, whose sensational success at Microsoft has given him super-visionary status, said in 1981, when forecasting the future of personal computers, that '640k ought to be enough for anybody'. But this couldn't even begin to cope with the latest versions of his Windows.

Gates is in good company. 'I think there's a world market for maybe five computers,' said Thomas Watson, visionary chairman and virtual founder of IBM. The company then proceeded to miss the start of some major developments in the market. 'There is no reason why anyone would want to have a computer in their home,' said Ken Olsen, visionary founder of Digital Equipment, which was allowed a fourteen-year clear run before IBM entered the lush mini-computer market.

Note that all three men had vested interests in those forecasts. Watson had a stranglehold on the market for punched card machines, which were threatened, and eventually destroyed by computers. Gates had an equally strong position in operating system software, which stood to be destabilised by any rampaging developments in PC power. And PCs were a massive threat to Olsen's business in mini-computers.

All three indulged in wishful thinking, in other words. Yet in two cases the unforeseen developments proved lucrative beyond anybody's wildest dreams. IBM became the fastest-growing, richest and most admired company on earth as its mainframes, mini-computers and PCs multiplied fantastically in spite of the failures of vision mentioned above. The explosion of PC power created marvellous opportunities for Gates to sell other software, where his market position became even stronger than in operating systems.

Even Digital enjoyed many years of growth and prosperity before its failure in PCs became fatal. The Olsen/Watson/Gates mindset does eventually catch up with the company, however. IBM's desire to preserve the present ultimately destroyed its premier position in the marketplace. Microsoft and Intel, two companies whose rise to fame and fabulous growth depended intimately on IBM, are each worth far more than the hardware giant in stock market terms. Their growth has surged, while IBM has stagnated.

The Internet might have had the same harsh effect on Microsoft, where cyberspace ranked far down the list of corporate priorities. Gates successfully mounted a last-ditch fightback, but the threat of the Net to his quasi-monopoly has not disappeared. The outcome of the challenges, led by Sun Microsystems, to the Windows/Intel combination is still uncertain. But Wintel's domination of the IT marketplace is by no means assured. The future could go either way.

The final outcome could, of course, result in the middle position expected by our ex-engineer. But the underlying reason why Olsen, Watson and Gates were wrong is that they could not know, because no man does, what the future holds. Similarly, nobody could know exactly what the year 2000 would bring until it happened. Thus in 1999 one major software firm was doing all in its power to ensure that its own in-house systems were free from the millennium bug; that all the hardware and software supplied by third parties were compliant; that everything sold to its customers, and already supplied to them, passed muster. Its directors had assured themselves that everything in the company's power had been done. But what if a major failure of other people's financial systems stopped bills being paid and thus ended the inward flow of cash? Insolvency would follow.

The Future Present

This is a rare case where understanding the present is of limited help in projecting the future but, as Peter Drucker has shown, this understanding can enable you to dispense with futurology altogether. If you correctly interpret what is happening now, you will win a huge advantage over the competition. Most other people will misunderstand the present and will base their plans on continuity. This is likely to be fatal in discontinuous times.

Often the present is difficult to read, but this isn't the case with the Internet. For example, the received wisdom holds that electronic shopping will be slow to take off and not be a serious factor until well into the millennium. Our pragmatic engineer pointed to the fact that Amazon.com has yet to make a profit in spite of its colossal growth. None the less, its competitors have been forced to add websites to their conventional stores because of the huge inroads that Amazon has made into their market share.

Against the newcomer's lack of profits must be offset its great cash flow and the immense value of the customer database which it is accumulating. Which traditional bookshops know who their customers are or what they buy? Which conventional retailers of any kind have this knowledge? And which banks?

In his book *E-Shock*, Michael de Kare-Silver makes statements that sound like predictions, but are actually accurate readings of the present:

- *The revolution in electronic shopping is going to happen.*
  It is self-evidently happening, with US retail sales over the Christmas period in 1998 estimated at $3–5 billion.
- *This revolution will have a major impact on the shopping and retailing scene.*
  It already has. In activities as far apart as travel bookings and music, new cars and shares, spending over the Internet is large and growing apace.
- *This revolution will reach critical mass by as early as 2005.*
  In the industries mentioned, that critical mass has already been achieved.
- *From supermarkets to banks, nearly all retailers will be affected.*
  This is also already happening. In Britain, local organisations are taking orders for packaged goods over websites and making home deliveries; Internet financial services are plainly taking the lead from established techniques, partly because of their unbeatable cost advantages.
- *The electronic environment will demand new marketing skills.*

The last 'prediction', and the reality poses much difficulty. Take the banks. They have yet, for the most part, to acquire and apply the marketing skills required for their existing and largely traditional business. Now they are being forced to contemplate a new world for which they are woefully unprepared. The new market is driven by customer needs and enabled by new technology. The old style of banking, in which expensive High Street palaces formed a nationwide retail network, is obsolete.

Banks, like other financial services companies, have proliferated their services, which, adopting the language of fast-moving consumer goods (FMCG), they now call 'products'. But they lack the business foundations of the FMCG companies. Few customers can differentiate between these financial 'products'. They can differentiate between two very similar FMCG products, like Coke and Pepsi, because years of differentiated advertising and distribution have created a meaningful brand. But because banks, insurance companies, mortgage lenders, savings banks, etc. have offered the same 'products' in the same way for generations, their brands *per se* have little worth.

Attract, Retain and Maximise (ARM)

Another way of describing the banks' problem is that their products have no inherent value other than that supplied by the customers, who are the true 'product' in financial services. By gearing themselves to products, the financial institutions have grabbed the wrong end of the stick. Their prosperity depends on their ability to master a variety of the ARM formula. In human resource management, that means the ability to *attract*, *retain* and *motivate* employees. In commercial terms, it signifies the ability to *attract*, *retain* and *maximise* customer loyalty.

The M involves maximising the income flow from each customer over time, preferably a lifetime. The ARM formula has become much more urgent with the advent of e-commerce. Customers for both retail and commercial goods and services will have no need to use the existing channels. In many cases, they can already go to the website of their choice or can search, with the aid of a search engine, for whatever they want. The strategy of Amazon.com is to ensure that its customers come first to its website when they want books, or CDs, or movies, or whatever else it chooses to sell. And this strategic need must be true of all businesses.

In some businesses, you may be able to retain customers by superior service. Computer resellers take this route, although it will become less lucrative as computers become simpler and prices drop still lower. The real stock-in-trade is the customer, meaning the corporations that could buy direct from manufacturers or from discounters who offer a no-frills service. More and more, however, computer hardware and software sales will be – and are being – made without frills over the World Wide Web.

The proliferation of supply sources and customer choices is also not a prediction, but a fact. It helps to explain why so many orthodox household names are shocking the stock market with dismal results: their unconventional rivals are creaming off their marginal profits. Remember the point about wishful thinking. When business people look into the future, the conservatives and the pragmatists alike do not want to sacrifice the strengths of the past and present.

Like Digital with its mini-computers, IBM with its mainframes and Microsoft with its Windows, they want to believe that the foundations of the business – its historic product, selling and image strengths – will sustain success into the far future. Only the visionaries perceive that those foundations have become generally as shaky as those of the world's great banks.

Consider one household name, Marks & Spencer. No less a guru than Gary Hamel was praising its innovative powers as recently as the autumn of 1998 to a worldwide satellite audience. The basic formula has sustained excellent performance down the years. Provide exceptional perceived value for money by ordering goods to your own specification; control the quality of those goods through direct involvement with the suppliers; attract the customer by well-located, well-designed and well-managed stores.

In an age of proliferating choice, however, the formula has become tired. A visionary could have seen how IT, through an extranet connecting M&S with suppliers and customers, could have revitalised the old formula. But the management paid the price of believing that it knew the market better than its customers. From December 1998, a series of appalling setbacks, led to an unprecedented cull of senior managers. But culling by itself accomplishes little. M&S desperately needs to invent a new future – one in which, like it or not, the Internet is inevitably going to loom large. To invent that future, though, this corporation, and many, many others, need to invent a new company. That is not going to be easy, even for visionaries. For conservatives, it is impossible, while pragmatists will probably be too late.

Rewriting the Rules

The extent of the difficulty can be judged by looking at the 'Ten Commandments for Next-Generation Businesses' which Karen Southwick describes in *Silicon Gold Rush*. As her dust-jacket says, 'the next generation of high-tech stars' is rewriting 'the rules of business'. The new rules are:

1 Shape the company's culture and work ethic by nurturing and managing the company's knowledge capital.
2 Maintain a fresh perspective of seeing the company's place in the world as something ephemeral and transitory rather than assured and permanent.
3 Cultivate knowledge by distributing leadership so that each employee is entrusted with higher levels of responsibility and information management.
4 Develop 'mind share' by complementing product innovation with brand marketing initiatives.
5 Avoid formal structures and prefer forming teams to allocate resources, prioritise tasks and determine how to launch products, etc.
6 Place the customer, not the technology, at Number One, tailoring products to meet real customer needs.
7 Find the right partners, mergers and acquisitions to make the company an integral part of a web of relationships.
8 Embrace the unknown by preparing for the next gold rush, knowing that it could occur in an entirely unexpected place.
9 Behave in a paranoid manner, expecting to face a horde of aspiring competitors.
10 Act swiftly to cope with the speed of market change, technological advances, and emerging business opportunities.

M&S observed only the first of these ten commandments. Small wonder that it landed in such deep trouble. Its problems do not lie with management as a whole. Excellent recruitment and top-class career development have created leadership potential at all levels. But in autumn 1997, when a representative cross-section of managers attending an in-house course was asked if they could describe the company's strategy, not a hand went up.

Southwick's Fifth Commandment helps to define the need. When a company opts for teamwork it means that senior management 'acts much like a venture capital investor, assessing the merits of relative projects, assigning values, selecting the teams (or at least the team leader), and giving them budgets and deadlines'. This not only achieves invaluable flexibility: its greatest merit is that it devolves leadership and focuses the organisation's effort through groups addressing specific needs.

Removing top management from an operational role leaves them free to concentrate on overall strategy and long-term performance – in short, to invent the future. That means letting the visionaries explore new frontiers and find partners so that they can goad each other forwards to achieve extraordinary results. Success will in due course convince the pragmatists and eventually even the conservatives.

BOOK SIX

The Real Customer Focus

16

Finding the Target

Customer strategy is the only strategy. Product- and producer-driven strategies are dead though not altogether buried. Few businesses, even in retail, have reinvented themselves to achieve a truly customer-centric business system. Such a system starts with the customer, reworks all processes back from the customer, and aims them towards achieving excellence in the customer's eyes. One notable example is Dell Computer. A customer orders a PC over the Net and is told to allow four days for delivery. The computer will be configured to his precise wishes, but he recalls next day that he's forgotten to order the necessary feature for an ISDN telephone line. He rings up, and gets the same operator. No problem: the computer hasn't yet been loaded on to the factory. The PC arrives on the customer's doorstep, precisely as ordered, but in two days – not four.

Extremely sophisticated technology is required to delight customers so thoroughly. That technology is available to any other business. But to make the most of the hardware and software, any other business will have to manage itself differently. In his book, *Direct from Dell*, Michael Dell sets out the following recommendations:

- See the big picture.
- Run with the suggestions your customers provide.
- Always think of the bottom line, but not just your own.
- Go beyond selling, and make yourself valuable as an adviser too.
- Be a student. Learn as well as counsel.

Because a customer-centric system is geared to a close understanding of customers, it can give them what they want how, where and when they want it, and at a profitable price that they are happy to pay. All the rest of marketing won't make up for failures on these key strategic elements. Not only must the technology support the service, and the product support the promise, but quality must support the value proposition, and people policies must support the customer focus.

That is a key issue, underlined by the Sears research which shows that a 5 unit favourable change in employee attitude drives a 1.3 unit increase in customer impression, which drives 0.5 per cent increase in revenue growth. Such incremental improvement, however, is not enough. You can make real breakthroughs, like Dell, by the excellence of your systems, provided that they are truly focused on insights into what consumers 'want'. But what they 'want' is partly what *they* say, partly what *you* say. Most successful consumer businesses achieved their original breakthroughs by telling customers what they wanted before the customers knew themselves. Effective strategy leads the customers in new directions which they then come to desire, and go on desiring.

In IT, visionary scientists, engineers and managers first saw the technical possibilities of the PC or the World Wide Web and then brought them to the market. The great low-tech brands, from Gillette to Benetton, likewise sprang from entrepreneurs who gave no thought to 'gaps in the market', but rather created a new market where none had existed.

Listening to the customers, hearing 'what they say' is still vital, just as Michael Dell says. Their perceptions are the essential guide to setting and meeting quality standards and achieving excellent customer retention. Use unstructured, anonymous interviews and you establish the 'perception gap' between what top managements believe to be true, and what their 'constituents' actually think (customers, employees, managers, suppliers, opinion formers). The perception gap is always great – far too great for any kind of comfort.

Customer perceptions are fundamental. According to a Xerox survey those customers who rate your service 'excellent' are six times more likely to buy from you again than those who consider it just 'good' or who are just 'satisfied'. Those are Xerox figures, but AT&T research is just as cogent. If the customers think your service is excellent, all but 10 per cent of your market share is secure – without any need for promotion. A 'good' rating, however, sees 40 per cent of the customer share depart.

Dying in the Past

Once you have listened to what your customers say, several planks of your customer strategy fall into place. But you will not expand market share without getting what *you* say right. How do you work out where to lead the customer? To know the future, you must understand the present. The bigger the perception gap, the less you know about the present (and still less the future). The usual course of extrapolating the past is not an answer. Managers who live in the past will die there.

Certain aspects of the future are ineluctably inherent in the present. Demography is a clear example. All the people who will be twenty-one in 2020 are already alive. The low birth rates of the present mean falling populations in the new millennium. According to statistics assembled by Paul Wallace for his book *Agequake*, 'populations in Europe are poised to plunge on a scale not seen in the Black Death in 1348'. Moreover, 'for the first time in human history, the old will outnumber the young'. The predictions which Wallace derives from these demographics likewise need no crystal balls. Many of the 'predictions' are already present and proved; pharmaceutical and biotechnology industries are growing fast, small businesses are flourishing as never before, private pension funds are expanding rapidly, and so is the leisure industry, etc.

The leisure boom is a powerful factor in the phenomenal expansion of traffic on the Internet. The latter is becoming a prime medium for entertainment of all kinds, opening up a gargantuan market whose potential has barely been tapped. Video shops, music stores, TV channels, video games, cinemas, magazines, and so on are all in the line of fire. In addition, cyberspace is creating new entertainment media all its own, such as chat sites. Since available leisure hours are limited, every participant in the new media represents a loss to the old.

The Net also offers suppliers new ways of cracking what in many industries and nearly all services is the biggest strategic problem: differentiation of your company and its products from others. The customer cannot differentiate for you. Yet what can management do when virtually all the key elements in the value proposition are the same? This is as much a problem for supermarkets as for banks. However, there is a potential solution: you can achieve lasting marvels by internal differentiation, radically reforming internal processes as Dell has done.

Competitors either won't follow internal differentiation, or will follow late, probably providing further proof of the law that says 'they never catch up'. Even so, you still need an external Unique Selling Proposition (USP) to consolidate your market position. The internal, Web-based abilities of a Dell or an Amazon.com in books can become an external USP, a reason for the customer to buy from you and nobody else. There is only one winning choice: to be different and better.

Being better at the same thing is not enough. IBM's followers in mainframes often made better machines at better prices. It helped not at all. Being similar on all counts also leads nowhere, while being worse is plainly hopeless. Most companies have failed to establish any degree of real differentiation. When the Royal Society of Arts team was conducting the study that led to the 'Tomorrow's Company' report, it found that few of the chief executives it visited could name anything that made their companies distinctive. Most customer strategies are 'me too'.

All industries tend to move in step in the same direction. Look at the banks, for example. They merge, they downsize, they make the same bad loans, they sell the same kind of insurance, they sell the same kind of investments, they advertise in much the same way, they sell much the same mortgages, they close branches, they proliferate 'products'. But what does any bank do for the customer that differs from its competitors' provision?

Why Contrarians Win

It is blindingly obvious that only contrarians, people who go against the crowd, can hope to achieve successful differentiation. They can also gain a lead-time that lasts for years, if not for ever, thanks to competitors who refuse to believe that contrarian strategies will work – or even are working. This is a powerful reason for the earliest possible entry into the world of cyberspace marketing. Not only may IP technology provide instant differentiation, but it also offers the prospect of lasting competitive advantage, if you exploit the constant innovation and extension that Web technology encourages.

Me-too companies cannot escape the need for differentiation by heavy brand advertising. Branding minus differentiation equals nothing. Retail branding, demonstrates the point: the business is the brand – even if it sells no own-brand products. The retail 'brand' embodies the total perception of all the company's audiences. But just as the product must support the promise, so the business must support the brand: otherwise, decline can be sudden and sharp. Analysis will spotlight the defects, and IP technology can cure them. The following quotes are from investigations by the Strategic Retail Identity consultancy into supermarket chains. After each one, we suggest the solution that IP technology might offer:

- *'They are understaffed. Always so busy. Everybody gets irate. You have to wait for ages'* – shopper
  Better information, checkout and pricing systems will speed shopping and free staff to look after customers.
- *'Senior management doesn't speak to the staff. We're invisible'* – branch employee
  An intranet with internal Web pages can provide updated information and facilitate an interactive response from staff.
- *'They could save themselves a fortune if they used us properly'* – supplier
  Extranets can effectively unite supplier and customer, making possible collaboration all the way from initial design to delivery.

- *'The head office is completely hierarchical. We should push responsibility down the line'* – head office manager

  The intranet gives head office clear contact with all units, whose managers can easily access the information they need to accept their delegated responsibility in a flattened management structure.

The effective strategic response to the perception gap is simply stated. Be first. Be fast. Be fanatical. Big no longer automatically means best when on the Net. The small, fanatical, fast pioneer can defeat the largest incumbent in almost any market. But fanaticism demands the exercise of self-challenge. If you don't challenge your own customer strategy, then a new competitor will. So never stop looking critically at your business, and changing it – radically if need be. Stability is far less important when customers are volatile. If you don't stay with your customers, they will not stay with you.

Too many companies have yet to adopt this new mindset. They still treat the customers' needs as secondary to their own. The conventional suppliers want to supply customers on their own terms. In conventional hands, the approach is obviously wrong. Paradoxically, however, that degree of customer control is what results from a successful, innovative, customer-leading, truly customer-centric strategy. The wants of customer and supplier become identical. The secret lies in the power and speed with which you generate and apply new ideas to overjoy your clientele.

The new rules mean that you simply haven't got time to take your time. Traditional internal processes, deliberate, thorough and slow, are too deliberate and too slow. If you really are customer-centric, you must be geared to rapid change and to experiment. The revolutionary company constantly tries new approaches, developing those that work, and discarding those that do not – a simple strategy, but highly effective.

Fanatics look continually for evidence that they are not selling the right things, nor supplying them in the most effective way. They seek ways of becoming the lowest-cost producer, while being fully aware that they must match or beat their best competitor not on price alone, but on every aspect that matters to the customer. They constantly open up wider markets, geographically and in applications of their products and/or services. They refocus as necessary to retain the edge that makes customers buy from them rather than from the competition. Above all, they revise and reform their strategies and tactics to ensure that they remain highly effective in the years ahead.

Customised Service

Once again Dell serves as an example. *Business Week* recently reported on its new customer-service plan: to use the Internet to automate and customise service, in much the same way that Dell streamlined and customised PC production. Dell plans to give non-corporate customers personalised Web pages, which will result in 'communications links over speedy private networks and the vast Internet'. The company then hopes to be able to answer tricky service questions from customers 'with the lightning speed only the Net can deliver'. By building on the individual file that every customer already has, Dell intends to deliver 'a new kind of direct-service model', in which company and customer are in continuous contact.

Cyberspace in such ways opens up whole new vistas of innovation which nobody can afford to ignore. But such opportunities are more likely to be seized by newcomers than by large established companies. Is this inevitable? It is if managements shy away from cannibalisation, putting the demands of established business ahead of the new and placing present profit ahead of future pay-offs. Being good, even very good, at serving the customers you already have is not enough. Eventually your existing customers will desert, if you are not also satisfying the new.

Recent history is full of disrupted industries, where established companies faced by new, disruptive competition have not just lost out, but disappeared completely. It happened in disk drives and mainframe computers, steel-making and earth-moving equipment. By and large, it has not happened in the front line of the new IT. Although companies like Compaq, Microsoft and

Netscape have had nasty wobbles (the latter's caused by Microsoft, just as Microsoft's were caused by Netscape), they have shown a remarkable capacity to right themselves.

They have applied the power of what we call zero-based strategy. Zero-based budgeting starts from the assumption that the company doesn't need the activity under scrutiny. Zero-based strategy starts from the assumption that nobody needs you or your business. The question is this: if you were a wholly new entrant in the sector, what would you do to win and retain customers? In effect, what would you do to beat yourself? That is a revolutionary mindset. But it is also the way to win.

17

Informating the Relationship

Companies have tried to focus on customers all through the 1990s, often with little idea of what focus demands or even what customers want. The IT revolution makes it far easier for everyone to understand those wants; to create customer loyalty through continuous feedback; and to achieve the elusive 'customer focus'. IT has come to the fore in boardroom after boardroom as, consciously or not, top managements have reacted to fundamental, far-reaching change in their markets.

Reacting is one thing, acting another. Only a few companies are taking the decisive actions that change demands, and it is these companies that will win in the Customer Age. Managerial mindsets are still heavily conditioned by the Service Age, which saw the previous production orientation give way to marketing. Now, while companies are still struggling to achieve service excellence, customer power is rapidly moving into the driver's seat. Customer focus is not a new buzz-phrase, but a practical and inevitable transition.

To focus on the customer means to orient all business processes to customer wants. The driving force of the company becomes meeting these to the fullest possible extent in the most effective possible way. But what do 'fullest possible' and 'most effective possible' mean? Information technology enables companies to answer these questions with an unprecedented precision.

In the Industrial Age, and to a great extent the Service Age, the focus lay on internal processes. Customers came second to the wants of those inside the company. Boards were content to leave the choice and supervision of processes to operating management. That option is disappearing. If the company's focus is genuinely shifting to the customer, top management must change its own focus. The 'what' and 'why' of corporate strategy have become inseparable from the 'how' of execution.

Redirected focus at the top has profound consequences for the company as a whole and for information systems management in particular. The primary corporate task is to ensure that all functions (sales, marketing, manufacturing, service, even finance) and all line managements shift their focus from internal to external – that is, from the needs of the company to those of the customer. Information technology is an intimate part of this process.

Leading-edge companies are using IT not only for future benefit, but also to achieve a sharper customer focus *now*. A proactive use of information resources provides management, from the board downwards, with the ability to make better decisions and build operational superiority into the system by:

- Obtaining detailed knowledge and understanding of their customer base.
- Manipulating the data to divide the customer base into meaningful segments.
- 'Informating', using IT to automate processes, to achieve the effect of intimate customer relationships by remote means.
- Using information to provide customised products and services at prices that customers will happily pay.

None of these four critical missions is IT-driven. Rather, top managements use IT to support the strategic ambitions of the Customer Age. Some new developments are state-of-the-art, such as smart cards. In many other applications, leaders are using IT to make easier what successful firms have always done: for example, exploiting the fact that a few customers contribute most of the turnover.

IT is the key to understanding customers better, and adjusting service to meet their wishes. But it requires a sophisticated use of data acquisition and analysis. This seems to be beyond many firms. They may be able to make a sophisticated analysis of sales and financial performance by market and product, but be unable to do the same analysis by customer.

In conducting such an analysis there are two basic questions. 1. How much does each customer contribute to turnover? 2. How much does each customer contribute to profit? The analysis may not produce the classic Pareto split: 20 per cent contributing 80 per cent. In fact, Jan Curry of consultancy MSP Associates found one white goods maker that derived 70 per cent of sales from 0.3 per cent of customers. The results of analysing profit are even more startling: Curry finds that '20 per cent of customers often generate 150 per cent of the profit!'

The IT Management Programme's (from which this chapter has drawn substantially) has confirmed this finding. To their astonishment, researchers found many top businesses 'do not know how many customers they have, let alone calculate the value of individual customers'. Perhaps they are swamped with incompatible customer data (a common dilemma in financial services companies, which cannot link information about, say, mortgage holders with that on savers); or they lack useful 'identifiers' of their customers (like most retailers). Either way, the result is loss of opportunity and profit.

Loss-making Customers

Suitable analysis will accurately reveal sales by customer or customer groups, and although it is harder to estimate costs accurately, an intelligent approximation will highlight those customers who, *prima facie*, are making a loss. Do you drop them, put up with them, or seek to move their account into profit? Termination is sometimes the right option, however disagreeable. A plastics moulding firm, Nypro, reduced its customers from hundreds to just thirty, each contributing at least $1 million to annual sales. Turnover trebled after the cutback, and profits soared. The terminations enabled Nypro to concentrate on providing its remaining customers with superlative service.

The issue isn't only current profitability. Dropping customers can be counter-productive if they contribute anything at all to overheads, or if, having been dropped, they go on to make money for a rival. Identifying future customer profitability is an underused approach of great value. Many techniques for charting the gap between current and potential profits and then closing it, are available for managements that have the necessary will.

Changing the balance of costs and revenues is another winning strategy: leading companies focus on optimising the return from their most profitable customers, while gaining bigger bangs per buck from the unprofitable. Savings on sales and service are the key: low-cost sales channels and call centres are powerful, IT-enabled tools for bettering the economics of the business.

Although analysing customer profitability offers rich pay-offs, it doesn't go far enough. Sharper customer focus means abandoning the mass-market mindset and segmenting customers according to how they actually behave. The whole business can be restructured round the identified segments. In one case, segmentation studies had to be undertaken by the retail department because the IT function focused on financial and operational issues and was unresponsive to marketing needs.

The benefits of identifying meaningful segments, and thus increasing marketing and sales effectiveness, are so great that few sizeable businesses dare ignore segmentation. It should be a key dimension of strategies and planning. Modelling customer behaviour through a variety of techniques will define segments, microsegments and individual targets. Moreover, the cost of such analysis is falling with the rapid advances in IT.

Direct mail and telesales have long been ideal tools with which to identify and reach more precise market segments, but the advent of the Internet has added enormous new capability. And these techniques of differentiated marketing become even more effective when they have truly differentiated products or services to promote. With the aid of new IT, systems product, position in the market, place of sale and price (the famous '4Ps') can be quickly varied to satisfy different segments.

The object is to answer the key question: 'Why should this customer buy from me and not from somebody else?' In the process of finding the answer, intimate customer relations are in effect being achieved by remote methods: not only by call centres, but, even more, by the Internet and other interactive electronic media, such as multimedia kiosks. At these new levels of sophistication, customer and supplier can achieve a dialogue going beyond the dreams of yesterday's managers – and many of today's.

Tailoring a business to the customers' needs has always been the foundation of great commercial success, but most companies lost sight of this principle as their customer bases swelled. Now thanks to IP technology, they can combine mass-marketing with the more individual treatment that today's customers increasingly expect, while suppliers themselves, eager for differentiation, seek to treat mass customers individually.

Impersonal Relationships

Obviously, in a mass market, this can't be achieved through personal relationships, but IT's provision of impersonal contact can be highly effective. Most people have used call centres by now, so managers know from experience that the centres are an excellent remote means of improving customer relationships. What customers may lose through such impersonal service they more than regain in 24-hour availability, as well as better and more consistent information.

Are impersonal relationships enough? Or are personal ones obligatory? Is the customer so large and profitable that intimate relationships become essential? IT can enhance even those relationships that still require personal or intimate contact. The technology makes feasible and economic the otherwise impossible: like enabling customer and supplier to work in harness to create shared success.

Airborne Express is a case in point. It provides customised express air services for business customers worldwide. For large-volume customers, Airborne developed bespoke systems. When Technicolor challenged a long-standing monopoly in Hollywood film distribution, Airborne and its subsidiary, Advanced Logistics

Services, worked with Technicolor on a new system using two warehouses, an easy-return airbill system and electronic links to customers. Development teams in each company worked together constantly to get the service operational. Its share rose to 40 per cent of the market.

Mass customisation, another way to strengthen the customer relationship, is set to become the norm in many sectors. The idea of customised sales tactics is to choose via a 'sales tactics system', the sales approach most likely to work for each individual customer or prospective customer. A potent example is 'event-oriented prospecting' or EOP: a US financial services company has identified nine 'life events' (out of a total of 29) that give it selling opportunities – for instance a birth in the family.

In such ways, customisation can satisfy unique customer needs at costs which need no longer be prohibitive. IT is lowering the premium for mass customisation. Not surprisingly, the lower the premium charged for a customised product or service, the greater the proportion of buyers who choose the customised product or service. IT systems have already proved their ability to:

- Reduce the costs of customised manufacture.
- Reduce the costs of special operations.
- Allow customers to customise the service or the product for themselves.
- Use feedback to improve the match between service and customer.

Motorola, as an example, found it could afford to make one-off pagers: customers were able to choose from a million-plus combinations of features. A tailored personal pair of Levi's jeans, costing only $15 extra, had obvious attractions for customers. Bank of Scotland's Personal Choice mortgage allowed borrowers to vary payments – and write cheques on the mortgage account. There's a personalised US newspaper that adjusts content to the individual subscriber's expressed preference. Websites offer similar customisation possibilities.

Customising the Product

Customisation can occur by assembly, integration or design – each with different implications for IT, on a rising scale of sophistication. Customisation by assembly involves a combination of predetermined elements that don't interact, as when you buy composite home and car insurance from Norwich Union. Customisation by integration is where alternative components and features must work together, as in the case of a PC. Customisation by design occurs when the product is uniquely tailored to the individual customer – like Levi Strauss's jeans.

Managements dare not take it for granted that the changes necessary to turn potential gains into real wins are being made. Customer focus has deep implications for corporate strategy in general, and IT strategy in particular, and must be led from the top. Focused chief executives spend time with customers large and small, commission qualitative as well as quantitative studies of customer response, and ensure that customer issues are always on the agendas of the board and the executive committee.

Once the passive focus of operations, the customer is becoming an active participant across the board. That presents a growing challenge to traditional ways of doing business. Mobilising all resources, including IT, behind true focus on the customer is the only way to meet the challenge proactively as customers stake out the new ground:

- Large businesses will expect to have intimate relationships with major suppliers who attend to their every whim.
- Smaller businesses will demand customised services at mass-market prices.
- Other businesses and consumers will call the tune by using agents – people, other businesses or computer software – to handle their procurement.

The consequences for management are clear. In an age when highly competitive markets are the norm, businesses must go beyond customer satisfaction to surpass expectations. That won't be done with yesterday's information. The future will depend still more on new means of collecting, analysing and exploiting data. They are the foundation of the strategies and tactical operations, employing the full powers of IT, that are making customer focus a winning reality.

18

Customising the Service

The concept of the all-powerful customer is nothing new. Peter Drucker wrote long ago that 'there is only one valid definition of business purpose – to create a customer'. Having created customers, the next step is to satisfy them. 'Customer satisfaction' has become the great watchword of business, largely because of acute external pressures.

One such pressure has been over-supply. Historically, this was created by over-expansion in boom periods and the slumps that followed rectified the situation. But with the globalisation of markets, over-supply has become a constant fact of business life. When everything from micro-circuits to motor cars can come from anywhere, efforts to control that supply are futile. The sensational, 85 per cent collapse in memory chip prices in 1998 clearly illustrated this problem.

A contributory cause is the revolution in manufacturing processes. Old plant, using new methods, becomes far more productive. Moreover, new technologies, including those of production management, allow smaller producers to compete, often with brilliant innovations that reinforce another important factor: segmentation. Innovators have helped to fragment markets into multiple segments. So the economies of massive scale of established companies have ceased to be reliable barriers of entry to newcomers. The new entrants not only add to supply, but intensify competition as they seek customers.

The competitive heat has also been turned up by deregulation. Financial services epitomise the customer revolution. Where once a few oligopolies limited choice, now deregulated banks compete with mortgage lenders, mortgage lenders with banks, both with insurance companies – and all are under attack by supermarkets, chain stores, branded entrepreneurs, etc. 'Product' variants have multiplied as, once again, over-supply (this time of money) stimulates proliferating competition.

The customer is no passive bystander in all this. Across the world, customers have become more demanding, more capricious, more promiscuous, more volatile. In part, this reflects the rise in disposable incomes fuelled by economic growth. Customers are also responding with a will to the increase in the quantity, sources and variety of supply. Think only of the welter of offerings in consumer electronics. Customers demand choice, and their pressure on producers stimulates variety.

The pressures are also socio-economic. Rising affluence and education have bred a race of highly active consumers. Ralph Nader, with his whistle-blowing on the manufacturing failures of Detroit car-makers, was seen as a disruptive radical. But consumerism has since become politically powerful, defended even by right-wing politicians who espouse free market capitalism. Consequently public services, too, have had to become user-friendly, to talk the language of consumer goods and to 'compete' for public income.

This new supremacy of the customer emerges as a dominant theme, whether in academic tomes, business magazines, company reports or guru lectures. Managements increasingly pre-occupy themselves with 'customer focus' exercises, tracing 'value chains' back from the satisfied customer through the various corporate processes. These are then redesigned and refocused to meet the customers' perceived needs, and outdo the competition on every factor that the purchasers hold dear – in theory.

In practice, the production-led mentality that dominated industry post-war more than lingers on. Given half a chance, manufacturers and service businesses alike will do what suits their managements best. Service provides an acid test. It has emerged as the key differentiator: sooner or later, products lose any superiority in specification, quality, or production methods.

Quality of service is much harder to imitate, but also much harder to achieve.

Companies don't, however, try hard enough on this vital count. That statement may sound strange, given the fortunes spent on tracking customer satisfaction, and the high proportions (usually two-thirds and upwards) of customers who find service 'very satisfactory' or 'satisfactory'. But the usual numbers are meaningless. How many of the 'very satisfied' or 'satisfied' customers are likely to patronise the company again?

How Service Quality Pays

The 'buy again' numbers are crucial, since it costs far less to retain old customers than to attract new. That partly explains the clear correlation between higher quality and superior financial results. As Sweden's Customer Satisfaction Barometer shows: 'Companies capable of increasing [on the CSB] by one point every year for five years improved the average return on assets during the period by 11.33 per cent.'

Since giving the customers what they want is clearly the secret of success, why do most companies pay 'customer focus' lip-service rather than real service? The reason is that customer satisfaction isn't a separate stage in the value chain. It reaches deep into the heart of the corporation, and any weakness within that core will damage the final outcome. How do companies with genuine achievements in delighting customers manage to do it?

The answer is that they really do 'manage to do it'. An American expert, travel management entrepreneur Hal Rosenbluth, in his book *The Customer Comes Second*, expressed the paradox that to put the customer first, you must put employees first. Discontented employees won't generate contented customers. This common sense has been vindicated by statistical research: as noted earlier, American retailer Sears found that employee and customer attitudes truly are umbilically linked.

The better customer and employee felt about the company, moreover, the better the financial returns. Sears found that employees want to feel good about the company's future, know that necessary changes are being made, understand the business strategy and believe that their work is helping the company towards its objectives. Very few managements meet these four basic demands, which require a near-reversal of the traditional top-down, autocratic style. It's hardly surprising that most managements therefore lag in customer satisfaction which, anyway, isn't their top priority.

Consultants Bain & Co, together with the Institute of Management, looked at the top ten management tools used in 1992–6 in Germany, Japan, the US and the UK. Compared to the previous five years, 'customer satisfaction measurement' had actually dropped one place across the four countries, to fourth. Ahead were strategic planning, mission statements and benchmarking. Only the Germans and Japanese included customer retention, and no list included any people policies other than pay for performance.

It could be argued that other tools and techniques, like strategic planning, mission statements and bench-marking, include awareness of customer needs; and that Total Quality Management (sixth in the list) is essentially a means of aligning individual, company and customer aims.

But TQM is used by only a minority of companies. And it's singularly pointless to form customer-based strategies, write mission statements to match, and compare customer responses against those experienced by other firms without having the means or the will to turn words into deeds.

The means, however, are becoming more powerful than ever, thanks to the digital revolution. The World Wide Web already has examples: around the clock customers can order books for next day delivery, buy personal computers configured to their choosing, have technical problems resolved at any hour of the day or night, conduct financial transactions round the world – all at the click of a mouse.

As *Fortune* magazine says, 'Mass customisation is going to forever change how products are made and services are delivered.' The Web may be the most potent, but it isn't the only electronic means of revolutionising customer relationships. Buyers of industrial components, sharing computer links with suppliers, can specify requirements and changes while the work is in progress. Customers can order home delivery of items (from Barbie dolls to vitamins) tailored to their individual requirements.

The danger is that customers may want less choice than they get. Using their new technological prowess, many companies have been over-producing new models and reducing product life-cycles (with PCs as example) to only a few months. Such embarrassment of choice can cause sales resistance. Researchers at Harvard Business School have already found opposition to excessive 'relationship marketing', another form of mass customisation. Companies want to treat mass consumers as individuals and to create loyalty by exploiting information about their profiles and tastes. That's fine. But how?

Harvard's Susan Fournier is plainly right: 'A relationship is not getting a newsletter, responding to a questionnaire or holding a frequent buyer card. It has to do with product quality, consistency, image.' Add service quality, and you have the perfect mix for the age of consumer power. That era is not about to end. Rather, customer sovereignty will wax still stronger. As each market coalesces, a few firms will dominate. But the forces behind consumer power make it impossible to prevent alternative and credible competitors from emerging.

Leading Responsiveness

Their success rests on sensing and leading customer responses. The extraordinary responsiveness of modern customers, in turn, is their guarantee of continued power. That responsiveness is often stigmatised as promiscuity or fickleness, but the customer's right to change his or her mind is paramount. The exercise of this right has been enormously strengthened by the Internet, which has multiplied channels, expanded customer information and widened the purchasing reach across the chartless oceans of cyberspace.

Front-line suppliers are by no means the only firms under threat. Pity the poor (or rich) middlemen. The nature of their business has changed, to their disadvantage. The Internet has already become everybody's go-between, from mighty corporates to schoolkids. The commercial go-betweens who want to survive and prosper must reinvent their businesses. E-commerce will damage other middlemen as it is already undermining travel agents, who stand to lose $7.4 billion of air ticket sales in 2001.

Even before the World Wide Web, resellers were being squeezed, as more retailers linked directly to suppliers and more suppliers went straight to customers. Paradoxically, though, the Web offers a potential escape from the squeeze. Wholesale markets can be recreated or invented electronically with unprecedented ease and breadth of coverage. In the US, successful Web wholesalers now deal in surplus electronic parts, used cars, software, and a myriad other goods and services. Few middlemen will flourish without some involvement on the Web.

But the exchange economy (see chapter 24) threatens to be a low-margin commodity business, in which the first and largest sites will make life extremely difficult, if not impossible, for the competition. Suppliers will join the battle. Nothing can stop them from putting their catalogues online, or becoming intermediaries themselves. Johnson's Wax, for example, stocks Wal-Mart's shelves, not only with its own products, but other brands. Both suppliers and distributors will be jockeying to capture more of the profit chain, and they will not stop at the traditional boundaries.

That must involve stealing customers from the traditional retailers. Retail cyberstores, says *Business Week*, are already booming by exploiting ultraconvenience (24-hour, 7-day operation, unlimited shelf space), customer clubs and low, low prices. Wholesalers must do the same to defend their existing sales: creating the necessary Web structure immediately unleashes new retail opportunities. There's no sense in a distributor allowing others to invade his market without retaliating – or retailing – in kind.

Many middlemen will seek – and need – to preserve their status by excellent personal service which genuinely adds significant value. Corporate PC customers will go direct to a website unless the resellers who are currently enjoying their business act as consultants, taking full responsibility for meeting the whole customer requirement. This breed of middlemen will rely on expertise and efficiency to keep their markets, and on websites to widen them.

Tomorrow's successful middlemen will be super-convenient, super-stocked, customer-focused, price-competitive, highly expert in their lines and rapidly responsive to customer command in both cyberspace and on earth. The same recipe applies to the retailer, whose place in the supply chain is just as threatened as that of the middleman. Increasingly the boundaries between the traditional roles in that chain are getting blurred – both in business-to-business markets, and consumer markets.

Outsourcing to the Customer

In their book, *Unleashing the Killer App*, Larry Downes and Chunka Mui describe how to 'outsource to the customer'. The functions of data collection and customer service 'can now be outsourced, not to other firms, but directly to the customer. Customers take on these tasks willingly, extracting value of their own by doing them.' The authors give the example of Holiday Inns, whose global reservation system is now on the Web. The customer finds the right hotel, checks availability, 'tours' the hotel virtually and makes the reservation: letting the customer tap into the system, moreover, isn't costly:

> For a small investment, you can have the customer perform many of the expensive activities you do today, including basic customer service, order entry and tracking, training, purchase order management, product configuration and even product development. The data you collect has far fewer errors, because it has been handled only once, and then by the originating source.

The secret of this outsourcing is that the customer benefits, too. It's a win-win outcome. Both sides make savings on money and time, and enjoy gains in convenience and accuracy. The customer base becomes what it should always have been – a marketing tool of great power. The Net entraps customer information in readily available and usable form, as customers willingly give information that most organisations would kill (or even worse, pay) to get their hands on.

Downes and Mui cite Travelocity. In return for all your data about travel needs and preferences, this business will give you a choice of itineraries, providing the best price and the most convenient schedule. That's one of the reasons why conventional travel agents have been losing business at so startling a rate – with the air ticket volume carried by the Net rising by 10,000 per cent in a single year. Familiar office processes cannot compete with networks whose marginal costs are next to nothing.

Examples of customer-oriented business transformation are burgeoning even faster than Internet access itself. According to Intellact, the number of residential connections worldwide, 70.3 million in 1999, will double by 2003. The number of corporate Internet users, 53.4 million in 1999, will treble over the same period. As business-to-business traffic expands exponentially, so customer-to-business transactions will mushroom in its wake. More power to the customer means more strength to the business which succeeds in harnessing that customer power.

BOOK SEVEN

Mastering the Market

19

Changing the Rules

The revolutionary company aims to own its market not by sheer muscle or unbeatable technology, but by control of the business system within which it operates. This requires the company constantly to change the rules of the game, forcing its competitors to react to its initiatives instead of being forced to follow theirs. As difficult as this may sound, it is, of course, the way most truly successful businesses have developed in the past. As their industries coalesce, though, so these path-finders become part of the establishment, and vulnerable themselves to the disrupters.

The Information Revolution has made the disruptive game easier to play by undermining existing patterns of distribution, widening the circle of potential contestants, and narrowing the gap between sitting tenant and attacker. The old business system relied on a series of stages, involving middlemen of many varieties, held together by pieces of paper. The paper transactions took far longer than the movement of goods through the system. Out of a total cycle time of nineteen weeks, non-manufacturing activity typically took eleven.

That's half the life-cycle of a new model of PC. That explains why their manufacturers, who can't afford the waste of time, have been in the forefront of using technology to eliminate paperwork, cut out middlemen and to minimise both transit and time spent in the factory. Competitors who change the rules in this way are very difficult to dislodge, because they are updating their systems to new pitches of efficiency when most of their opponents are installing the new IT for the first time.

Changing the rules accounts for much of the upheaval in the Internet market. This strategy had its most extraordinary manifestation in the rise of Netscape. When the infant company gave away its browser for nothing, it sounded like commercial suicide to conventional ears. But revenue was far less important than rapidly achieving a viable customer base so large that no competitor save one, even by using free distribution, could hope to take more than the crumbs from Netscape's table.

But that one exception was huge: Microsoft. Perhaps no other company has better exemplified the strategy of changing the rules to stay ahead of competitors. Microsoft's exploitation of its dominance in PC operating systems has been ruthless: first, it ensured that MS/DOS was vastly cheaper than other operating systems; second, it built other software on to the MS/DOS base; and third, after turning Windows into a new industry standard, it bundled its software into the Windows operating suite. Other suppliers were competing with at least one hand tied behind their backs – until Netscape.

Then Netscape changed the rules to put Microsoft on the rack. Through Netscape's browser, users could gain access to software over the Internet, much of it free; they would thus have no need of Bill Gates or any of his works. Microsoft's counter-attack was based on the same strategy that had worked so wondrously in the past. If its own browser, Explorer 3.0, was bundled into Windows, Netscape would automatically and rapidly be shut out of the market it had created. That would remove the colossal threat to Microsoft presented by the upstart.

But Microsoft pushed its retaliation so far that a highly embarrassing antitrust suit followed. Microsoft was reacting like the incumbent it has become, with a massive market share, huge assets to protect and too broad a range of territory to protect itself against all raiders. It has been forced to confront a truth pronounced by Gary Hamel, co-author of *Competing for the Future*: 'Never has incumbency been worth less.'

Hamel points to the savage attrition of the banks, if you measure their market by share of financial assets, which, in the

US, is dropping towards half. Time is running out on the banks. They cannot afford to follow the US car industry, which, Hamel says, 'every year for 40 years has missed every paradigm shift'. 'Paradigm shift' or what Andy Grove, chairman of Intel, calls a 'strategic inflection point', are just two more phrases to indicate a change of the rules. This happens, says Grove, when '10× forces', ten times more powerful than the normal forces in business economics, hit an industry.

The 10× Forces

Some of these 10× forces, like the superseding of the transatlantic liner, are the result of technology: the railways and the talking picture are other examples. Intel has faced three sets of 10× forces in its history: the large-scale integrated circuit, which it exploited brilliantly; the microprocessor, which it invented but whose potential it was slow to recognise; and the Japanese challenge in memory chips, which forced Intel to leave the business altogether.

Intel is trying not to make the same mistake with the Internet. Writing in *World Link* magazine, Grove called the Internet a strategic inflection point, 'a commercial and broad-based communications vehicle' that was the 'biggest technological change in the past decade'. If anything, this is an understatement. In his book *Inside Intel*, Tim Jackson questions whether the company has reacted as rapidly and strongly as it should: 'Intel would look very different in a networked world in which individual users had less computing horsepower and fewer bloated software packages on their desks, relying instead on smaller, simpler and faster pieces of software downloaded across the Internet as needed.'

The threat will not be wished away. As Grove himself has commented, such changes are unstoppable: whatever can be done will be done. Like it or not, the rules will be changed, 'if not by the incumbents, it will be done by emerging players. If not in a regulated industry, it will be done in a new industry born without regulation.' This is what happened with satellite

TV in Europe. By going extra-terrestrial, and loading his channels with highly prized sports events, the unregulated Rupert
Murdoch changed the rules, with severe effect on the revenues
of land-based, regulated broadcasters.

Grove comments of the computer industry that the Internet
has brought 'fundamental change in its structure, distribution
systems and pricing models'. What has happened in computers
is also having a heavy effect on communications:

> These changes may not occur overnight on a worldwide
> basis, but the evidence of change is everywhere. From free
> Internet calls in the US to government-sanctioned Internet
> connections in China, a global network is emerging. More
> people than ever are connecting to information and e-mail
> through computers. Those countries, businesses and indus-
> tries that embrace this new method of communication will
> emerge with a stronger competitive position than those that
> hoped it would go away.

If the strategy of changing the rules starts by accepting that
technological change won't go away – and on this Grove is
plainly right – the next step is to understand the change
thoroughly and look for what it enables.

Nine Key Conditions

The existing rules can be challenged successfully under nine key
conditions:

1 The practices and products of an industry have not been
  changed for a long time, and all players use the same methods
  to create similar products and services (mainframe computing
  before the PC era).
2 There is a latent need for functionality that doesn't exist at
  present (instant cameras or personal computing).
3 What's on the market has plain drawbacks or deficiencies
  (having to use telephone kiosks instead of your own mobile).
4 There is a genuine gap in the market (laptop computers).

5 Existing products or services can be used to drive others (Microsoft's bundling of its other software with its operating system).
6 Technological breakthrough has occurred (e-mail as a faster, more convenient, cheaper alternative to fax).
7 A success in one geographical market has not been replicated elsewhere (importing cable TV from the US).
8 A cheaper way exists to satisfy market needs (IP telephony instead of land-based connections).
9 Changes have occurred in economic circumstances (the rising affluence that enables the masses to buy new gadgetry).

Because of its revolutionary impact, the Internet has seen an unprecedented outburst of disruptive, aggressive strategies exploiting these nine opportunities. Some of the companies involved have mutated at least once. *Business Week* gives the example of AllApartments, which began life by listing apartments for rent right across the US. After only two years, the site was still listing apartments, but was also offering furniture, moving trucks and loans. It wasn't charging for any of the services: but its three dozen 'business partners' were coughing up commissions to AllApartments, at $4 and upwards, for each customer hit.

You can earn Web money through commissions, like All-Apartments, or ads, or subscriptions, or transactions, or of course direct sales, which can be pursued with a new flexibility. A Malaysian company called Biztone.com sells enterprise software; its price varies according to how the software is used. Intuit makes money not only from sales of its financial software, but also from subscriptions, usage, advertising, transaction fees and mortgages: loan partners pay Intuit a fixed fee on mortgage business booked by its Internet customers, which reached $600 million last year.

'Free' is a magic word in the context of changing the rules. The only way you can compete with free is by paying the customer to take the product or service – which will no doubt, one day, be somebody's preferred strategy. But the free route is actually nothing new. Countless newspapers and magazines are distributed to their readership for nothing. The revenue stream comes from advertising.

Selling something for nothing is a contrarian idea. Being a contrarian is an excellent, simple way of changing the rules. If the established companies sell cars in basic form with loads of costly extras, bundle all the extras into one price. If competitors operate from expensive premises, sell from the Web, with no branches at all. If the competition is selling through wholesalers to retailers, go direct to the latter; if the competition is selling direct to retailers, then sell direct to the customer. Michael Dell has built a $130 billion company on the simple principle of cutting out the middlemen, wholesalers and distributors, on whom his competitors depended.

Information technology may play a critical role in changing the rules, but it is not specifically required. Take the magazine *Loot*, for example. Traditional classified ad papers charged the advertisers. *Loot* didn't: it sold the paper, but printed the ads free. That rapidly made it the largest, and therefore most purchased, source of small ads.

There are obvious parallels between *Loot* running free adverts and Netscape giving away its browsers. Win the market, and the revenue will follow. The aim is to achieve the dominant 'share of mind', to be the first name that comes into the customer's thoughts. Amazon.com has the dominant share of mind in book-selling. Dell has the same dominance in the direct-selling of PCs.

Traditionally, share of mind resulted from share of market. Now it is the other way round. The Internet is an incredibly economical way of winning mind-share: it is instantaneous, vivid, easily accessible, responsive. Its gossipy nature has given rise to what Gary Hamel and Jeff Sampler call 'word of mouse'. Web-users rapidly spread the word about valuable sites and the companies to which they belong. The word-of-mouse will not spread, you may be sure, to sites which tell clickers about the company's products, but don't – following the rules of the old game – provide a means of purchase.

You can never change the rules if you obey them. That is obvious. You begin by becoming disobedient, by valuing con-trarian ideas precisely for their contrariness. Phrases like 'It will never work' or 'That's been tried' or 'If it was any good, somebody would be doing it' are your battleground. Because most people will agree with this conventional unwisdom, disbelievers have a golden chance to be dynamically different, and to win.

Creating the New

Once you accept the imperative of dynamic difference, the necessary strategy becomes clear. You establish a unified idea (a 'vision', if you will) of the future, and you put in place a clear framework for realising that vision. Then you identify the key processes and radically reform them by applying new tools and techniques. That's the high road to the key aim: a 'killer app' company that directs its energies to the creation of new rules, new methods, new markets, new opportunities, new products and services, all with new efficiencies.

But most companies and most managers get stuck 'in the box', swallowing the conventions and obeying the rules of their organisation and industry. When the industry leader turns, they all turn, thus missing a marvellous opportunity. The situation has been well described by Michael Bloomberg, founder of the financial services upstart bearing his name: 'Whenever you see a business that's done the same thing for a long time, a new guy can come in and do it better. I guarantee it.'

Food retailing since the war is a perfect example. The new supermarkets elbowed aside the old retailers, large and small; the superstores then intensified this campaign; only a very few established businesses – above all, J. Sainsbury – jumped out of the box to share the stupendous spoils. But there's another box in which unwary giants can get stuck: staleness. They get locked in by their very success. The entire organisation, together with the careers of those inside, becomes geared to doing very well what they have always done – obeying their own rules.

New and dynamic thought does exist in food retailing, but not in packaged goods. The star thinkers today are brilliant at selling prepared food and drink. Café chains like Starbucks in the US, or Pret a Manger in the far smaller British market, have caught the mood of the millennium. Although the formats are carefully standardised, the 'stores' give the perception of difference and fun. Their success demonstrates that even in crowded markets, today's customers are as open as ever to a new 'total experience'. Achieving the perception that you are different changes the rules, and wins the game.

Paradoxically, the giants have the most to gain from differentiating the total experience, because their size gives far greater financial leverage. Marks & Spencer created a massive business 'outside the box' with smaller, central, food-mainly stores that flouted the conventional out-of-town, superstore wisdom. Yet breaking the rules never became absorbed into the corporate lifestyle: no further innovations followed.

Today's marketplace battles will hinge on who best behaves like a new guy coming in. Success will depend on developing the vital brand – the business itself – by finding new-guy, radical, rule-breaking ways of exploiting the established strengths. The odds are overwhelming that those who behave most like new guys will be the new guys themselves. The old guys thus face a tremendous challenge.

20

Envisioning Uncertainty

When markets are changing rapidly and unpredictably, strategies and tactics must be flexible. So revolutionary companies, within a broad visionary context, delegate strategic planning to business units which are able to adapt swiftly to shifting markets. Using IT, the centre controls without interfering. One of the key controls is planning itself.

President Eisenhower once famously observed that he had never found plans any use, but that planning was indispensable. These wise words are an essential guide to exploiting the Triple Revolution. The leading companies of that revolution (including Microsoft) still make business units construct three-year plans, even though they know that realisation of those plans, as written, would be a miracle.

The success of these companies depends upon a devolved strategy. Top management remains the guardian of that strategy, but it is no longer the sole dictator. Senior management may decide to engage fully in the Triple Revolution, to convert old businesses to online operation, to develop new ones, to bind the company into a whole, linked internally and externally by the latest technology. But a devolved strategy means that the decision is confirmed by discussion with those who must implement it.

The implementation is left in the hands of the business units, but the centre is kept fully informed of progress, and may need to give a push from time to time. The main strategic function of the centre is to close the gap between knowing what must be done and (the absolute necessity) actually doing it.

Company boards and executive committees have been among the main culprits – and victims – of the Unclosed Gap. For example, Western car manufacturers knew they needed to emulate Japanese methods to raise quality and speed up new model development. But for years nothing was done – most of the firms concerned still lag behind Toyota in significant respects. Complacency and inertia are natural but unacceptable concomitants of the cloistered nature of top executive life.

It's hard to evolve an intelligent Internet strategy if you have never used a PC. Nobody can blame a middle-aged director for ignorance of cyberspace technicalities and technologies. But ignorance of their business relevance is inexcusable, and, as the Internet becomes increasingly dominant, could well have fatal consequences. So far, the ignorant and the apathetic have been protected by the ignorance and apathy of their competitors. Sooner or later, however, someone breaks out of the pack, or breaks into it: and disaster must follow for the unwilling and the unready.

In theory, a typical board could revolutionise itself. You can teach old dogs new tricks, but getting them to teach themselves is another and more difficult canine strategy.

Soichiro Honda, the brilliant and eccentric strategist who, against all the odds, transferred his success from motor-cycles to cars, retired at only sixty-three. Even though his role had not been operational for a decade, Honda thought that his unfamiliarity with computers deterred him from carrying on. That act of abnegation took place long ago. The same shortcoming would rule out perhaps the majority of today's board-level managers.

Some very large companies may well have digital war-rooms, capable of displaying and manipulating the latest statistics and asking 'What if?' questions, etc. These can be mightily impressive. One chief executive spoke with awe of the whole company 'coming alive' before the eyes of the board when the chief technologist unveiled the war-room. we later learned how often it had been used: once. As it happens, this group's strategy has so far failed conspicuously, despite (or because of) some violent changes of direction. The more dominant the influence of the top stratum of an established company on the formulation and execution of strategy, the harder it is for that strategy to succeed. Even so plainly able a chief executive as John Sanders of Cisco cannot conceivably devise the strategy for every one of his hundreds of business units, and it would make no sense to try.

Monitoring the Strategy

With the aid of a 'digital nervous system', however, the CEO can find out what is happening on the strategy front – and on all others. That is in itself one of the key strategic issues. Can you monitor strategies and their outcomes whenever you want, wherever you want? The answer cannot be yes unless the nervous system is comprehensive, meaning that you can answer yes to twelve other critical questions:

1 Has e-mail become the major internal communications system?
2 Can you get sales data online?
3 Are PCs used for business analysis?
4 Does the network enable teams to work together across functions, departments and units?
5 Are you using the digital system to eliminate paper and bureaucracy?
6 Have you redesigned processes to eliminate single-task jobs and adopted multi-functional tasks?
7 Does the system monitor and improve quality and efficiency?
8 Do you have and use customer feedback in real time, online?
9 Are your customer relationships built into the system?
10 Do you communicate via the digital system with all suppliers and partners, sharing the aim of shortening cycle times and accelerating processes?
11 Have you eliminated the middleman, substituting direct, digital control of deliverables?
12 Have you automated customer processes so that, wherever possible, they are handled digitally?

The questions are adapted from Bill Gates's *Business @ the Speed of Thought*. They are not what are commonly thought of as strategic questions. It requires no understanding of the technology to see the advantages that getting the right answers must confer. It needs no remarkable business awareness to see that having the wrong answers greatly reduces the effectiveness of an organisation. Nor do you have to be a great strategic thinker to understand how the right answers underpin strategic efficiency.

This is the platform for zero-based strategy. You devolve the zero-based strategy to the business unit managers in the front line of implementation. Possessed with full information, they can place themselves in the position of a newcomer who's tackling your market without preconceptions, without fixed assets, without the hampering baggage of the past.

It has to be said that the example of a relatively small piece of strategy given by Gates shows that the system can result in centralised over-management. The issue was where to direct Microsoft's sales activities among small to medium-sized customers. It took two months to work out the answer with great precision, using the in-house data warehouse, the Internet and much work on PCs. The answer? The best strategy was to invest in new marketing programmes for cities where there were currently no Microsoft marketing activities at all.

To be brutally honest, that should have been obvious intuitively. A simple test of the proposition would have checked the viability of the intuition, and roll-out would have confirmed the conclusion. Great care is needed to ensure that the powers of the system are used economically, and that thought does not come to a halt while you grind out data. But Microsoft even had Steve Ballmer, the company's president, 'critiquing plans' for the above project 'by e-mail from Europe'. That is evidently the Gates way. It isn't the new way. In the new methodology, units work out their own strategic objectives in the light of the general strategic direction agreed by and with the top management.

The Threefold Strategy

Take a financial services business – Fuzzy Financial – which is losing old customers at a rate of 600,000 a year and gaining new ones at only 400,000 a year. The figures represent a substantial loss of profit. Not only does it cost more to recruit customers than to retain them, but the old departures have more profitable contracts than the new recruits.

In this situation, the strategic need is obvious and threefold. Stop the bleeding, increase the recruitment and raise the profitability. The business units within the organisation each develop their own strategy to achieve the threefold target.

If they cannot meet the dozen Gates criteria above, however, they start with tremendous disadvantages. Typically a financial services company will hold details of the same customers on different databases that cannot communicate with each other. The company may not even know that the customers are the same people. And the customers have no efficient means of contacting the businesses. As Gates told some banks in Canada, the condition could be cured:

> Today [banks] have back-end database systems that store information, and they have applications for people doing customer service on the phone and for tellers and for branch banks. Now they're looking at adding new systems to present customers with data over the Internet. They said, 'We don't want to pick up the additional cost and complexity of still another interface.' I told them that the solution was simple: They should build a great interface for customers to see data over the Internet, then use the same interface to view data internally.

The 'new interface becomes the bank, both inside and out,' comments Gates. Without such a solution, financial companies cannot optimise their strategies. With the necessary information, though, they can use the customer data, and facts about the popularity and profitability of existing products and marketing methods, to construct plans for both new and old customers.

They can test those plans by simulation before incurring any real costs. And they can monitor the results of implementation in real time.

The centre will tap into the monitored results to get an overview of progress, and to ensure that the units are sharing their experiences and helping one another, where needed, to meet their individual targets. Above all, the centre will check that the plan is being constantly revised as actuality tests assumptions and expectations. In uncertain times, nobody expects outcomes to be exactly according to plan, but management must react to the certainty of uncertain events.

They must operate in the spirit of Gates's 'two years from disaster' which he regards as Microsoft's perpetual condition. Every strategy has the same inherent weakness: the conditions under which it was formed will change, perhaps profoundly: the switch to digital technology, for example, caught Motorola napping and gave its world market lead in mobile phones to Nokia. Since such Titanic changes are inevitable, constant monitoring of the strategy and the marketplace – an iceberg watch – is essential.

Collection and analysis of the data will establish the dimensions of the problem and reveal its root cause. In Motorola's case, the cause almost certainly stemmed from a phychological and financial attachment to the old technology, coupled with a refusal to take seriously enough the inroads of upstart digital competitors. Any firm, of any size, can kill or be killed through:

- New technological developments
- New forms of competition
- Different methods of supplying and serving the market
- Emergence of new customers and channels
- Alternative market and product strategies
- Emergence of new markets

Compaq is one company that explored these strategic icebergs, not when it was in crisis, but after five years in which sales had risen five times, profits ten times and its stock eight times. The purpose was to prove that dominant firms can fight the inertia of success, and that 'stretching the organisation brings out the

best in it'. In *Straight from the CEO*, a collection of pieces orches-
trated by Price Waterhouse, Eckhard Pfeiffer, then CEO of Compaq, drew on experience when he wrote: 'People respond to a
bold, well-defined vision and adjust swiftly to its demands. Don't
rely on incremental steps – they're just an excuse not to change.
When you reach one goal, pursue an even bolder goal.'

Boldness, escalation and speed are vital to the killer apps
approach. Typically companies take a long and leisurely look at
these matters. If you take eighteen months to study your strategic
options, say, the obvious drawback is that nothing will be the same
in eighteen months' time. If radical change is needed, you have
lost eighteen months of valuable time. You can't afford that in any
business, electronics above all. In personal computers, with their
life-span of six months or so, eighteen months is three generations
– the equivalent in human terms of a century.

Project Management

Eckhard Pfeiffer of Compaq didn't want to wait that long. So
he gave his strategic renewal project, code-named 'Crossroads',
just eight weeks. The technique applied, mentioned earlier in
this book, is called 'project management'. Its principles are
simple: our KAITs (Killer Apps Implementation Teams) take a
very similar approach. It is the epitome of devolution. You divide
the task into separate components and give each to a cross-
functional team. The teams (fifteen in the Crossroads case) are
co-ordinated and facilitated by higher management, but are self-
contained and responsible for meeting their own deadlines and
targets.

Crossroads findings gave top management the material with
which to debate and devise 'a new three-pronged strategy' for
the company, which worked brilliantly for a while. But the
planners failed to devise a 'digital strategy for market dominance', and Pfeiffer was ousted from Compaq in April 1999,
partly for failing to match the sensationally low costs of direct-
seller Dell; partly for other failures, including the halting
execution of the mega-merger with Digital, a top-down strategy

which the fifteen Crossroads teams doubtless did not consider.

Compaq has floundered against Dell's killer app: what founder Michael Dell calls 'virtual integration'. He argues that a normal $15 billion company – the size that Dell has reached in merely thirteen years – would employ 80,000 people, but Dell actually employs only 15,000 (a mere sixth of Compaq's size). As Dell sees it, the more people you employ, the more time you spend managing them, as opposed to managing the business.

Moreover, not building your own capacity to cope with expansion dodges what MIT professor Peter M. Senge calls a limit to growth. As Dell says, 'If we had to build our own factories for every component of the system, growing at 57% per year just would not be possible.' Virtual integration is more than simple outsourcing. It is finding reliable partners who act as part of your business system. Dell adds that 'regardless of how long these relationships last, virtual integration means you're basically stitching together a business with partners that are treated as if they're inside the company'.

You share information with them in real time, which is how you place your very specific orders: 'Tomorrow morning we need 8,562, and deliver them to door number seven by 7 a.m.' Using state-of-the-art IT, 'supplier-partners' can be incorporated into the system in a way that 'creates a lot of value that can be shared between buyer and supplier'. Much of that value is created by speed. Taking supplies on a daily basis, Dell fills customer orders with only five or six days of lead-time, while its on-hand inventory of raw materials is measured in a few days, even a few hours.

So Dell doesn't get caught by falling prices or rising stocks, and can move much faster. Dell told the *Harvard Business Review* that if 'I've got 11 days of inventory and my competitor has 80, and Intel comes out with a new chip, that means I'm going to get to market 69 days sooner'. No matter what Compaq or any other competitor does, it won't be able to match Dell without matching its corporate model.

The very word 'model', though, can be a trap, which Dell is determined to avoid. People in his company talk about 'the model' as if it were 'an all-powerful being that will take care of

everything. It's scary because I know that nothing is ever 100%
constant, and the last thing we should do is assume that we're
always going to be doing well.'

The paramount issues are not the specific challenges and
changes (which you should, of course, respectively meet and
make), but whether you are prepared to kill your old systems
with new apps – and when. The inhibition is understandable if
you are serving the existing customers brilliantly in every respect
with highly profitable products, so that there is no immediate
economic case for change at present. There never is until rivals
with better systems have taken over the market. By then, of
course, it's too late (as for Pfeiffer's regime at Compaq) for anything but epitaphs.

21

Racing for Speed

'The race is not always to the swift, nor the battle to the strong.
But that's the way to bet it.' Thus wrote Damon Runyon, the
poet of Broadway, author of *Guys and Dolls*. In business terms,
his message has always rung true – until now. Strong companies
were strong in physical assets, strong in financial resources,
strong in market share, strong in technological depth. Naturally,
enough, they ruled the business world.

If all else failed, the strong could use their superior financial
muscle to buy up smaller businesses, to enter new markets in
great force, or to merge with other Goliaths. But the enormously
strong Goliath, remember, was slain by the much smaller, much
swifter David. This has become the compelling metaphor for the
revolutionary era whose intensive phase can be dated back to
1993.

That year saw the world's first website, and, unperceived,
the business revolution swung decisively away from the strong
towards the swift. Speed and strength, in fact, have become
synonymous. The competitive advantage of Dell Computer
doesn't lie in its hardware, but in its speed: speed in serving the
customer, in turning over inventory, in reacting to demand. It
is a business basic, moreover, that time is money. The swift can
take on the financial superiority of the massive.

In 1998 IBM managed to lose $1 billion on its PC business.
Dell, with a lower market share, made $1.5 billion of profit.
That is one measure of the financial chasm between the fast-
movers and the slow. But the gap yawns wherever the slow-

mover turns. There's no contest between a website that enables buyers to order what they want in minutes and the traditional round of telephone enquiries which takes hours.

The contest would be desperately unequal even if the website conferred no other advantages, such as giving commodity buyers the certainty of obtaining what they want at the lowest available price. But the time advantage is the key factor in cyberspace, even for a non-profit organisation like Amnesty International. In July 1998 *CIO WebBusiness* magazine selected Amnesty as one of its fifty best sites. Its website cuts costs for printing and mailing materials supporting its efforts to protect human rights. But managers say the site's greatest value is in 'enabling instantaneous global action, such as letting visitors sign online petitions or send e-mail protesting individual human rights violations.'

'Instantaneous' is a magic word in marketing. Another champion site, Innvest, matches buyers and sellers of 'hospitality' properties: listing, updating and deletion of online ads is instantaneous. Even if delay cannot be wholly abolished, greater speed of decision, speed to market and speed of response can all be killer apps. The top speedsters depend vitally on advanced communications for their key strategies: making only against orders, relying on suppliers to hold inventories, outsourcing everything they can and using the Internet to the full.

The greatest time-saving stems from eliminating stages in the supply cycle altogether. As noted earlier, the conventional progress of a factory order requires a total cycle time of nineteen weeks. Of that, three weeks are taken up by processes at the retail outlet. After three and a half days in transit, the order reaches the distributors, where another two weeks pass before the order moves on, taking another three and a half days in transit, to the factory. There eight weeks are taken to complete an order that may require only hours in manufacturing time.

The return journey back down the supply chain takes another three weeks. The customer finally has the order, but out of nineteen weeks, eleven have been wasted on paperwork, and there's still more to come. The customer has to complete the cycle by filling in a warranty card. Inventories and book entries are required all along the line. The disadvantages of these cumbersome, costly routines were obvious. 'So I guess it's not surprising that I started a company based on eliminating the middleman,' Michael Dell would comment. Dell sells computers 'directly to our customers, deals directly with our suppliers, and communicates directly with our people, all without the unnecessary and inefficient presence of intermediaries.'

Eliminating the Middle

Economies do not arise just from eliminating the middleman. The 'middle process' itself is also generally inefficient and unnecessary. Using the Web, the customer can with one click place the order, which immediately alerts the factory, prepares and distributes all the paperwork (including the warranty) in digital form, and books the transportation. A single process has replaced multiple stages. It is as near to instantaneous as manufacturing and movement allow.

'Lean manufacturing' complements lean ordering. The basic and very simple principle is to make in a day only what is sold in a day, thus eliminating inventory and giving rapid delivery to the customer. Yet even new organisations vending the new technology do not exploit its power. In March 1999, for instance, On Digital, whose digital TV service was only a few months old, expected customers to wait ten days for delivery not of the set-top box, but just a package of information.

The package should, of course, have been waiting, needing only a label, which should have been printed automatically from the information that the customer had already given. The package could have left the On Digital premises within the hour, possibly making the difference between gaining or losing a customer. Whatever convoluted route caused the ten-day delay inevitably cost money, as did the human being who, instead of the Web, took the enquiry in the first place.

But speed is not its own justification. It must have a purpose. There have been cases where speed-ups have proved counter-productive: accelerated vehicle schedules, for instance, which cut transport costs but displease customers who like to chat with the delivery men. There have also been instances where setting time targets led to huge expense but no positive results. Levi Strauss launched the Customer Service Supply Chain initiative, with the praiseworthy ambition of reducing the time taken to deliver jeans to stores from 21 days to 72 hours. It also wanted to market new products in three months, an 80 per cent improvement on its old performance. The effort involved 200 company executives and, according to *Fortune* magazine, 'at least 100 Andersen consultants'. After two grotesquely disruptive years, and an expenditure of $850 million, the initiative was aborted by the board. In 1998, worse still, it took 27 days for Levi's to deliver to retailers, against 20 for rival J. C. Penney.

The company should have taken the 'killer apps' approach, identifying the major causes of supply chain delays, looking for simple uses of IP technology to remove the bottlenecks, and buying the applications off the shelf. That would have produced great time savings in two senses: the deliveries would still be made quicker, but also the benefits, instead of failing to be achieved in two years plus, would have been actually won in weeks or months. Moreover, vast costs would have been saved.

But then, Levi's project had not even been designed to cut costs as well as time. Quite the reverse. 'Amazingly, no one seriously considered the possibility that getting a pair of jeans to stores in 72 hours might double or triple Levi's costs.' The whole fiasco, a milestone on the sorry road to shutting twenty-nine factories and losing over 16,000 jobs, was an example of fat thinking – the opposite of *Lean Thinking*, the title of a book by James P. Womack and Daniel Jones.

To get the best from any technology, including that of information and communications, you look before you leap, think before you act, and aim to make improvements in the three crucial elements of time, money and efficiency, cutting the first, saving the second, and increasing the third. The authors recount what happened at one plant in a day, not two years, and pose the obvious question:

Production activities for a specific product were rearranged in a day from departments and batches to continuous flow,

with a doubling of productivity and a dramatic reduction
in errors and scrap . . . yet the great bulk of activities across
the world are still conducted in departmentalised, batch-
and-queue fashion fifty years after a dramatically superior
way was discovered. Why?

Lagging behind Potential

On Bill Gates's estimate, 'The typical company has made 80 per
cent of the investment in the technology that can give it a
healthy flow of information, yet is typically getting only 20 per
cent of the benefits that are now possible.' Womack and Jones
explain that lean thinking is 'counter-intuitive' (it contradicts
the established norms); and that it doesn't fit into the frame of
conventional financial measures, even though a 'dramatically
superior way' self-evidently improves the financial prowess of
the firm.

Managers similarly under-use IP technology, or don't use it
at all, because it requires a wholly different mindset, and even
different measures. How do you measure the return on investment that flows from giving customers what they really desire?
This is the starting-point for Jones and Womack, as for any
effective application of IP technology. The processes are
identical:

> Identify the value stream for each product or group of prod-
> ucts, moving through the three critical tasks of (1) problem-
> solving (design, engineering, production) through (2)
> information management to (3) physical transformation
> (the progress from raw material to finished product in the
> hands of the user).

Identifying the stream 'almost always exposes enormous, indeed
staggering amounts of *muda*' (the Japanese word for 'waste').
You eliminate this waste by converting to a flow system. Next
the customer 'pulls' the product from you, rather than being
fed at your convenience. And, finally, another virtuous circle

develops as you find that 'there is no end to the process of reducing effort, time, space, cost and mistakes while offering a product which is ever more nearly what the customer wants'.

One of the biggest wastes is time itself. The cost of waste when people can't get the information they need when they need it is estimated at between 25 per cent and 40 per cent of the total cost of an organisation. The calculation of this gigantic sum is simple. Ask a sample of people at all levels in the organisation to keep a record of the time wasted in their day-to-day jobs from being unable to find the information they need. Bear in mind that information from a good IP application is immediate – that is, available within three mouse clicks.

After a week's feedback, add up the sample population's wasted time and work out the average hours wasted per employee. Multiply this by the total number of employees to give the wasted time for the week. Multiply by £20 per hour to provide the week's cost of waste. Multiply by 50 to give the total cost for the year, and you will see the massive return available from effective investment in IP technology. And that's without taking into account the factor stressed in *Business Week* by Ira Sager: 'Speed kills – if you don't have it.'

There's an astonishing contrast between imperative words like those and action. During the 1990s, the world of business, led by the US, began to come to terms with the Internet. The growth of usage and traffic over the Net could hardly be ignored by managements, governments or the media. The press, in particular, went to great lengths to explain, report and encourage the revolution. Yet despite all the sustained and increasing publicity, and the mounting commercial importance of cyberspace, executives have stayed reluctant to accept the consequences.

In March 1999, a survey of 500 US and European board directors, conducted by the Institute of Directors and Oracle, 'showed that few business leaders in Europe had grasped the cost-cutting opportunities offered by the Internet'. Even fewer had any idea of the exciting opportunities for business transformation. If such opportunities go unseen, so, too, do competitive threats. The top managements in the UK and France, the report concluded, were in a 'state of denial'.

Fear and Ignorance

Fear and ignorance of the technology are prime causes of denial. The information specialists have done little to tackle these causes. Often they oppose developments which will weaken their own hold over IT strategy and implementation. After all, an unaided home worker can now buy, for relatively little money, a full-feature, state-of-the-art system for global communications and information.

You wouldn't want every employee to order his or her own system, but that is how you want employees to feel. Too few IT departments, however, have made it their mission to help create a new kind of company, bound together and animated by IP technology. This gives their bosses an excuse for dangerous inaction.

An Andersen Consulting partner, Rudy Puryear, told the *Financial Times* that even in the US, where clients are much more aware of the strategic need, most of them lack the requisite sense of urgency. He urged the world's top thousand companies to adopt three related steps:

1 Link electronically with suppliers and customers.
2 Re-engineer the workforce, processes and strategies to exploit the new network.
3 Reposition the company in the new world of electronic commerce.

You can envisage these three stages as a pyramid. At the base, most major US companies have websites, intranets and extranets. Some have advanced further up the pyramid by instituting changes that use their new technology. At the apex of the pyramid a very few of these large and sophisticated organisations have actually transformed their businesses. It's the age-old problem. How do you persuade corporate managements to abandon the systems and strategies that have made their companies, and themselves, rich and successful?

You can try to frighten them with bogeys like Scott Blum. His company, Buy.com, has been trading since November 1997. It could be worth about $4 billion on the stock market, even though monthly losses were running at $2 million a month in early 1999. Using the slogan 'the lowest prices on earth', Buy. com sells computers, software, books, videos and electronic games. Blum aims to offset minute gross margins (1 per cent) with massive advertising revenue and ancillary sales. His target, he told *Fortune*, is to reach $10 billion in sales by 2003.

Sceptics and conservatives can laugh Blum off, and he could, of course, fail. But there are hundreds of contrarian Blums already, and their number is swelling. Their activities may expand markets. But they will inevitably steal sales from the hides of major competitors – even giants like the car moguls. Detroit is already under threat from websites that sell new cars. Even if manufacturers' own websites are successful, their dealers will suffer slashed margins. The old industry model must collapse in front of the new rules.

The lesson of all technologically driven change is that the new order always wins. The operators of transatlantic liners may have known that airliners were a threat, but did not believe that the airlines would destroy their businesses altogether. They thought that, at worst, the two modes could live alongside each other. That almost never happens. Big business is still reluctant to accept the obvious conclusion. The current state of transition will be resolved not by evolution, but revolution.

BOOK EIGHT

The E-Commerce Boom

22

Joining the Unstoppable Surge

Commerce over the Internet, even though it is expanding at a phenomenal rate, remains small in relative terms. Yet already bookselling, personal computers, travel, car retailing and many industrial markets are being transformed by direct selling via websites. No business can afford to neglect the potential, and new Net-based businesses are being born every day.

You can express this unstoppable surge very simply. Open a site on the World Wide Web, and your business is automatically international. Through your site you can link up with suppliers, (who may make everything you sell), tell customers in detail about your products, and arrange for their purchases. Make your products and services available to this worldwide audience, by direct selling or distribution via partners who are linked over the Net, and – hey presto! – you're a fully-fledged global business.

This process, moreover, doesn't take the thirty years that was the traditional time needed for a company to become a big-time player. Thirty days is ample for the start-up, and thirty months could achieve a gratifyingly high turnover. The website may be all the company has at first, as when Amazon.com launched the first global bookseller. You also need money (which the investment community is delighted to supply) and brains, both commercial and technical. But that is all.

Such start-ups intensify the pressure on the wealthy old order. Their initial backing is adequate, and public appetite for their equity is such that, even in a much less hysterical stock market, they will rapidly generate all the wealth they need. Established companies can observe this phenomenon, but they cannot join the unstoppable surge without radically changing their established formats. The latter may work for present purposes, but not for the future.

Multinationals in particular have reached a Rubicon. On one bank of the river sits a vast, habit-ridden national corpocracy with affiliates abroad. On the other beckons a truly global, lithe organisation which knows no frontiers and no obstacles. Can the former cross the river and transform itself into the latter? The managements are certainly trying to make the journey. But their progress towards the future almost always reflects, and is restrained by, the lumber of the past.

This is not a theoretical issue. The boom in e-commerce is a reality, wonderful for some, harsh for others. In *Virtual Finance*, meaningfully subtitled 'A Survivor's Guide', consultant John Ginarlis observes that the costs of virtual e-commerce are falling fast while physical branches are becoming ever more expensive. This produces 'a scissor effect'. You could also call it a squeeze, but the impact is the same: irresistible.

So far technological limitations have kept e-commerce penetration in the US, easily the most developed of consumer markets, to below 10 per cent. But the finishing touches are being swiftly applied. When mobile phones connect to the Net, to be joined by ordinary TV sets, the gates to cyberspace will be flung wide open. Ginarlis's prediction, that this will happen within five to ten years, seems highly conservative to us. But he is absolutely right in saying that the triumph of virtuality is inevitable.

Ginarlis is referring specifically to the finance sector, but no business is immune. Writing in the *Financial Times*, Barry Riley observed: 'Anxious strategic planners in all kinds of businesses . . . are grappling with the challenges of keeping up with the e-commerce revolution.' In his view, stock markets, even when there is a speculative bubble in Internet stocks, are reflecting the underlying realities of the changing world. He cites the threefold rise in BT shares as an example: 'The stock market now perceives that BT is well plugged into both of today's phenomenal growth sectors, mobile telephones and the

Internet, and has become an international growth stock.'

As Riley notes, the growth action will not be in Internet portals, 'surely not an activity that in itself will make huge profits. But somewhere, in a linked business, *somebody* will.' To become that somebody, a great company remaking itself for the new world order has to scrap its old business model and build a new one – or new ones, because it will almost certainly be operating in many markets. Yet, if you believe the 1999 report, *The Competitiveness of Global Firms*, published by FT Management, the old, US-dominated order is still good enough.

The 'Best' Globalists

Twenty-three of 'the best' globalists are incorporated in the US, followed by nine from the UK. The list includes some eyebrow-raisers: the two brewers Bass and Whitbread, the electronics manufacturer GEC, the finance house 3i and household goods conglomerate Reckitt & Colman. GEC, long excoriated for its lack of innovatory zeal, has used its cash resources instead, paying $6 billion for what Riley describes as 'a modest pile of all-American communications wizardry'.

As for Reckitt & Colman, its strategy had just come apart at the seams, despite some expensive consultancy designed to turn the group into a truly European powerhouse. The same kind of disappointment has affected several other stars of competitiveness, including one-time cynosures Hewlett-Packard and Electronic Data Systems, the computer services firm originally established by H. Ross Perot. In April 1999 EDS reported dismal figures as it struggled, under new, imported leadership, to perform more effectively in a high-growth marketplace. The company had fired 5,200 employees, abandoning 'underperforming' businesses, and losing $20.6 million in a single quarter.

HP, still more dramatically, had recently decided on bifurcating in a belated effort to exploit cyberspace. These traumas show how violently the Internet has changed a global game, which is evidently moving too fast for the calculations of INSEAD's Jean-Claude Larréché and his competitiveness team. In an amazing omission, the report's key measure, Overall Market Effectiveness Capability (OMEC), does not specify information and communications technology among a dozen 'global dashboard' dials, ranging from 'mission and vision' to 'planning and intelligence'.

Nor do any dashboard features, save 'international', distinguish global from local firms. In the age of the Internet, that distinction is dying. True globalism makes similar brands available in similar ways in worldwide markets, managed by an organisation that sees no difference between home and away. By these criteria, Amazon.com is a more global company than the OMEC champion, Unilever. The Web is spawning similar revolutionary globalists every day.

As it happens, global champion Unilever also reported disappointing results in April 1999. Almost every business must be touched, and many damaged, by developments such as the rise of the 'infomediaries' (see page 212), database sites which act as exchanges for purchases on an ever-widening front. Because they offer total information and complete price comparison, these sites offer a stark choice to companies in the affected industries: you either join the infomediaries or cede to them your profits.

If you simply continue with business as usual, the infomediaries will gradually take over your customers. You may be able to add value to the purchase through significant elements of service or consultancy. This may offer some protection to your custom and profits, but the low-cost, low-price Web rivals will still be a continual threat, especially if they offer their own value-adding options. It would be much wiser to become an e-commerce force yourself, as Dixons, the UK electronics retailer, did when attracting 1.3 million users in seven months with a free Internet access service – leading to a £1.7 billion share flotation.

Established corporations had best get their global retaliation in first. The first necessity is to get fully wired. The whole organisation, and everybody within, must be linked by networks that make maximum information universally available in real time. The expense of doing this is not prohibitive, while the cost of doing nothing may be lethal. The network cannot become globally effective, however, without revolutionary changes in the way the organisation is managed.

The Catch 22 is that the traditional organisation goes about its revolutionary purposes in the traditional way. A typical multinational giant, deciding to connect all its people and businesses worldwide, spilt forth documents and presentations, explaining to its people how they were going on 'a transformation journey which will require each and everyone of us, (you), to commit to and take individual ownership for the Business Principles and the Values in order to achieve the breakthrough performance that will be required'.

Five Fatal Faults

This 'breakthrough performance', the company declared, would be accomplished by 'working in innovative new ways, combining the expertise of our highly talented staff to develop and implement world class best practices, serving our cross border customers more effectively, sharing and valuing diverse ideas across the globe'. The company identified five fatal faults of the 'current reality':

- Excessive internal focus
- Excessive bureaucracy
- Limited sharing of information
- Information-is-power culture
- Limited sharing of resources

Given this certainly accurate analysis, there was an inherent difficulty in moving to a 'future reality' of sharing best practices through 'virtual distributed teams' in a 'culture committed to learning' in which common activities would 'cluster', and which would feature 'partnering with customers and suppliers'. The company (or its directors) clearly wanted to move in the directions urged in this book. But the organisation being asked to make the move was the very machine exhibiting those five fatal faults.

The actual programme to which all this verbiage referred was the installation of a global information and communications system. But the would-be revolutionaries were anxious to downplay the significance of the IT. It was 'the enabling component for enhanced communication, collaboration and working in new ways. However, it cannot be over-emphasise [sic] that this is not an IT project'. The project leaders sounded almost apologetic when saying that the project 'does however need a common infrastructure'.

None of the 'mandatory' equipment changes were particularly challenging: local and wide area networks, a global intranet, e-mail, and a standardised desktop. But a sprawling, elaborate training and 'coaching' programme was devised, complete with a large range of communications 'designed to inform and educate everyone who will be effected [sic].' There was no mention of specific applications of IT or of the precise business results required, although 'local business representatives' were told that they 'should network with other business representatives to share best practices for working in new ways and to identify opportunities to deliver faster to market, more effectively to market, or identifying new venture opportunities which are common across lines of business'.

This apparently ambitious programme did not impress us. The chances of curing the giant's self-confessed Five Fatal Faults seemed very poor. A lumbering process is hardly the way to speed up and reform a lumbering giant. The company's subsequent financial results were terrible. Its management had not understood that an information and communication system that, like the Web, is shared around the world of itself creates wholly new norms.

The truly global system doesn't just inform and communicate; it also engenders collaborative action, which, because of the transparency and universality of the medium, can be initiated anywhere on earth. This means more than, say, having a common platform for all cars produced round the world. The Holy Grail is to have a common platform for management. But this cannot be provided by a structure founded on national head offices staffed by omnipotent, although not omnicompetent, chief executives and their cohorts. The essence of true globalism is the dissipation of central power and its replacement by widely dispersed, shared responsibility. The giant multinationals are having real trouble in adapting to this formula. One response,

is to contract to spin off businesses or (as global champion
Unilever has has done) to sell them. But this in no way rides
the revolution. The opposite response is to grow through merger
or acquisition. Neither response does anything to improve – and
may actually retard – 'Overall Marketing Effectiveness'. For both
put off the necessary step of adopting radical change – not in
the structure, but in the management. But it demands changing
behaviour, abandoning 'the way things are done round here'
for new ways of doing things – led by IT.

From Awareness to Action

The problem is not a lack of awareness. An IDC survey of fifty
senior directors in Britain showed that 96 per cent of companies
were making or planning to make changes in both their
businesses and technology. Two-thirds had already done so. But
you have to question the extent of the changes. The real pace
is being set by what the e-commerce innovators are actually
doing now to change the nature of global business.

Consider the implications of a phenomenon like e-Bay, the
Internet auction house which became a Wall Street sensation
after going public in 1998, with the share price multiplying ten
times in ten weeks (a process that took Microsoft ten years).
The site brings together buyers and sellers for over 900,000
products in 1086 catalogues. It gets 140 million hits a week, and
in just three months, between October and December 1998, its
registered users rose by half to 1.8 million.

The stockmarket début of Priceline.com, which mediates
between airlines and customers, was another sensation. It rapidly
rose to a market value higher than that of American Airlines,
making its founder worth $4 billion on paper. There's no reason
why the auction and intermediary principle shouldn't spread to
other markets – perhaps to all markets. The customers will pay
precisely what they are prepared to pay. The oligopolists will no
longer be able to control prices, and their profits will depend, not
on their control over markets, but on their efficiencies.

As the external forces of the unstoppable surge come to bear, internal forces should also drive managements in a revolutionary direction. Marketing, finance, production, R&D, human resources and innovation must be linked in real time to achieve leading-edge performance. The leaders of the Triple Revolution consciously function within wider business systems, to which extranets hold the key. Intranets (spreading fast) likewise provide vital internal linkages. Treating these as 'infrastructure' misses the whole point. They are developing, powerful tools for action and interaction.

Regarded as infrastructure, the systems simply add an electronic layer to the bureaucracy. Indeed, the systems can separate the company from its own people. According to *Fortune*, in the course of the doomed Levi Strauss Customer Service Supply Initiative, 'all over the company people had to reapply for their own positions'. The company's handbook, *Individual Readiness for a Changing Environment* (all 145 pages of it) can't have eased the pain of inhuman resources management, applied, what's worse, by a company dedicated to 'aspirational' management and values.

Applying the digital revolution to the supply chain is not enough. You have to change behaviour radically from the top to the bottom of the company. Otherwise you get unhappy staff and impaired performance – not just the financial figures, which come in after, sometimes long after, the real damage has been done. Against a revolutionary background, it's easy to lose touch with customers – even while making determined efforts to serve them better. They will vote with their business (and their credit cards) to join the e-commerce boom. if people have access to information, they will expect to use it, whether they are inside or outside the company.

Since information is power, senior managers have tended to cling to the stuff. But since information is also the prime competitive tool, to clutch at it is self-defeating. Intranets and extranets cannot thrive on secrecy. Anyway, they defeat it, just as the unstoppable surge of e-commerce will defeat any company, however great, that cannot find an escape from the past into this all-embracing future.

23

Retailing's New Format

Shopping has already begun to move in some force out of the High Street, the mall and the superstore and on to the website. Traditional retailers have no option but to join a revolution that will cut costs, increase variety and make home delivery – which largely vanished in retailing's previous upheavals – the norm for countless products. Many retailers will find this an uncomfortable transition. But they have no option, since the fundamental economics of their traditional business are under attack.

The most valuable fixed assets in retailing have suddenly become vulnerable: the stores. Major multiples, still expanding vigorously wherever they can find sites, should take serious note of what's happening to banks and building societies. Their High Street assets are becoming liabilities. Branch handling costs for transactions are vastly higher than automated processing. Not only are their branches uneconomic, but also the extremely low costs of electronic networks have opened doors to new, direct-marketing competitors.

Retailers may downplay this analogy with 'money shops' which have nothing to display or stock. But the startling rise of Amazon.com ('Earth's Largest Bookstore') can't be dismissed. With no shops to its name, Amazon had 2 million visitors in 1997, generating $148 million of sales. What is happening in books can happen anywhere. Retail outlets could easily mutate into nothing but showrooms and warehouses.

Until recently the banks could justifiably be criticized for their lack of retailing skills, but now such skills are becoming redundant anyway. Nor can the financiers hope to escape the retail squeeze simply by offering backroom services, such as investment. Five million people traded stocks on the Internet in 1998, a total that was predicted, according to the *Financial Times*, to double or triple by the millennium.

Obviously, you might think, the Internet's financial bandwagon is one on which everybody wants to jump, because of its huge profit potential. You would be wrong.

Indeed, what on earth would persuade you to invest in this product? You have no idea of how to make money from the thing. You know just as little about which customers, if any, might want the offering. Plainly, this is a non-runner. Yet banks worldwide are 'rushing to invest large amounts' in just these circumstances. The product is Internet banking, and the evidence of this weird 'gold rush mentality' – without any gold – comes from Ernst & Young researchers who interviewed 100 banks in 26 countries.

Management at large shares the bankers' ignorance. One recent survey found that only 3 per cent of UK managers considered themselves well-informed about the Internet. A year later, in early 1999, their level of awareness had improved by a spectacular two-thirds – to 5 per cent. The majority differ from the banks only in the propensity to invest. No gold rush here: 54 per cent of UK companies with turnovers exceeding £100 million, according to another, contemporaneous survey, have no intention of developing websites.

These companies presumably feel that the Web offers no worthwhile commercial benefit. As they will soon discover, they are wildly wrong. The banks may be investing heavily, but they take an equally pessimistic view, believing that electronic commerce will increase its share of banking transactions by only a wimpish 1 per cent annually. If that unlikely estimate proved true, banks would lose out on the tremendous transaction savings mentioned above.

Banks and other businesses are not blind to the revolution now developing apace, but the Internet is changing the rules for all the processes of management. The awful fact that 54 per cent of the surveyed banks wait a full day before processing online messages from customers shows how wrenching a transformation is required. It's far more comfortable to stick to the old ways and hope that the revolution will pass you by.

Business-to-Consumer Markets

But the revolution is here to stay. Despite the expressed conservatism of many retail leaders, all business-to-consumer markets offer the richest potential on the Internet. That's the verdict of an IBM–Economist Intelligence Survey report. An obstacle, more marked in heterogenous Europe than the homogenous US, is that complex and fragmented markets increase the required investment of time and money – another fact that managers find off-putting.

But they can only hold back until somebody forces the pace, like Amazon.com in bookselling. The book interloper was busily remaking the sector, even when its profits lay only in a ludicrous stock market valuation. With the Net fast becoming the most frequent means of purchasing books, other consumer goods such as recorded music and films are bound to follow suit. But many companies in other sectors are racing along the same disruptive path, many, like Amazon.com, newcomers with no old ways to preserve.

The newcomers' investment in new ways is helping to double Internet business-to-consumer commerce every year, in Europe as in the US. The implication for orthodox retailers is that they will inevitably lose market share. The Net's present tiny proportion of total consumer purchases will grow rapidly, maybe eventually matching the growth curve of business-to-business sales (doubling every three to four months, according to Price Waterhouse). How much share the stores retain will depend on their ability to innovate, and to change at speed.

Retail managements have never previously had to challenge the reasons for their existence or expansion. Now the size and usage of added space need the most searching scrutiny. Once, cataloguing operations were peripheral. Now mail order and conventional retailers alike should be contemplating a long stride into a future where selling by electronic catalogue is the norm, and stores become places of entertainment, demonstration, assessment and wonderful service. Failing that, many of those retailers' fixed assets will disappear like so many of the High Street banks.

The shadow and promise of the Internet hang over every store. The sweeping changes now afoot will change the face of the retail sector. The potential for the Internet to eliminate the distributor cannot be overlooked. Many retailers have recognised the danger and taken sensible steps, like opening their own experimental shopping sites. The traditional retail management structure, with its hierarchical pyramids and fixed ideas, is ill-suited to this new world. But the technological revolution offers the chance to create flatter structures, linking everybody in stores and head offices on intranets. All can share not only information, but ideas, expertise and experiments instantly and in real time.

Such collaboration is badly needed to exploit the still uncertain, but vast potential of online shopping, and to develop enticing store formats and operations that will tempt shoppers away from screens into real shops. But the electronic share of retail business must surely rise. Established retailers must address this fact or risk redundancy themselves. In *E-Shock*, Michael de Kare-Silver outlines the strategic options that face retailers:

- They can simply supply information only, using a website which deliberately sells nothing.
- They can 'export' the business, retaining their traditional outlets, but expanding into other geographic or rich markets over the Web: Oxford bookseller Blackwell's has followed this route, investing in a major expansion of its existing wholesale business and venturing via the Web into the US market.
- They can try to subsume electronic shopping into the existing stores. Customers will order the requirements electronically, but come into the stores to pick up the purchases and perhaps make others.
- They can be more ambitious and see what is plainly true: that the Web is another channel altogether. Full-blooded develop-

ment of the new channel may well lose business from their existing channels. They can, however, hope to offset the losses by attracting new customers.

Cannibalising yourself is more comfortable than being eaten by others. British supermarkets, with their palatial sites paid for by high margins, are already being challenged by local operators who are offering home delivery and who can compete on price thanks to their tiny overheads. The policy of opening another channel, though, is less ambitious than that of attacking on all fronts – call centre, home delivery, e-mail order, website, stores.

The Trouble with Stores

The nature of the traditional store will inevitably change, as store traffic diminishes. Silver describes a 'mixed system' solution. You concentrate on a flagship site (perhaps a mall) which supports an online plus home delivery service which is based away from these centres – 'shopping, leisure entertainment meccas which will reach out into wider catchment areas'. Part of the entertainment, no doubt, will be Internet shopping.

In some cases, though, the shops will disappear altogether as the Net takes over. The Automobile Association's 142 High Street shops vanished for this reason, and other shops are bound to follow. Others still will dwindle into kiosks with Internet access. But the pace in retailing will be set by the dedicated e-sellers who concentrate on home delivery: 'Unencumbered by existing physical sites and with a lower cost because these organisations are learning how to take advantage of their position in the market.'

Can retailers have the best of both worlds, combining Internet and physical locations in 'a store for the future'? Can conventional stores 'revitalise and buck the trend'? These are two key questions that de Kare-Silver raises in *E-Shock*. But there are very few examples from other industries where established leaders have been able to give birth to new ventures in the same field and to become leaders in the new technology as well. The example of Woolworths in the US is deeply discouraging. Confronted by the disruptive technology of the discount store, Woolworths set up its own Woolco chain, while continuing to invest in the traditional business.

The Woolcos eventually all closed down: and so, in time, did Woolworths, becoming a sports shoe chain under a different name. To our eyes, the choice is starkly simple. Either carry on as usual, and lose first profit and then the business. Or plunge as eagerly as you can into the Web world, setting up the business as a separate operation with its own finances and management. Existing stores can be maintained so long as they earn their keep, either in their own right or as feeds and supports for the e-commerce operation. But most conventional retailers will never reach this destination, because they are starting from the wrong mindset.

Typically, the chief executive of one leading British fashion manufacturer, speaking in March 1999, argued that fashion couldn't be sold over the Net. Customers could look at what was on offer, he said, but they would have to use the firm's printed catalogue to order the clothes. In the same breath, he revealed that the company had badly misread the market, offering high fashion when the market had turned to classic merchandise.

A printed catalogue is an expensive hostage to fortune. Prepared many months in advance, it locks the offer into its pages with no hope of revision. A Web catalogue, in contrast, can be changed and extended on an hourly basis. Switches in fashion therefore hold far less fear. Moreover, Web ordering is simple; the catalogue can have moving images and sound; it can be as long as you like. What would be hopelessly unwieldy on paper is easily manageable on the Web. Users see only the page open before them, swiftly reaching the next wanted page with a simple click on the mouse. As time goes by, the website will become the automatic choice for anyone who wishes to bargain-hunt or simply browse.

Part of the reluctance to embrace e-commerce may stem from the over-hype that probably dates back to *The One to One Future*, a book written by Don Peppers and Martha Rogers. Their concept was revolutionary: the market of one. Companies would use the technology (as they certainly will) to sell to tens of thousands of people, but would tailor every sale to the specific desires of each individual customer. The authors were simply ahead of their time. Apart from anything else, customers were then uneasy about giving their details to suppliers. That no longer applies.

The Active Customer

The Net turns customers into active participants. They can now take control of what they buy, where they buy it, and how. A consumer revolution is under way whose impact will dwarf supermarkets, discount stores, department stores and shopping malls put together.

Writing in *Fortune*, Gary Hamel and Jeff Sampler describe how the mass market customer has become unfaithful to the Mass Media which fed customers with product and service ads. 'Online customers simply aren't going to be pushed around', say the authors. They cite the example of an extraordinary company named Yoyodyne and its 'permission-based marketing'. In 1997 a million players signed up to play Yoyodyne games and contests and thus gave permission to be used as customers for Yoyodyne's client websites.

Not surprisingly, Yoyodyne has been bought by Yahoo!, the leading search engine. Other bright ideas have also put customers in the driving seat. CompareNet gives them the opportunity to compare and even discuss competing products in which they are interested. Junglee and CBB act as giant comparison shoppers: they guide customers to the best buy, and then enable them to make their purchase through an online auction. The traditional definition of shopping has been thrown out of the window.

The response is not just a matter of investing in the new technology. The experiences of one of the greatest names in retailing are a powerful warning. Marks & Spencer built a brand that seemed well-nigh invincible until in 1998 profits went sharply into reverse on sales that barely inched ahead. Yet M&S has an ardent fan in Gary Hamel, the most incisive critic of big-time corporates. He placed M&S high in his management pantheon, lauding its pioneering innovations, and above all its development of supplier partnerships.

The business how long rejoiced in being a 'manufacturer without factories', whose suppliers, like those serving Dell, were an extension of its own business. But Dell is not a manufacturer without factories, it is a 'retailer without shops'. As more and more manufacturers make this transition, finding direct ways to the customer, retailers will face a painful choice: do they take on their suppliers in mortal commercial combat by going back down the supply chain? Or do they subside gently into oblivion?

The answers are plainly not obvious to retailers themselves. In *E-Shock*, Silver quoted Robert Tillman, chief executive of Loew's, who commented that 'retail saturation combined with growth coming in electronic commerce represents the biggest challenge facing our industry today. How do we grow shareholder value when we can no longer grow what we are doing and what is growing is something we are unfamiliar with?' The paradoxical answer is that only by becoming, thinking and acting like 'retailers without shops' can tomorrow's retailers hope to make their shops succeed.

24

Purchasing the Future

Suppliers to industry and commerce face a new world in which their customers can tap sources far and wide in search of the best and cheapest answer, whether they require small components, commodities or huge machines. Buying over the Net already saves leading-edge companies hundreds of millions of dollars in annual costs. Indeed, the long-established function of purchasing is a dying trade. Like many bastions of the old management, it is crumbling before the onslaught of the new.

In the process, whole industries are being reshaped. As the purchasing revolution develops via the Internet, companies will no longer need expert purchasers with deep knowledge of markets. Instead, a few clicks on the mouse will establish the sources of supply and the best available combination of price and availability. The purchaser's fabled negotiation skills are useless in this context – not that they were ever as marvellous as companies supposed.

When a large retailer took over a privately owned chain, it was startled to discover that the smaller business had won consistently lower prices from its suppliers. So much for economies of buying scale. The same thing happened when Compaq's chairman, Ben Rosen, sent an undercover two-man team to the Comdex trade fair to check the cost of building a cheap, entry-level PC. The pair, posing as tiny start-up entrepreneurs, got better quotes than the great Compaq.

All the hit and miss of purchasing, however, disappears when you have complete transparency. The slogan of the John Lewis department store chain, 'Never Knowingly Undersold', gets reversed, as 'Never Knowingly Overcharged' becomes standard operating procedure. But cost is not the only path to profit. There is another powerful alternative to traditional purchasing: the supplier partnership. The principle is as old as W. Edwards Deming's famous fourteen quality points, of which Number 4 is 'End the Practice of Awarding Business on Price Tag Alone'.

Instead, Deming advised that you should seek a supplier who provides perfect quality with totally reliable just-on-time delivery. This may well produce lower costs, even at a higher price, but 'price has no meaning without a measure of the quality being purchased'. Although perfection is not, of course, given to man or manager, today suppliers routinely get brilliantly near to Deming's ideal thanks to the quality revolution that he did so much to inspire. This is still not enough. You want suppliers who are also intimately involved in every aspect of specification and production, and who make a contribution that goes far beyond meeting orders.

The traditional relationship between supplier and customer was at arm's length. The customer gave orders to the supplier and ordered him about, squeezing him on price, blaming him for failures of quality or delivery, threatening to take the business elsewhere, and playing one supplier off against another. The supplier in turn sought to appease, concealing both his resentment and the various stratagems he used to defend his margins against the customer's pressure.

Deming gave the example of cost-plus. As Deming described it to Mary Walton, 'A supplier offers a bid so low that he is almost certain to get the business. Midway into production the customer discovers that certain changes must be made. The supplier obliges, while boosting the price of the items. It is too late for the customer to make other arrangements.' In Deming's own words, 'With a single supplier and a long-term relationship of trust, such pillage does not occur.'

In most cases, the warring parties in the traditional relationship, where several mistrusted suppliers were kept to short-term contracts, each achieved worse results than were available to them had they worked together. Deming's philosophy still stands, but the Information Revolution has made its implementation much easier. By linking their computers, customer and supplier can have full information about each other's requirements and costs in real time. Price issues become transparent, and the two business systems become one.

At one extreme, the customer–supplier partnership creates the 'virtual company', which controls but does not produce what it sells. Companies like Sun Microsystems rely on outsiders for everything from whole assemblies to delivery. Their proprietary edge rests on design, management and marketing. Virtual and near-virtual companies like Dell Computer take their outsiders deep inside. They will only expel suppliers if forced to do so by technological change or inadequate performance.

Virtuality Pays

The examples of both Dell and Sun suggest that virtuality pays. Since 1994, Dell's sales have risen sixfold to $18.2 billion. Net income – $250 million in the red in 1994 – is today around $1.5 billion. This puts Dell right at the top of the fabulous microelectronic league. Sun, with $9.8 billion of sales, has doubled its return to investors every two years since 1988. Conservatives may protest that what prevails in Silicon Valley has no relevance outside, but they are as wrong as the Western car-makers who argued that Toyota's production methods had no application outside Japan.

The Toyota system naturally became the norm, but only after the West's car manufacturers had lost billions in market share. The same suicidal tendency is operating now. Managements are slow to move to cyberspace purchasing, despite the evidence of booming trade. Total business-to-business purchasing is already over $100 billion, and is expected to reach the trillions by 2003. The industrial world is splitting into those who intermediate between suppliers and customers, those who deal with the intermediaries and those who do neither.

The only obstacles companies face to adopting true supplier partnerships and web purchasing are internal. Managers have to make radical changes in their processes, including the way they think. E-commerce demands a very different attitude to supply, suppliers, markets, information systems, value chains and everything else. Minor changes are not enough. Only those companies able to make a major break with the past will seize the opportunities as many already have.

The volume of one area of business-to-business trade, purchases over third-party websites, had become enormous by 1998. That year, according to Forrester research, volume achieved by these 'infomediaries' reached $43 billion. This was a drop in several oceans compared to the torrent of trade expected by 2003, a 34-fold rise to $1.4 trillion. In February 1999, *Fortune* reported that infomediaries – or industry exchanges – had sprung up for 'steel, paper, research chemicals, hospital suppliers, marine equipment, home equity loans, even bull semen'.

A whole new business sector has emerged to exploit and expand this market of markets. Basically the infomediaries deal in information. The efficiency of websites depends on the scope and accuracy of their databases. If they can provide the necessary facts about suppliers, prices and availabilities, finding the right product at the right price can take minutes instead of hours. The infomediaries can also drastically reduce cost to the customer. The Career Builder, for example, finds over a million people for jobs every month at a claimed cost of $900 per placement, compared to a US national average of $8,000.

Since the infomediary's needs for capital and stocks are minimal, many entrepreneurs will be tempted into so vast a market. They cannot all succeed. The rich prizes will continue to go to those who are 'fastest with the mostest'. The lesson of the infomediaries applies generally in the world of e-commerce: get in fast, get in first, and get in fully. Waiting to see and half-measures are disastrous. Don't wait for anything, not even the establishment of standards.

E-Commerce Standards

As Louise Kehoe pointed out in the *Financial Times*, important issues of standardisation in e-commerce had yet to be resolved as the millennium neared: 'The 10-wheelers of electronic business-to-business commerce are getting up to speed – with suppliers and buyers of all manner of goods exchanging orders via the Internet – but nobody has defined the rules of the road.' Firms are exchanging data as they exchange goods. However, 'each industry or vertical segment is creating its own set of standards for how to exchange data, but most do not take full account of the standards created by others'.

Her fear is that 'e-business may be heading toward a pile-up of immense proportions'. An endearing and crucial characteristic of the Information Revolution, though, is that its problems encourage rather than retard revolutionary progress. Eager companies gather round the problem like bees round a honey-pot, offering the solution that may create a fortune. They do not wait on those associations of companies which from time to time, and usually over a long period, seek to bring the warring standards together.

Kehoe pointed out that by 1999 many versions existed of XML, 'extensible mark-up language'. An order form could carry an XML tag specifying price, quantity, product description, etc. It would make sense to merge all the XMLs into one fully compatible language, as Microsoft and others have proposed, on which everybody can standardise. But well before any such agreement could be reached, some upstart will probably have stolen the prize – perhaps it will be Ariba.

Already Hewlett-Packard, oil company Chevron, General Motors, Cisco Systems and 'a host of other big companies' have put Ariba's software on their intranets. You simply connect with Ariba to order 'anything from fuel oil to office notebooks'. This intranet marketplace for business is a harbinger of the revolutionary future. It's a short step from the passive receipt of orders to their proactive execution. Automatic replenishment of supplies, raising automatic payment, will plainly become routine

– with safeguards against over-ordering, under-fulfilment and crime built into the system.

This is the essence of the real time supply system. Its objective has been well described by Bill Gates: 'Capturing and analysing data in real time can create an information cycle between a business, its partners and its customers that can reshape a company's entire behaviour.' The idea is to tie the company 'so closely to consumer buying patterns [that they] will drive its business processes in real time'. You transcend historical data because, however skilful the analysis, it won't forecast demand accurately enough to stop under-stocking or its evil twin, over-stocking.

But if you know what customers are buying right now, you can operate a 'just-in-time' system with your suppliers, who can supply the goods in demand when and where they are demanded. The advantage for the suppliers is that they need only make what is actually being sold; the gain for the customer is fast response. Both sides benefit from lower costs, while the information collected by the supplier is invaluable for planning future products and production.

The digital documents used in the new supply chains are *intelligent*. James Martin uses the word in *Cybercorp*. He pours rightful scorn on conventional purchase orders, which have to be 'laboriously filed, searched for, and sent by snail mail'. This procedure is even less defensible when the pieces of paper have actually emerged from a computer:

> It does not make much sense to have a computer print paper documents and then have humans stuff them in envelopes, deliver them to the postal system where people sort them, put them in sacks, deliver them to places, sort them again, missort some of them, until eventually they reach a destination where they are manually keyed into another computer system with a 1 per cent error rate.

When computer speaks direct to computer, the supply chain can be automated. The intelligent computer at the customer end responds to production schedules and inventory records and arranges for delivery of the required goods. The equally bright computer at the supplier's establishment 'monitors the customer's needs or production schedule and supplies goods appropriate for a changing production mix, in the correct sequence, just in time'. And all this starts from turning a dumb purchase order into an intelligent one, and building on that change as simply and cogently as possible.

Complex and costly systems are not required to achieve this end. Phillip Jackson, who formerly directed worldwide operations for De La Rue Cash Systems, stresses this: 'It is now cost-effective to stream customer delivery throughout the total enterprise by going online through a distribution chain in over 30 countries and a supply chain with over 300 suppliers.' The great benefits in lower inventory and improved delivery performance, leading to increased revenues and margins, can be achieved with simplicity and speed, 'in time-scales which match the critical need to achieve and maintain competitive positioning in an increasingly crowded and competitive marketplace'.

Kill or be Killed

Jackson is not exaggerating when he uses that word 'critical'. Remember that in the world of the killer app it's kill or be killed. As Shikhar Ghosh has observed: 'The opportunity for those companies that move first to establish electronic channels is a threat to those that do not.' He cites 'ten of Cisco's largest customers' who 'are installing new software in their own computers to tie their inventory and procurement systems to Cisco's systems'. That gives them the same kind of advantage that Johnson & Johnson acquired by linking its computers with those of Nypro, its supplier of plastic mouldings for soft contact lenses.

Such purchasing linkages could force companies into the Information Revolution technology even if their managements have failed to appreciate the opportunity. The infomediaries are by no means alone in changing the rules of purchasing by opening new websites. Large corporations are centralising purchases in a way which puts immediate pressure on suppliers. At General

Electric, for example, huge savings are expected in both money and time (with the purchasing cycle halved) as suppliers bid for its business over the Web. In the affected product groups, you either trade with GE over these sites, or you don't trade.

Writing in the March–April 1998 issue of the *Harvard Business Review*, Ghosh was prescient about the sales and profit troubles that were to hit Compaq and force out its one-time hero, Eckhard Pfeiffer, in the spring of 1999. What if GE wanted to buy Compaq's PCs over the Net? Compared to Dell's direct selling, Ghosh observed, Compaq's business model of selling through distributors meant that its 'costs were higher, its pricing and information systems are designed for conducting business through distributors, and any move Compaq makes toward accepting orders over the Internet could threaten those distributors'.

At that time, Dell's Web sales had already reached $3 million a day: a year later they had more than doubled. By moving to the Web, the supplier gains from internal efficiencies which offset its lower prices. There is no alternative to joining the game, and not only because of the pressure of giants. As Ghosh says, 'Ultimately the risk of Internet commerce for established businesses is not from digital tornadoes, but from digital termites.' In the digital business itself, relatively small distributors such as Ingram Micro and MicroAge are using the Web to muscle into the territory of their retailers, who in turn are using electronic ordering to make own-brand computers.

Ghosh describes these activities as piracy. The pirates 'are essentially eliminating layers of costs that are built into the current distribution system'. Should you pirate your value chain? Ghosh proposes four key criteria to consider in reaching an answer:

- Can you realise significant margins by consolidating parts of the value chain to your customer?
- Can you create significant value for customers by reducing the number of entities they have to deal with in the value chain?
- What additional skills would you need to develop or acquire

   to take over the functions of others in your value chain?
- Will you be at a competitive disadvantage if someone else moves first to consolidate the value chain?

The answer to the last question is more than likely to be yes. Value chains in the affected industries (for which, eventually, read all industries) are being taken apart. The car giants like General Motors will find Internet companies like Auto-by-Tel stealing their end-markets and their margins. The giants in turn will seek greater economies by integrating their purchasing with their suppliers: the US car industry is already linked to components suppliers by one of the largest extranets. From every direction, new forces are at work to turn cyberspace into the world's dominant market. It is impossible to avoid the consequences.

BOOK NINE

The Knowledge Powerhouse

25

Resourcing the Revolution

Guru after guru has pronounced that capital, labour and raw materials are no longer the key resources. Knowledge and information have taken over. The new kind of company is built around information flows and the mobilisation of knowledge in every corner of the organisation. IT transforms the data that every corporation collects into a knowledge powerhouse, a unique source of competitive advantage.

The power of these developments is so obvious that the 'information society' has become a truism. But behind the clichés about the knowledge economy, the knowledge company and the knowledge worker, lies the reality that is reshaping the world – above all the world of business. In his book, *Intellectual Capital: The New Wealth of Nations*, Thomas Stewart writes of 'the end of management as we know it'. He delineates accurately how management must change in order to manage not one but three varieties of intellectual capital.

'Human capital', which consists of individuals' mental powers and resources, is the most widely understood of the trio. But 'structural capital', the accumulated knowledge and know-how of the organisation, is at least as important. The third form of capital, 'customer knowledge', is the most difficult to pin down. As Stewart says, it is 'probably . . . the worst managed of all intangible assets'. Clearly, you cannot afford to mismanage any of the three varieties. To manage them well, however, requires what we call the New Business Model. It contains only four elements and, used to help apply new technology, it is the antidote to unnecessary complexity, while providing necessary consistency and stability. The elements are:

- Strategic direction and vision (human capital)
- Customer focus (customer knowledge)
- Products and processes (structural capital)

  which together form the fourth element:

- Culture.

All four elements revolve around the core of applied technology. Any one of the four can generate killer apps. Some apps will produce significant improvement rather than sweeping reform. But the latter is the ultimate objective: the killer application that not only leads to a transformation of the killer company, but transforms the entire industry in which it operates. Once a company sees what can be done with the first apps, it can see and seize the 'killer opp' – the killer opportunity to reposition itself and win sustainable competitive advantage in a world of ferment and constant change.

Speaking of the 'killer app', Steve Merry, formerly European director of IT for Kodak, now with H. J. Heinz, observes: 'It sounds dreadful! It sounds as though you are going to attack somebody, but it is actually well-named, because that is what we are using them to do.' Kodak is among the early users of the killer apps process, which the Leading Change Partnership consultancy has developed for BT and its customers. The development grew out of two regular seminars, which we call 'Winning Market Acceptance' and 'Riding the Revolution', at which BT personnel and their customers are introduced to the rich opportunities of IP technology.

The two seminars lay the foundations for the Partnership Approach, in which BT and the customer work together to exploit the abundant opportunities that lie in collaboration. The whole programme is a demonstration of knowledge management. The combined knowledge and know-how of the customer, BT and ourselves is applied to products and processes in order to find successful uses of IP technology. Two essential criteria need to be met: speed and simplicity, which go hand in hand.

The traditional broad-band approach to IT systems is too bureaucratic and takes too long (and too many consultants and too much money). If you have to think about the application for too long, and then spend seemingly endless months in preparation before delivery, you will probably miss the killer opportunity. The companies that have been the first to take new technologies into the marketplace over the past decade have often won such a clear advantage that nobody else has been able to catch up.

Industry Transformation

Amazon.com is a clear case of industry transformation produced by the killing application of existing technology. Its success, like the killer approach as a whole, lies not in inventing some wonderful new technical advance, but in exploiting the capability of existing technology and getting to market faster than the opposition.

Our killer apps programme is therefore founded firmly on a key principle: the application of IP technology is a strategic issue which must be led by business, not technology. By definition, a killer app achieves and sustains a sharper competitive edge, increased revenues, higher margins and/or expanded market share. We believe further that senior managers need practical help, not months of strategic studies followed by expensive consultancy solutions. It is surely much more useful to deliver benefits quickly by using the skills and experience of the people in the company.

The business framework and implementation process are also simple. If the customer is not already wired up, he starts by going online with a standard, inexpensive, effective system: we helped to develop BT's Freedom product for precisely such a system. Then, after a two-hour customer briefing, we stage our half-day Killer Applications Workshop (KAW). This takes the management team through its business needs and the ways in which IP applications can meet those requirements. Initially, the workshop is likely to concentrate on 'building blocks', standardised BT applications, which can be applied step by step to achieve business transformation. The standard products include:

- The real time information system
- The real time supply chain
- The customer loyalty programme
- The direct-to-market model

A real time information system seeks to eliminate the waste caused by inaccuracy and poor availability of information. In money terms (see chapter 21) the cost can run at anything up to 40 per cent of the cost base of the business. Giving people the information they need when they need it significantly reduces this hidden expense. It also creates opportunity. Recognising that access to information is among the most powerful weapons in Microsoft's armoury, Bill Gates sings the praises of his central Web location called InSite: 'At the end of each consultancy engagement we require a Microsoft consultant to post technology solutions [to InSite] for the benefit of other technical employees, and we evangelise the use of InSite to reduce preparation time and risk in consulting engagements.'

An InSite-type solution, pooling and updating key information, is simple in concept, provision and cost. Giving people what they need when they need it is also the secret of the real time supply chain. The process of speeding up supply is one of streamlining, eliminating unnecessary stages and cutting out waiting time while documentation is processed. The Killer Apps Workshop challenges the long lead-times that many businesses take for granted. For example, getting fashions into a large store chain can take a whole year. The Killer Apps approach takes nothing for granted – particularly not so long and risky a delay.

The programme's building blocks of applications obviously must be aligned with the company's strategic direction and vision, which senior management must explain in a simple mission statement and slogan that everyone in the organisation can understand and agree. Typically mission statements fall short and sound much like everybody else's: viz, 'To be recognized as the leading supplier of [whatever], continuously improving our products and services to meet customer requirements.'

The Gates Vision

Gates's long-standing vision – 'a computer on every desk and in every home, running Microsoft software' – is a far superior mission statement – clear, concise and hard-nosed. It was not improved by the later omission, presumably on public relations grounds, of the last three words: 'running Microsoft software'. The original statement, and any mission statement worth the paper on which it is written, answers the question famously posed by Harvard's Ted Levitt: 'What business are we in?' And the next two questions follow logically: 'What do we need to be good at? Where must the organisation excel to achieve its business objectives?'

One answer to the third question will be the same for all companies. You have to excel at retaining existing customers and attracting new ones. Without customers, after all, there is no business. The power of customer process, however, has been transformed by IP technology. As Steve Merry says: 'It is very simple to communicate and to transmit data very quickly, and capture and keep a customer.'

For example, effective use of the new technology will easily accomplish an essential task that many companies today find near-impossible: getting a breakdown of where the company really earns its revenues. The 20/80 rule invariably applies: a small proportion of customers will account for the bulk of the revenues and profits. IT will quickly tell you which customers are among the significant few. The technology then enables you to turn the critical relationships into permanent assets.

At Advance International Group, chief executive Tony Belisario discovered that one of his companies was earning 93 per cent of revenues from only nine customers. Mike Peacock, the quality director, followed up this information by using IP technology. It enabled Advance to share information with the nine key customers, saving time and improving communication on both sides. This system of shared information simultaneously develops and strengthens customer loyalty: a very severe failure is required to break the bonds created by jointly installing browser-based information systems that are simple and effective in use.

Shared information systems are much better than customer surveys in achieving customer satisfaction and loyalty. The Internet facilitates continuous, two-way communication in a way that no other technology can match. You share key information online with your customers, working together to develop the Web pages. The feedback is then built into both your operations and those of your customer. You can far more easily achieve the perceived 'excellence' of service which provides a six-to-one advantage in customer retention, even over competitors whose rating is 'good'.

BT's experience with Kodak in Europe illustrates the power of the killer apps approach. Like many other organisations, Kodak is going through a revolution in the types of product it makes and markets, in this case particularly in the digital arena. The revolution requires a wholly different way of selling products and dealing with end-users. The issue was how IP technology could help to resolve the many issues created by strategic upheaval. The programme started from a sensible appreciation of where to start. To quote Steve Merry: 'One of the difficulties with what people are calling Internet trading, is that senior management, if I'm being honest, are not so good and well educated at these things. There are a lot of people who don't understand it, and that's the bottom line.'

Past failures have burnt the fingers of many managers, some of whom remain sceptical about investing in IT. But Kodak was determined to educate management about the IP opportunities. Considerable effort was required. Just assembling the busy regional business unit managers from across Europe was a major exercise. The briefing that followed, however, convinced managers that the killer apps approach was the best suited to Kodak's needs for speed and directness. So the company moved on to the next stage: the Killer Applications Workshop.

This session developed a long 'want' list from discussions with the Kodak managers. BT's Chris Downing and the authors then demonstrated some simple answers, applications that got to the customer quickly and promised to generate new business, growth and profits. Several examples of successful uses of killer apps were shown: 'They were so damned obvious!', was one comment. 'What was possible with this new medium . . . was an amazing revelation to us.' For example, digital products are typically high-value items with a six to nine-month life-cycle. One such Kodak product had reached the end of its life: an ad on the Web sold 400 units within two to three hours.

Killing with a KAIT

Turning a want-list like Kodak's into working applications is the task of the Killer Apps Implementation Team, the KAIT. The team, which tackles a specific app, is multi-disciplinary and multi-level. BT experts participate with the customer's staff, who thus understand the impact of the changes and take full ownership of the project. It is a genuine partnership: a shared commitment to the continuous identification and achievement of business benefits afforded by the killer applications which are unique to the Internet revolution. Creating a working partnership has three stages:

1 Who are they? Who are the senior managers who will take responsibility for applying Internet technology to achieve business benefits?

2 What they are like? Who are the visionaries who will enthusiastically adopt the new? Who are the pragmatists who want proof that it works? Who are the conservatives who oppose change? The task is then to build the leadership position through the visionaries: they will convince the pragmatists, who in turn will shift the conservatives.

3 What do they need? What product features and functionality? What service quality? What business benefits? What killer apps can deliver these benefits fast?

With these questions resolved, the Partnership Approach provides the continuous relationship vital to developing and maintaining customer loyalty. It turns strategic direction and vision into strong customer focus by developing products and processes in shared ways which, by the very act of sharing, develop the revolutionary culture demanded in the Age of the Internet. Intellectual capital, in both structural and human forms, comes together with customer knowledge. It is a winning combination.

26

Running the Cybercorp

The information-based company depends on two nervous systems: the private and secure intranet for internal use; and the external network linking customers, suppliers and the general public to the central brain. That brain is everywhere and nowhere, acquiring, storing and processing the knowledge which runs the 'cybercorp', or the 'E-corporation'.

As a *Fortune* headline put it in December 1998, 'The smartest companies are using the Net to create a whole new way of doing business. Call it the E-corporation.' The accompanying article by Gary Hamel and Jeff Sampler insisted that 'a real E-corp isn't just using the Internet to alter its approach to markets and customers: it's combining computers, the Web and the massively complex programs known as enterprise software to change *everything* about how it operates'.

The word 'cybercorp' was coined by James Martin, a famous industry guru, and used as the title for his book on the 'New Business Revolution'. His paragon is the virtual company, 'virtual' meaning 'that something *appears* to exist . . . when in actuality it does not'. This entity, which also merits the description 'everywhere and nowhere', is only one of the state-of-the-art transformations in progress in millennial business. Most could happen (and many have) without the Internet; yet most cannot be fully grasped without understanding the impact of cyberspace.

The IT revolution has vastly enhanced management's ability to deploy new, accelerated processes. The companies that most avidly embrace the new technologies of management and information are putting irresistible pressure on the laggards. The pace-makers, writes Martin, 'think of business opportunities in terms of cyberspace, radically changed marketing, value streams reinvented for real-time interaction, agile intercorporate relationships and new employee teams'. The internal and external nervous systems, in a very real sense, are the company.

Bill Gates also uses the metaphor of the nervous system in his 1999 book, *Business @ the Speed of Thought*. This is the summation of Gates's conversion to the Internet, one of the great U-turns of business. When he published *The Way Ahead* in 1995, the master entrepreneur, acclaimed as a technological seer, seemed oddly oblivious to the world-changing importance of the Net. But in the second edition, published in 1996, the Internet had taken centre stage. Microsoft, which might otherwise have suffered total eclipse, had grasped its importance just in time. Gates has undergone a truly Pauline conversion to cyberspace, and every manager needs to understand why.

The regular use of PCs at work and at home, the routine employment of e-mail, the spread of personal digital devices and the rapidly increasing number of Internet users are enlarging and changing the boundaries of the wired world all the time. In the last year of the old millennium, free Internet access spread like a bushfire through Britain. At the same time in the US, as noted earlier, the first PCs were being given away to people signing up for Internet access. You need no great prophetic powers to see the consequences of this sea change.

As people's lives change, so will their work. Riding the Revolution demands changing the organisation, and how it is managed, in order to meet fast-changing and more imperious demands from customers. Their use of the World Wide Web still seems peripheral to many managers, who, despite the Internet's astronomical growth, take comfort in the still relatively small size of Internet transactions. But they can't take comfort for long. Gates rightly regards the killer apps within Microsoft as the indispensable foundations of the equally effective apps that customers can make using his software.

The phrase 'killer app', though, contains one trap. It suggests that once the application is in place, the 'kill' has been made. IP technology, however, allows constant revision, without which the best of apps may lose its killing edge. *CIO WebBusiness* magazine describes this revision as an 'imperative', adding that 'Web work is never done'. Exactly the same imperative applies to intranets (the core of Microsoft's 'digital nervous system'). The magazine's champions in all varieties of application adopt continuous and radical change.

Scope and Service

Its 1998 website rankings featured three 'returning champions' from 1997, who all demonstrated that 'they'd significantly improved their sites' scope and service'. They included Cisco, the biggest Webseller of them all, which derives over half its revenues from its site. Cisco demonstrates the truth that once a site is established commercially, the key to sustained success is to widen the offer to attract new customers and increase the business won from existing users.

That one-two combination punch is the ideal of all marketers. Some businesses will find that Web customers are being converted from existing sales. This prospect (the dreaded 'cannibalisation') frightens some companies away from using the Web at all. Their fright may rob them of a far bigger prize, getting new customers and business on a significantly greater scale – exactly what Charles Schwab won after adding an Internet service and sacrificing $124 million through lower commissions.

Another champion website in *CIO WebBusiness*'s rankings belongs to the US Corporation Co., which provides one-stop shopping for research, retrieval and filing of public business forms covering all fifty states. The corporations and law firms who patronise the service used to buy only the company's proprietary software. Many of them have converted to the firm's IncSpot Website. In fourteen months, IncSpot registered four times as many customers as the software product had acquired in five years. In other words, by cannibalising its own product, IncSpot hugely expanded its overall business.

Well into 1999 we wave still talking of visionaries who have the 'courage' to take their organisations into the new era. But how much courage do you require to buy £100 notes for a pound coin? Benefits like those won by IncSpot or Charles Schwab are the equivalent. It takes foolhardiness to throw such opportunities away. Absolutely no courage whatsoever is required to appreciate the folly of the following:

- Sticking with paperwork systems when digital text will execute the same tasks far more efficiently.
- Making team members and teams work independently when they could use the same data simultaneously.
- Having out-of-date and incomplete information about sales and customers.
- Keeping suppliers and customers in the dark, and being equally ignorant about them yourself, instead of developing a true, close business partnership.

The digital office, genuine groupwork, the real-time information system and supplier partnerships are all readily available. Moreover, if you're quick, you still have a chance to catch up. All the other laggards who have yet to transact any serious business on the Internet have left gigantic openings for others. Less than 1 per cent of US gross domestic product will be transacted on the Internet by 2001. That, however, represents an eightfold increase over 1997. As the number of connections with the Internet mushrooms, achieving saturation quite soon in the millennium, the pull to the Net will become irresistible.

There's another harmful side to the four follies listed above. The customer actually wants what the company is denying. Dealing with a company over the Web has great advantages over personal shopping, including greater convenience and faster service. Dealing with people who know all about you and your needs, and have the information literally at their fingertips, is far superior to the alternative. Not only your treatment, but what you are buying can be personalised. The new phrase 'customer-centric' is acquiring real meaning as relationships are strengthened by the new technology. Managers have been told for years to achieve 'customer focus', to begin and end all processes with the customers, first defining and then fulfilling their needs, and constantly changing as markets and competition change. Managers, by and large, merely paid lip service to customer strategy. In the age of the Internet this option no longer exists. But the cybercorp is not just a conventional corporation with some cyberspace technology grafted on. The cybercorp is a whole new kind of organisation, which works, not because of its systems, but through them.

Gunk in, Gunk out

The old GIGO saw about computers ('Gunk In, Gunk Out') still applies. Microsoft's own 'digital nervous system' (DNS), for instance, hasn't prevented a whole series of mishaps and mistakes, from the failure to grasp the early significance of the Internet to its weak competition against Intuit in financial software. The explanation may lie partly in the ultimate autocracy of the organisation: Gates has been used to taking all the large decisions, and many of the small. Furthermore, a proliferation of digital systems, and the insistence on their use, can mislead people into thinking that the system is the business. It isn't, even for Amazon.com.

Several of Gates's examples of excellent, path-finding use of the DNS are unconvincing, given the actual marketplace and workplace results. He heaps praise on Marks & Spencer and its use of IT to 'respond immediately to customer preferences and to achieve the kind of personalised service that's impossible to get at a typical supermarket'. But the praise sounds very unconvincing after the Christmas 1998 season, in which M&S pitched its demand forecasts far too high. It thus oversupplied a market which, in any case, had turned away from the company's fashions and foods towards those of other suppliers.

When analysts and journalists looked at the resulting débâcle (which coincided with an embarrassing public squabble over who should be the next chief executive), they criticised M&S heavily for failing to meet customer preferences. A senior executive blamed the company's troubles in part on the screens:

managers had become so intent on studying the data that they had forgotten to study the customer. Far more important, however, was the effect of a top-heavy corporate structure, which still managed the company in conventional, bureaucratic ways.

Gates also praised Boeing's use of IT. But its system didn't prevent Boeing from taking on far more jetliner orders than it could meet with its existing production capacity and methods. In 1998, this had disastrous results. Now, says Gates, a 'new digital process will . . . drive Boeing's entire production': but that is slamming the stable door after the horse (and with it the boss of airliner production) has bolted. With only one competitor, Airbus Industrie, in a booming world airliner market, Boeing in March 1999 was valued at $34 billion, a humiliating 40 per cent less than its sales.

Even more humiliating, this valuation is 60 per cent less than that of Lucent Technologies, the spun-off manufacturing arm of phone giant AT&T. Lucent is half Boeing's size and earns less profit. The Seattle aerospace company could take lessons from its neighbour, Microsoft, in the vital characteristics of the cyber-corp: outsourcing everything but its core activities to outside suppliers, keeping full-time employment as low as possible, having its work done in the best and/or most economic location, and (unlike Boeing) continuously acting to shorten cycle time and improve process speed.

As James Martin writes in *Cybercorp*, the question to ask is 'What should my corporation look like if it takes maximum advantage of cyberspace, cybernetics and superhighways?' The answers 'for many in traditional companies . . . are startling.' The crucial point, in Martin's view, is that the cybercorp standing alone is far less powerful than cybercorps linked electronically:

An order placed in Spain with an order-entry computer in France triggers manufacturing planning software in New York to place items into a manufacturing schedule in Dallas, which requires chips from Japan to be built into circuit boards in Singapore, with final assembly in the robotic factory in Dallas and computer-controlled shipment from a warehouse in Milan.

The cybercorp has no boundaries. But it does have rules, and they do not change, even within a corporation that is built round change. Martin calls this 'fundamental wisdom'. What he lists under that heading wouldn't surprise anybody at a business school, whether professor or student: 'core values, strong cultures, clearly articulated vision, audacious goals, continuous process improvement, and management who pay careful attention to detail'. These fit perfectly well with the eight attributes that Tom Peters and Robert Waterman enunciated in *In Search of Excellence* in 1983. So what's new?

Martin's answer is a charter for corporate subversives. The 'fundamental wisdom' is the wisdom of stability, which no longer exists. The cybercorp has 'different clockwork, different architecture, changed marketing'. It is virtual in operation (that is, using outsourcing and direct connections to customers and suppliers). It is 'as fluid as mercury' and can 'dynamically link competencies from agile webs of associates'. This is an organisation 'designed for very fast evolution', which needs 'new thinking'. The chances of a traditional, conventional business developing these attributes are virtually nil.

Ten Behaviour Changes

You can't expect General Motors, ICI, Siemens, Philips or Renault to throw in the towel and wait to die. Right down the corporate scale, the imperative is to change behaviour, because if behaviour changes sufficiently so will culture. Martin lists ten key behaviour changes, which we would strongly endorse:

1. *Eliminate delays where possible*. IP technology can be used to reduce delays through just-in-time techniques, continuous flow manufacturing, real-time information exchange, etc.

2. *Link causes and geographically distant effects*. Internet or intranet systems will enable you to see the consequences in Asia of a marketing decision taken in East Anglia.

3. *Link causes and time-distant effects*. The system will watch out for consequences remote in time and relay them instantly.

4. *Combine responsibility for cause and effect*. Ignore hierarchy: reorganise activities round value streams, and use electronic links so members know what is happening all the way down the stream.

5. *Stop feedback before it becomes dangerous*. Design processes to react to feedback before problems escalate dangerously.

6. *Simulate the system dynamics*. Use simulation to teach managers how the system operates and to experiment with variations in safety.

7. *Facilitate learning about system behaviour*. Simulation helps to establish systems thinking, and to show managers how to recognise 'counter-intuitive' situations – for example, when increasing promotion to meet sales targets results in less profit, not more.

8. *Build closer interactions among trading partners*. Close relationships between trading partners 'prevent overswings, delays and harmful feedback'.

9. *Simplify systems and their human interactions*. Multi-stage processes can often be replaced by one team with digital information. So start replacing.

10. *Stop building stovepipe systems*.

It's the tenth Martin recommendation that strikes home hardest. In company after company, departments and functions and profit centres act as if nobody else existed. Outside, retailers and distributors operate independently of the supplier. Their separate IT systems seek to optimise their individual performance, but in doing so not only undermine the whole, but threaten to destroy it. Using IP technology to create shared systems will not by itself create a cybercorp, but you will have taken a long stride in the right direction.

27

Managing the Knowledge

'Knowledge management' has become the latest technique, an essential part of the 'learning company'. The latter absorbs and acts on proven knowledge and feedback to provide a basis for action. Linked over the internal and external networks, people exchange, incorporate and apply knowledge to achieve shared results. But what exactly is that knowledge? Probed more deeply, it seems, in the words of Dr Myrna Gilbert, 'very complex, difficult to define, difficult to hold on to, slippery'.

'How then are we going to manage knowledge?' Gilbert asks. A visiting professor at Cranfield University, she has been closely involved in a joint research project between Cranfield and BT, which has developed a new diagnostic tool to map information flows at the operational level. The idea is to highlight the main channels and to remove the constrictions and blockages.

As Gilbert says, 'knowledge management is about people and processes ... interactions, acquiring and transferring knowledge'. Some companies confuse this with databases and communication, which sets them off in the wrong direction. Other managements worry about whether in this soft environment, they can get answers to hard-nosed questions like these:

- What are the competitive advantages?
- What are the tangible benefits?
- How much does it cost?
- Can the cost be justified?

These pragmatists also worry about the available frameworks and approaches, and, critically, whether the decisions that result from knowledge managers will make a receptive environment. Will the future take too long to happen? One British database company, for example, observed the rise of the Internet and concluded, like many other businesses in publishing, that the future lay in cyberspace. It took decisive action, at great expense, converting its database information from hard to soft. A comprehensive website was set up, which was a huge improvement on the company's old twice-yearly loose-leaf binders. The clients loved the idea, but when the project started in the late 1990s very few large UK companies were Internet-friendly. They might have a website themselves, but they had not gone interactive.

Even as the millennium neared, the idea of using the Net for daily business transactions remained for the most part just an idea. Yet everybody, from customers to IT suppliers, recognises that one day the digital revolution will take over the bulk of transactions, just as it has already seized communications. So a yawning gap has opened up between present-day potential and practice. But it will close.

In 1997, a seminar on the business uses of the Internet was packed with managers who had plainly been attracted by its potential, but hardly any of their companies had even a single Internet project in hand. Moreover present-day potential runs far behind developments: future technology is still advancing at lightning speed. According to Richard Howard, director of wireless research at Lucent Bell Laboratories, the pace of change is actually accelerating. The next two decades, he feels, will 'see explosive growth of communications, computing, memory, wireless and broad-band technology'. Inevitably, these advances will have a powerful impact on business.

The Universal Linkage

Internally, intranets will become the universal electronic linkages for organisations, not only bringing great improvements to basic functions such as communications, database apps and reporting, opening the door to the decisive corporate power: knowledge. This requires, as Chuck Lucier of Booz Allen Hamilton has observed, getting staff to share best thinking; use other people's ideas; collaborate with other experts; and evolve their thinking. These four elements, while brilliantly facilitated by networks, don't come naturally. Knowledge management is essential. The breakdown of departmental and disciplinary barriers that its implementation involves, and their replacement by a horizontal, fluid, organic culture is a test of management. The companies that pass this test to exploit their internal accumulation of knowledge, as well as their access to external sources will win in the marketplace.

Major adaptation could be required, endangering many current operations. Bill Joy, head of research at Sun Microsystems, told *Business Week* that the likely changes would 'carve middlemen out of transactions'. As we noted earlier, in the PC business firms like Dell Computer have already carved away the intermediaries, but many of Joy's other predictions have also become fact: online auctions in real time, for example, undermine the differential pricing that forces business travellers to pay more for airline tickets than occasional fliers. Networks give people access to what things are really worth, defined by what people will pay at that minute.

Since the cost of networks is dropping as fast as they spread, no management can afford to stay on the sidelines. As a fascinating survey by *Business Week* shows, research is growing apace in all directions and could result in computers very different from today's boxes, with their windows, icons and often clumsy programs. The future promises much easier computer use and the ubiquity of knowledge at much lower prices: the cost of a given amount of computer power is halving every eighteen months.

Business managers can with confidence ask for the moon, so

to speak. What level of information and communication do you ideally require? Almost certainly, it's yours: if not today, then early tomorrow. The strategic programme is clear. Plan ahead in full awareness of the impact that the digital revolution may have on the business, internally and externally. Ensure that the corporate and information strategies are tied closely together. Make sure that current systems are state-of-the-art quality to provide a solid foundation for the future, while planning future systems to fit in with strategic needs.

If you do this, then you've created the ultimate in knowledge management. 'The most successful corporation of the 1990s will be something called a learning organisation, a consummately adaptive enterprise.' This forthright prediction, made by *Fortune* magazine, is based on the latest preachings of the management gurus. Not content with virtual corporations, time-based competition, total quality management, etc., the gurus are now demanding that organisations become gurus themselves and take charge of their own education.

As usual, it was Peter Drucker who first signalled the trend. He spotted that information had replaced physical assets as the backbone of business. In today's competition, what you know determines what you can provide and sell, and how. Therefore, the competitor who knows most and uses that knowledge most effectively, must win. Moreover, information is being constantly outdated: so winners will update their knowledge continuously to retain their lead.

This general truth is illustrated by the ups and downs of information technology, where knowledge differentials have led to rapid changes of leader in every field from spreadsheets to supercomputers. It's not just a matter of technology. The power of learning affects every activity inside the company, and dictates its ability to succeed outside in the marketplace where the customers live.

'Today leading firms seek to understand and meet the "latent need" of the customer – what customers might truly value but have never experienced and would never think to ask for,' commented Peter Senge, the MIT professor who has become heavily identified with the concept of the learning organisation. But companies, argues Senge, don't only need to be *adaptive*, they must above all become *generative*.

To illustrate the difference, he cites the comment of a Detroit executive on Mazda's fun sports car: 'You could never produce the Mazda Miata solely from market research. It required a leap of imagination to see what the customer *might* want.' That's an example of generative learning, in which the learner 'acquires new ways of looking at the world, whether in understanding customers or in understanding how to better manage a business'.

Adaptive Learning

By contrast, the adaptive learner essentially reacts to changing circumstances. Many companies, of course, have failed to react to change, some through utterly failing to compete with Japanese rivals which produced new models faster, cheaper and to far higher standards of quality. Now, of course, everybody left in the affected industries has adapted or is adapting: it's do or die. But the stable door is being shut well after the horses (billions in lost sales) have bolted.

Manfred Perlitz of the University of Mannheim points out that the West's adaptive learners have been busy winning the last war. The race will now be won, not by the most efficient user of the 'just-in-time' principle, with the lowest rate of defects and the highest output per man-hour, but by the leaders in creativity. Senge makes the same point, and so too do the Japanese. They've even invented a perfectly awful word, 'creagement', to describe the creative management processes which are needed.

What does all this mean for management and managers? In the first place, the old targets expressed purely in financial terms have become even more inadequate. Perlitz warns that the high rate of innovation needed won't be achieved unless companies set specific goals for, say, the annual earnings and sales to be generated by new products. Reward systems must recognise that reality, partly by becoming less systematic. What carefully calibrated yardstick can you put on creating the future of the company?

The learning organisation seeks to generate the future it

wants. Its philosophy is totally opposed to out-worn defences of the *status quo* like 'That's the way we've always done things round here'. Senge instead calls for 'creative tension' – 'seeing clearly where we want to be . . . and telling the truth about where we are'.

Corporate strategists and total quality companies have long been accustomed to establishing the gap between 'vision' and 'reality' in this way. The difference is that Senge challenges the realism of most ideas on reality. Managers, like everybody else, focus on isolated events rather than patterns of behaviour. Even if they look at the latter, they rarely look behind patterns to the systemic structure that is the ultimate reality.

The car industry serves as an excellent and chilling example. Western manufacturers quickly spotted the rise in Japanese car sales, for which all kinds of irrelevant explanations were offered, from cheating to unfair cultural attributes. Then they noticed the patterns of behaviour – the way in which the Japanese produced and marketed cars. But Westerners have only recently realised that their own defective methods flowed from rigid corporate systems in which design, marketing, production and finance were separate, warring camps.

In contrast, for its new Omega executive range, GM Europe, for the first time in its history, formed thirteen teams for each part of the car, each manned by all ten functions, from design to finance. By working together, people learn from each other. That's one way in which the learning organisation is becoming reality. More and more, managers (and other employees, for that matter) are forming self-directed teams in which know-how and information are pooled. More and more, too, management development itself is founded on team-working, tackling real-life corporate problems – from strategy downwards.

Shifting the Burden

Many real-life problems, on analysis, tend to be of the type that Senge calls 'shifting the burden'. An agonising symptom shows up – say, falling sales. You can respond in two ways: attacking the sales shortfall directly, or finding the underlying cause and treating that. Human nature being what it is, most managements treat the symptom and not the disease. So, to take our example, they launch a marketing promotion drive to boost the sales. But even if that succeeds, the problem, since its cause remains, will recur, possibly in a more virulent form.

In one case cited by Senge, a management team looked beneath the symptom to find the underlying cause of recurrent sales difficulties. Curing the symptom had indeed worsened the disease. The real defect was lagging introduction of new products – the company had never heard the Perlitz message. But, as a side-effect, the reliance on marketing expenditure to save the day had inevitably promoted the saviours to high positions in the company. They knew masses about marketing, but nothing of new product development, which had languished accordingly in a vicious circle.

Three chief executives in succession had come from advertising. The remedy for the firm's decline turned out to lie as far from the consumer as possible – in the boardroom. Even if pursuing the symptoms and not the cause doesn't worsen the problem directly, it always does so indirectly by delaying the necessary action. This may seem obvious, but what has it got to do with *learning*? Shouldn't common sense alone have spotted the new product lag, or the advantages of the Japanese carmakers?

Not by itself: *informed* common sense is the catalyst for effective change. Xerox was shocked into a massive effort to change its ways by *learning*, through a team of line managers, that Japanese competitors in copiers were winning, not because of skulduggery, but because of superior methods of production and management.

To accomplish the vital change and reverse its calamitous loss of market share, Xerox had to resort to learning in the traditional sense. Every one of 28,000 Rank Xerox employees, for example, was trained in the principles and practice of total quality. Exercises in radical reform of specific activities such as 'continuous improvement' or 'business process re-engineering', provide a double education. First, the participants have to learn the tools and techniques with which to tackle the process. Second, they learn from the experience of undertaking the project as a team and driving it to a successful conclusion.

It's a truism of total quality, though, that the emphasis must lie on the *total*. Unless everybody, from the summit of management to the shopfloor, is involved in learning and improvement, the organisation ends up with pockets of excellence. Its parts will add up to an unsatisfactory whole. In the learning organisation, everybody learns, which means that everyone is taught – an idea that many senior managers find personally uncomfortable.

But if they don't learn, the discomfort will eventually prove much greater, for themselves and the organisation. The organisation *per se* can't learn: it's amorphous and inhuman. But the humans who animate the organisation can create an environment that is both adaptive and generative. Companies need that, no matter which of the gurus or change programmes they follow. For without that environment of successfully managed knowledge, managers who seek successful change are wasting their time, and their greatest, human assets.

BOOK TEN

The Winning Way

28

Leading the Revolution

The Triple Revolution confronts companies with only one real way to win – networking the company within a networked business system and regarding the state of the art as purely temporary. Such an approach will alter management in all aspects and lead to ambitious, shared strategies. It is no panacea, however. The network leaves management open to abuse and abusing, unless top managers themselves can radically change their behaviour patterns. Leading the revolution is what it says: a leadership issue.

Bad, ill-led behavioural patterns confine major corporations to their over-prescriptive, over-restrictive ways. Writing in *Fortune*, Michael Schrage gives a chilling example of the old mentality at work in the new clothes of the IP revolution. Intranets enable collaborative working and information flows across the entire business, from top to bottom. They also, however, allow the bureaucrats to impose new rules and to check on obedience.

Major intranet users like General Electric and ABB 'now store databases enumerating the performance standards and process practices deemed "best" . . . [which] create brave new infostructures that effectively enforce employee compliance with organisational norms'. A brilliant new idea for re-engineering customer service stands less chance of acceptance if 'best practice' is already enshrined on the database, and controllers can discipline you for departing from the 'best'.

'Just how sustainable are "best practices" in a world built on the premise that change is the one constant?' Schrage's question plainly begs a negative answer. The network must be a living entity, which guides managers not towards the controlled environment of the past, but towards the directed anarchy that responds to new stimuli all the time and sets nothing in concrete. The network is a neural system, not a rulebook. Abusing the network is a dereliction of leadership, and a misuse of its power.

Visit a comprehensive intranet like BTs, and you quickly become aware of that power. Start with the Directory: enter someone's name, and in a flash you get the person's phone number and what he or she (one of 75,000 employees) is doing that day. If he's away or at a seminar, the intranet tells you, and you won't waste a phone call. Another click or two, and fuller details of the person flash onto the screen. Anybody can have their own home page. In the case of a particular manager, for example, it describes his team's work and provides access to the department's management system, meeting minutes, training records, and so on. All the department's documents and templates are available as well. These savings in paperwork will be repeated thousands of times over through the organisation.

Then, there's BT Today, which contains new information significant to the company. Items range from the CEO, Sir Peter Bonfield, addressing US investors (with a complete text of the speech) to secretaries drawing attention to missing messages. The share price is the permanent top item. There's also an unofficial Website giving further information about the shares (the system crashed when to the huge interest of the employee/shareholders, the price went through £10).

Another intranet feature, the ISIS Library, is an enormously rich source of information. Type in 'creosote', for example, and the Library will produce every reference to the subject. Technical information is thus available in seconds, where it once took weeks. ISIS can be accessed in any BT office, anywhere in BT, and also out in the field. In mid-1999 multi-media kiosks, a relatively primitive and unsatisfactory system, were still being used for this purpose: palmtop PCs will take over in due course.

There are believed to be two million pages on the BT intranet. Any such quantity would be grotesquely prohibitive in printed form. They are handled with consummate ease in a digital format: you see only a single page at any time, and the system guides you at a click to where you want to go, efficiently ignoring everything else. Such efficiency doesn't happen by itself. There is a steering group, with a manager, and there are 'franchise holders' responsible for different sections, but the system really revolves round 'information owners' and 'information providers', who sign up to abide by the guidelines.

Among the multitude of Web services is 'Job News'. Employees can see what jobs are available, what skills they require, what the jobs pay, how to apply, and so on. Then there's multimedia: one of the services here is 'Superoute 66', which shows you the position of buses travelling between BT's labs at Martlesham, Suffolk, and the train station. Satellite TV is the key to this minor marvel. You can also summon up a video picture of traffic conditions around the lab – very useful in the rush hour.

The Intranet Millions

The business benefit of BT's intranet has been put at the extraordinary figure of £750 million. The saving from the first application, the Directory, came to £900,000 on printing bills alone. Measured as a return on investment, the benefit has been put at 1,700 per cent. The precise figure may be arguable, but the point is that the cost of establishing an intranet is small compared to the huge returns if you go the whole way. *CIO WebBusiness* magazine defined five categories of wiring-up:

1 Broad operational application-supporting sites (addressing multiple operational areas or broad business processes).
2 Narrow operational application-supporting sites (addressing a single, narrow business process or application, such as benefits enrolment).
3 Intranet/extranet hybrids (intranets that selectively admit customers to password-protected areas).

4 Customer-care extranets (full-featured customer service/self-service or commerce-supporting sites).
5 Advanced knowledge-management sites.

True leaders encourage their networks to evolve. Intranets and extranets customarily begin with what *CIO WebBusiness* Magazine calls 'fat, happy buckets of information' – this was true of BT's intranet. But companies can soon begin to tackle some serious business goals, providing – as the magazine puts it – 'some fairly ambitious transactional capability'. Of the fifty winning sites that the magazine announced in its July 1998 issue, thirty-one 'performed predominantly operational roles in the form of robust transactional, process-interaction or workflow-enhancing capabilities'.

Not that the remaining nineteen intranets were purely passive. Though mainly devoted to sharing information internally, decision support or knowledge management, 'most offered implicit (and some explicit) benefits to internal decision-making quality, employee productivity, customer satisfaction or product-delivery cycle time'. 'Nothing to sneeze at,' as the magazine commented. Plainly a successful intranet expands its powers exponentially. The result can be paradoxical, as an executive at the pharmaceutical giant, Glaxo, told the *Financial Times*: 'We think of the intranet as the telephone. It's just part of the fabric . . . The people who said it would never work now say that it was their idea.'

In other words, as more and more applications are put on the intranet or extranet, proof-seeking pragmatists quickly become converted into risk-tasking visionaries. *CIO WebBusiness* gives examples of some killer apps from the Chrysler Corporation: competitive intelligence, collaborative work group support, HR self-service applications (including records administration), financial modelling tools, company news, a vehicle-build tracking system, manufacturing quality statistics – plus a 'dynamic' stock market site.

The Net promises to revolutionise government as well as business. Transactions between the citizen and the state can be processed in cyberspace at a huge saving, and many of the bug-

bears of civil administration, such as overlaps and poor communication between agencies, can become a thing of the past.
Moreover, internal relationships can be greatly improved in
government, just as in business: here (for one example) the
Lucent Technologies site proved valuable in establishing the
company's separate identity after spin-off from AT&T.

Distribution networks can be transformed by keeping information current and available to all participants in the supply
chain. Allied Van Lines, for example, estimated that its 500 agencies had saved over $6 million annually through the installation
of its intranet. Geographic dispersal can also be managed far
more effectively with intranet help. Houston Industries thus
gives its electric and gas facility managers real-time data for use
in power generation and transmission and in buying fuel: 'The
availability of this operational information has created a flatter
process-management structure that delivers improved efficiencies.'

One of the most striking intranet operations has been built
by Perot Systems, which H. Ross Perot founded after parting
with General Motors and EDS his original company in the same
computer services business. Perot's TRAIN system, a knowledge
management intranet, is reported to have cut the time taken
over developing proposals for customers by 40 per cent; cost of
developing proposals by 45 per cent: travel time required for
business development by 35 per cent: and time to market for
new offerings by 40 per cent. The TRAIN traffic is enormous:
2.1 million hits weekly from 4,800 employees.

Joining up The World

The demands of such networks e-commerce and multimedia
communications are driving a revolution in the huge telecom-
munications networks that connect the world. User pressure is
growing all the time. Today, via mobile phone terminals, you
can access a corporate network from almost anywhere in the
world. As Nick Hampshire writes in *CeBITViews*, 'users are wanting to attach a whole range of applications hardware that is just

starting to come onto the market'. These range from advanced Personal Digital Assistants, which are likely to become as ubiquitous as mobile phones (and mostly allied with them), to 'sophisticated electronic white board systems'. Hampshire predicts a revolution: 'Out will go the network loop to be replaced by point to point switching, and out will go the client/server model to be replaced by the triple layer database/application server/thin client model. Indeed, out will go much that is familiar in networking to be replaced by a whole range of new and exciting ideas.'

Setting the technicalities aside, this means that computing power is moving back down the network as the service providers aim to supply much more bandwidth with greater reliability. For networks based on mainframes and mini-computers downtime is already negligible: three to four hours a year, even zero. But it's deeply unsatisfactory that PC networks can go down for three to four hours a month. The technologists are hard at work seeking solutions. A fundamental fact of the Internet age, remember, is that problems in use automatically create advances in applications.

In a sense, indeed, the technology can be left to look after itself. The real issues are not technological, but managerial. How are benefits like those listed above going to be realised? How are the choices between technologies going to be made? Only when technology is utilised fully and focused to support business objectives can it provide competitive advantage.

In the West too much technology has been applied for its own sake, rather than as part of a total business strategy. The UK has won twenty-six post-war Nobel prizes for scientific innovation, but has failed to capitalize on this achievement in the world marketplace. By contrast, Japan has won just four Nobel prizes, yet its manufacturers have wiped out whole Western industries.

The blame for the West's failures to exploit technological advance lies squarely with management leadership. While the West fell prey to fashionable management theories, ubiquitous consultants and questionable techniques, the Japanese quietly applied simple frameworks, simple structures, simple processes and simple tools in a consistent and determined manner in their manufacturing industries (but unfortunately not in their financial institutions).

It is important to understand that Japanese success is based on communicating appropriate techniques through every level of the company. According to M. Bensaou of Insead and Michael Earl, writing in the *Harvard Business Review*, this is as true of information technology as in any other field. If this seems a surprise, it's because of the prevailing wisdom 'that Japanese companies lag behind the West in IT and that Japanese management could learn from US and European practices. Some Japanese believe that themselves.'

The Japanese Solution

Bensaou and Earl 'were startled to discover that Japanese companies rarely experience the IT problems so common in the US and Europe'. The Japanese simply adopt the approach so strongly recommended in this book: their leaders know that the purpose of IT is 'to help the organisation achieve its operational goals'. In other words, they don't (as in the West) try to develop an IT strategy that 'perfectly mirrors the company's business strategy'. Instead, they base their IT decisions on 'simple and easily quantified performance-improvement goals'. The Japanese model is:

- Let the basic means of competition, especially operational goals, drive IT investments.
- Judge investments by the improvement they make to operational performance.
- Select the technology that helps to achieve the chosen performance goal in a way that supports the staff involved.
- Rotate managers through the IT function, have IT specialists and users work together, and give IT supervision to managers who also have wider responsibilities.
- Design the system to use the tacit and explicit knowledge that people already possess.

The Killer Application Workshops and Teams that we have

created in our work for BT (see chapter 9) follow precisely these principles. They go against the grain for Western managers, who not only expect IT to provide a strategic big bang, but also – as Bensaou and Earl point out – use inappropriate capital-budgeting processes to run and evaluate their IT investments. Furthermore, they put the technology before the need, try to make specialist IT management business-conscious, and 'design the most technically elegant system possible and ask employees to adapt to it'.

This approach leads straight to a dire situation reported by the Wentworth Management Program. It cites a study by Standish researchers which found that half of all IT-dependent projects in the US overrun their budgets by 90 per cent, and fewer than one in ten is delivered on time. As for business benefits, a Cranfield survey in Britain showed that potential benefits were fully identified by less than a third of respondents. Two-thirds inadequately quantified the benefits – not surprisingly, given that nearly half admitted overstating the benefits in the first place to get project approval. In any case the benefits are often not realised for the following reasons:

- Lack of business accountability for benefits
- No commitment to the project from the business
- Not enough emphasis on changes in working practices
- Unrealistic benefits claimed at the outset
- No explicit success statements
- No success criteria sought and measured after implementation
- Uncertainty about benefits as they become harder to identify and measure

To this depressing list, we would add lack of leadership. None of these failings would occur in successful Japanese companies, whose senior executives are trained in what is needed to achieve improvement through technology and who personally lead education and training. In the US and the UK too many managements stop short of taking this active leadership role and delegate responsibility to their juniors, in particular to technical specialists in the IT and engineering functions.

This amounts to management by lip-service, the most popular

and least fruitful of all management techniques. The need for a radical rethink of the business is implicit in the application of technology to convert the company from a hierarchy to a network. As top hierarchs, that involves some sacrifice from senior managers and from many below them. The sacrifice is essential: otherwise they risk sacrificing the company.

29

Making the Transition

The application of technology in the context of the Triple Revolution imposes major demands on senior management. It requires that they lead the implementation in their organisations. Failure to do so will place their businesses in grave jeopardy. Fortunately, a clear set of guidelines exists, based on best practice. Following these is essential if the application of IP technology is to be successful. The guidelines focus on three key areas:

- Understanding the technology
- Understanding what the technology can do for your business
- Creating the environment for success

Unless managers understands the capabilities of the technology, how can they use it to improve competitiveness? Alarmingly, surveys show that 46 per cent of British managers do not believe that IT can raise competitive prowess, while 12 per cent know too little about IT even to express an opinion. By contrast, a large majority of US managers (74 per cent) believe in IT's competitive power. The surveys also suggest that managers in Germany and Singapore are far more aware of the prowess of IT than their UK counterparts.

Many British managers clearly perceive the Internet as just an extension of existing information technology. They are sure to be overlooking many valuable opportunities for simplifying and re-engineering processes. Similarly, if management sees the Internet as predominantly an internal and technically focused tool, invaluable supplier and customer contributions will be ignored. Such a technical focus will also fail to spot the so-called people issues that lead to developing and implementing the most effective applications of the technology.

The inescapable fact is that IP technology is a strategic investment affecting all aspects of the business. When developed and implemented correctly, it will have a major short, medium and long-term impact on competitiveness. Its reach extends far beyond a single functional area. The effect on overall competitiveness will be dramatic. Because it is such a key factor in the company's future success, all levels of management must be actively involved in debating and reaching the vital decisions on IT development and implementation. A top-down operation will lead to inferior solutions which are neither fully accepted nor effectively operated by the users. The essence of the technology is democratic. Unless it is used as a liberating force, its impact will be blunted.

The investment, moreover, is continuous. Consequently, both current and anticipated future requirements need to be considered if the full benefits are to be realised. Because future requirements can never be identified with precision, the focus should be on continuous development of fast and effective applications within a clear business framework. Many of these applications will be mundane, like replacing fax with e-mail for specific purposes. Others will provide the kind of lasting, massive advantage that, say, Cisco has won with its Website sales and services.

Next, before applying IP technology, full attention must be paid to simplifying the business processes. One of the major reasons why companies fail to secure the full benefits of any technology is that they do not undertake a fundamental rethink of the business and its processes before application. The opportunity to reduce complex and inefficient systems to simple and effective operations must be taken. Otherwise new wine will be placed in old bottles, with the usual unhappy results.

Nor is it enough to bring all necessary staff into the Internet decisions. Suppliers and customers must also be actively involved. Internet development that is focused around internal operations but ignores the company's external relationships is deeply illogical. You cannot be a world-class company without world-class suppliers. And you cannot be a world-class supplier without world-class information links with your customers. Because supply is such a vital part of a successful enterprise, failure to involve suppliers is bound to lead to inferior solutions.

Companies ignore their customers at their peril too. You must know how customers feel about relevant Internet applications. The apps represent a fundamental change to operations, which, in a modern company, are geared to satisfying customers as a minimum requirement, and, better by far, exceeding their expectations. Decisions which adversely affect customers are therefore self-defeating. Try any website, for example, and you are unlikely to find a truly user-friendly, enjoyable customer process: getting exactly that should be the object of the IP enterprise.

Interactive Websites

Moving to the ideal of interactive websites, however, represents a step-change which will ultimately affect all aspects of day-to-day operations. That applies to any thorough-going application of IP technology. Its introduction must be carefully managed by senior management to avoid disruption to the business. You have to decide whether to proceed with implementation module by module, process by process, and in parallel with the existing system, or to opt boldly for once-and-for-all step-change. To use the Japanese terms, the choice is between *kaizen* (continuous improvement) and *kaikaku* (radical change).

Careful consideration of all the alternatives is vital. The benefits of IP technology can easily be outweighed by losses resulting from poor implementation. Unplanned training, delayed process change-overs, wasted time, etc. generate excessive direct costs. Indirect costs could be even more damaging: harm to the firm's reputation, or orders overdue and lost through failure to meet customers' needs. Whether you choose *kaizen* or *kaikaku*, you must operate within an organised framework and with a methodical step-by-step approach.

The first step in understanding what IP technology can do for the business is obviously to understand the business itself. What is the company's true competitive position? Armed with that knowledge, you can then recognise the Internet's potential contribution. To get the most out of the Net, seek out the processes that link into the key drivers of your business.

Many managers start from a position of double ignorance. Very few British managers consider themselves fully informed about the Internet. Managers are thankfully better informed about their companies' current competitive situation. But 'better' is not enough. Many are surprisingly ignorant about how well their products compete in the marketplace, the standards achieved by competitors, or the key business drivers which will create competitive advantage.

The whole object of adopting IP technology is to improve business performance not just by small degrees, but radically. To improve performance, you need criteria. What is current performance? What is best practice? What benchmarks should you set? Can you transcend the best to set new standards of your own? But be careful: too much benchmarking achieves no real competitive gain, and may leave you far short of attainable standards.

The business drivers can be thought of as the levers that need to be pulled to achieve the benchmark criteria and the required competitive advantage. In Dell's case, for instance, the system that enables building PCs to order within a four-day delivery cycle is a key driver. Many critical processes are involved in achieving this powerful result.

It is vital to identify the benchmark criteria precisely. Then realistic targets can be set, and you can establish the *raison d'être* for the IP applications. Getting wired is not an exercise in new technology for its own sake, a criticism which can be applied to the vast majority of corporate websites that we have visited. The principle that a clear business case should be established before increasing substantial expenditure applies to all investments, but it becomes much more important when the whole future of the enterprise may be at stake.

Delivering Capability

The first two stages are complete: you have identified the key business drivers that will create competitive advantage, and you know which business processes could be transformed by IP technology. The next step is to deliver the competitive capability. You are seeking a major return on investment. How are you going to determine that return? Form a realistic expectation of the benefits; you can then sensibly determine the level of your investment and measure progress. Gather together business information that will help to identify and focus on the key areas of competitiveness.

Next, cherry-pick. Agree the solutions that offer the best returns from Internet development and generate evolutionary growth – the killer apps. Once you know the key benchmark criteria, the business drivers and the processes, you can identify which applications will deliver the most profitable and speedy returns. Look at the first killer apps as building blocks on which evolutionary growth leading to revolution can be erected. In BT's experience, it's not uncommon for customers to start with an app costing a few thousands, but go on to spending (and earning) millions.

Completing the step-by-step process will not achieve the desired result unless the environment supports success. Since top managers are responsible for determining the cultural atmosphere, their proactive leadership is vital in exploiting IP technology. They must be the IP champions. They must show by their knowledge, enthusiasm, commitment and participation that they fully support the development and implementation of the killer apps.

With commitment goes full responsibility. Delegating the responsibility for strategy founded on new information technology to staff or to consultants is neither acceptable nor workable. Of course, people in the company should be involved in decision-making as much as possible. However, overall responsibility must lie with top management, whose commitment to the process has to be demonstrated by learning to use the IP business tools themselves.

No one expects senior managers to know all the technical aspects, but they do need to demonstrate their general understanding of the technology if they are to lead the implementation effectively. The screenless desks of chief executives, which have been common for too many years, are now inexcusable.

Putting into personal practice what you claim to be essential is basic to leadership. Without that demonstration of commitment and faith, you can hardly hope to win the essential support for a realistic implementation plan. Unfortunately, the same managers who had, or have, screen-free desks spend little time planning how to implement information technology. They lack a framework and a clear process to follow. The systematic search for and implementation of killer apps, however, provides both structure and process.

Leadership extends to personally communicating the Internet rationale to everyone in the organisation and the company's suppliers and customers. Genuine two-way communication is fundamental to successful implementation. Contributions from the sharp-end operational areas must be encouraged and welcomed. People need to understand clearly the strategic context of IP development – specifically, the competitive requirements that dictate it. With full information, each individual can understand his or her role and how to contribute to competitiveness by improving the service to the customer.

KAITs (Killer Apps Implementation Teams) involve all those affected by the change, whether staff, customers or suppliers. The lack of such participation inevitably results in opposition from users, low morale and a siege mentality. Strained relations will inevitably occur between users, system designers and operational management, and the investment is likely to run to waste, resulting in still more tension.

The Vicious Spiral

If people feel no ownership in the new IP system, a vicious spiral can result, which sometimes leads to complete removal of the innovation. This is often seen as a victory by the operational management and, not surprisingly, as a disaster by their seniors. In addition, the designers lose credibility. All too often, the chances of the organisation trusting in new approaches are reduced to nearly nil. But if you harness the contributions and creativity of all the staff, then (and only then) the optimum solutions can be identified and implemented.

The great advantages of moving to the new technology of product and process will guarantee that, in case after case, companies wedded to the old products and systems will lose business. There's no escaping this. Since the loss is certain, there is absolutely nothing to be said for sticking to the old. The profit margins on the old business may well be higher. But that's no consolation if the business disappears, as it surely will. The new technology and business model will win, and your business will be cannibalised by others. Your sacrifice will have been in vain.

30

Heading the Advance

A new breed of company is emerging to lead the Triple Revolution. These businesses are customer-driven in a new sense: they not only respond to customers' wants, but they place the customers in the driver's seat by leading them in directions chosen by management. This paradox springs from innovation. These companies are energised by brilliant ideas, conceived in quantity, realised at speed, and all aimed at both creating and serving the market.

These new leaders are inevitably steeped in state-of-the-art information and communication technology. They have shattered the mould of the world economy. According to a famous 1960s projection, that economy was supposed to fall into the hands of 300 mega-multinationals, but now it is many of the mighty who are in danger of falling.

They have tried to avoid their apparent fate. Whether the damage appears in shattered profits (Shell), or takeover turmoil (BMW), or inability to grow businesses (Siemens), the list of giant victims rumbles on and on. Some of their disarray reflects such passing afflictions as slumping oil prices, but chronic disease is also rampant. Many companies are still living in the past, although the future is rushing upon them at breathtaking pace. In that future, size is less relevant than speed, and muscle less important than litheness.

But the continuing orgy of mega-mergers on the eve of the millennium suggests that this lesson has yet to be learned. Management after management is still betting billions of shareholder wealth on the proposition that the battle goes to the biggest. In the real world, lumbering elephants are exposed by the aggression of speeding midgets. No matter how hard they try (witness IBM) the old-line companies, even those that have pioneered the new technology, cannot win the sprint championship – and that is increasingly the only race in town.

That places unprecedented pressure on the mighty. The Internet and all its works will affect them in two painful ways. First, cyberspace has brought global competitiveness within the reach of any entrepreneurial spirit, even with modest resources. Second, the same technology has become a decisive weapon for revolutionary companies, strong on people policies and low on hierarchy. Fluid and flexible, and often created by the entrepreneurial spirits mentioned above, these new competitors have decisive advantages over the mighty and muscle bound.

They even have money – in billions. The apparently insane boom in Internet stocks in 1999 had an eminently sane side. It enabled the new entrepreneurs to lay their hands on superabundant and cheap capital. The cash hoards of new heavyweights like Microsoft, moreover, rival or surpass those of the old leaders. Well-financed, well-staffed, and well-managed, the revolutionaries have nothing to fear from corporations which were once cushioned by their wealth and fixed assets.

Financial services show vividly what must happen on a widening front. Virtually every company in banking, insurance or home loans follows the same strategy. Nobody has genuinely new ideas. Nobody mobilises human assets to win growth: sackings (a.k.a. 'downsizing' and 'restructuring') are the favoured, wrong-headed strategy. Piece by piece, their profitable business is being chewed away by newcomers like First Direct, which pioneered telephone banking in Britain, or Charles Schwab, which has led the revolution in online broking.

Schwab's venture has been a stunning success: online banking is bound to follow. In every industry, many more upstarts are setting up every month, every week, probably every day. Whole sectors will fragment and reform, much like the computer industry itself, where IBM lost its stronghold in hardware (which none of its big-time rivals had been able to dislodge) to little PC and workstation rivals. It fell behind in third-party software, too, losing out to Microsoft and swarms of other midgets.

In services, beaten to the punch by upstart EDS and another tiny crowd, IBM is also confronted by converted accountancy practices. In microcircuits, start-up Intel has left IBM in the dust. The King's successful challengers seemed insignificant on entry, but the fastest have emerged as new giants, billionaire companies whose wealth is created by equity markets and predicated on the ability to mine still more paper gold.

Internet Over-valuations

Even Microsoft's Bill Gates regards the boom in Internet stocks with misgiving. In a speech he deplored their over-valuation. When he spoke, the price/earnings ratios of 350 for America Online and 1700 for Yahoo! did indeed look lunatic. But, just as significantly, Gates was threatened by what the lunatic ratings represent. He may be yesterday's man, 'the old-timer in a kid's game', to quote *Fortune*.

The magazine listed five threats to Microsoft's near-monopolies in PC operating systems and office software: tiny computers that do not use Microsoft software; best-selling début of the Apple iMac (also non-Microsoft); Sun Microsystems and Java (the language that bypasses Windows); direct Internet access to software programmes; the free operating system, Linux.

Each of these challenges is linked with a new array of upstarts. All of them represent a turning of the tide away from the Wintel proprietary dominance (for Intel faces its own challenges from Internet and manufacturers of cheaper microprocessors) and towards open competition – the same kind of flood that drowned IBM's monopoly. Nature abhors a monopoly, and so does technology. It is many-sided and no respecter of persons or the past. Both economics and applied science work against industrial establishments.

History tells that it is desperately difficult to reverse such rolling tides. Companies of historic success, buttressed by stupendous cash flows (Shell's was $15 billion in 1998), are headed by well-heeled managers with vested interests in the past. That makes it hard to contemplate, let alone create, a future that these men (no women) will see only as retirees. In contrast, the revolutionaries are led by a younger generation who make up their traditions as they go along, and discard them just as rapidly.

Netscape and AOL, now joined together, have metamorphosed continually, but the old companies in the establishment industries have great difficulty in changing at all. Metamorphosis is beyond their capability. Shell was deep into a long programme to change its culture – unrolled over years rather than months – when it was struck amidships by the massive drop in its profits. Ironically, the culture change was supposed to raise its profitability. Top-down change, yet again, had proved counter-productive.

Just embracing the new technology of marketing and selling will not avert nemesis. The technology is essential, and most companies have been abysmally slow in adopting e-commerce breakthroughs. But management processes also need revolution. Today you cannot afford to delay decisions for months while committees deliberate, back-burners get overloaded, and defensive people cover their backs. Nor dare you frustrate the young, bright and ambitious by resisting second-guessing and eventually killing their ideas. Do that, and they will react like today's promiscuous customers, and vote with their feet. The troubled giants stand to lose both their best clients and their best employees, very possibly to their start-up rivals, or to ventures begun by their former employees. A disturbing example should be SAP, whose enterprise-wide software systems have been installed by blue-chip after blue-chip. This German company was founded by four engineers who broke away from IBM when its management frustrated their project. The enormously expensive contracts that SAP now fulfils have taken its sales to $5 billion and its market value at the end of May 1999 to $38 billion, compared to IBM's $25 billion. Every SAP contract represents business that might have been IBM's.

The True Value

You can readily find big companies that right now are losing more (and more profitable) customers than they can replace. If they have outlived their usefulness, it is perhaps of little consequence. But hardly any have made a serious attempt to embrace and manage change: to ride the revolution. Shell's much-trumpeted culture change, for instance, merely nibbled at the edges before being finally derailed. But unless these companies do join the revolution, they risk the same fate as more than half the original British companies in the FT-SE 100, which have simply dropped out of the list after only fifteen years. The next fifteen years will be even deadlier for the would-be dinosaurs: on one prediction, 80 per cent of companies in the *Fortune* 500 will either dwindle or disappear over the next few years.

Bizarrely, the managements of these companies may be congratulating themselves on having raised 'shareholder value' (SHV) even as they head for a great fall. When the stock market creates billions of paper profits in a day, it generates huge advances in SHV. True believers in SHV, however, regard it as more than a mere euphemism for boosting share prices – easy to do in raging bull markets. It sounds much harder just to calculate, let alone increase, the 'present value of future cash flows discounted at its weighted average cost of capital less the value of debt'.

The Price Waterhouse tome which contains this definition of SHV inadvertently reveals that many of the managements pursuing SHV have no such calculations – or anything else – in mind. 'Perhaps your company has declared a commitment to shareholder value,' begins the book, 'and you want an explanation.' What kind of management commits itself to a prime directive that it can't even explain? Commentators, however, dispense with explanations. Thus, CEO Lou Gerstner was praised by one magazine for raising IBM's value 'more than $40 billion in four years': and that meant simply in the stock market.

Writing in the *Financial Times*, business professor Henry Mintzberg neatly skewered such claims with three well-chosen words: 'All by himself.' If Gerstner truly were the unique hero, he would also be the villain of every share fall. He would certainly be responsible for IBM's dismal sales growth in a dynamic industry: 3 per cent in 1997, 4 per cent in 1998. Harshly enough, *Business Week* calculated that IBM would enhance SHV by selling no less than five major business – including PCs – to focus on services, etc.

This analysis doubtless referred to the crude SHV, hinging only on the share price, which is what managers also really pursue. It is a wildly inappropriate choice for the prime objective of corporate strategy. All that happens is that managements twist and turn as they search for a new story that will galvanise the analysts and elevate the price earnings ratio: like the sale of assets (as advised for IBM) to concentrate on a new 'core'.

But sell-off exercises merely repair the devaluation wrought by past neglect of the real, intrinsic worth of the business. IBM's PCs once had an Intel-like quasi-monopoly. Successive PC managements (changed far too often) devalued the strategic strength of a marvellous brand. Sold off, the PC business, along with IBM's other suggested discards, might have remade itself into a revolutionary operation – a real challenger to the upstarts (notably Compaq and Dell) who were allowed by IBM to seize advantage after advantage.

Michael Dell is by no means indifferent to the share price which has given him a multi-billion dollar fortune. But his true success lies in the design and creation of business systems that achieve non-financial prodigies of performance. For instance, Dell has brought inventory down to eight days, a third of Compaq's. The proper target for management is optimisation of the system to achieve best-of-breed performance on all significant measures, internal and external. The true SHV thus created lies in the ability to generate superior revenue and profit growth over time.

The Knowledge Powerhouse

That will do wonders for everybody, including shareholders. Giving such priority to the business and its real value in this way must mean priority for information and communications technology. The simple reason is that moving an organisation from conservative to visionary demands reconstructing all its processes around the knowledge powerhouse.

If the leaders of the organisation cannot grasp this truth, then they are not visionaries, and the outlook for any reform plans is bleak. The acid test is whether senior management is ready and able to move into the strategy zone or out altogether. In that zone they look ahead, they oversee, they inspire. But they don't try to manage in an operational sense. Instead, they entrust younger men (and many more women) with the task of remaking the corporation, by removing hierarchical levels and customs, slaughtering sacred cows and speeding up all processes.

The operators will move towards the virtual ideal, in which customer, corporation and supplier are indivisible. This may sound complex, but is actually based on simple principles and activated by accessible and readily available technology. After all, what is more natural than sharing information with your business partners and your own colleagues? And what is more sensible than acting on that information to achieve optimal results for everybody engaged in the business system?

The most difficult obstacles to riding the revolution are psychological. Worse by far than all the technological, financial and economic inhibitions is the fear of the unknown. Managements cling to the past when they would do better to put aside their worries and take this simple ten-step route to future prosperity:

1 *Always put the human factor first.*
   Technology is useless unless it fulfils the requirements of human beings.
2 *Always use the technology to simplify.*
   Reduce complex issues to simple, common-sense principles.
3 *Work towards clear, significant objectives.*
   Develop aims that will inform and guide not only the technologists but everybody else.
4 *Spend money to defend money.*
   Lagging behind in expenditure on technology will boost short-

term profits but jeopardise the long-term viability of the business.

5 *Spend as long as necessary on the preliminary work of creating the set-up.*

Build a system in which people can operate effectively.

6 *Expect the investment to make an 'economic profit'.*

That is, a handsome return over and above the cost of capital.

7 *Use the system to delegate responsibility.*

Make people responsible for what they personally influence.

8 *Only invest in technologies whose business economics are sound.*

Keep commercial purpose constantly in mind.

9 *Always aim to produce the best long-term results.*

But also seek to optimise short-term performance.

10 *Remember that mistakes made in the cause of progress are no mistake if you learn and apply their lessons.*

Be prepared to experiment.

These principles animate a truly millennial management. But they are only a beginning. Faced with inescapable complexity, and constant change, managers have always sought immutable guidelines and permanent business systems. Hewlett-Packard's 'the H-P Way' and the innovation processes at 3M are respective examples, but in both companies immutability and permanence eventually produced unresponsiveness and conservatism: the length of 'eventually' depended on the personal strengths of the leadership. In the Age of the Triple Revolution, that is no longer safe.

Mutable, transient, responsive and revolutionary organisations are paradoxically the only corporate life-forms that promise to be lasting. They depend on an excellent infrastructure of information and communications, working in combination with killer apps that use the infrastructure to transform processes and businesses. There are no certainties in this formula. But an uncertain world provides limitless opportunities for internal and external breakthroughs, for phenomenal pay-offs at fractional costs. The winning strategy is just three words long: Ride the Revolution!

Select Bibliography

Bennis, Warren and Patricia Ward Biederman. 1998. *Organizing Genius: The Secrets of Creative Collaboration*. Nicholas Brealey Publishing, London.

Brummer, Alex and Roger Cowe, 1997. *Weinstock: The Life and Times of Britain's Premier Industrialist*. HarperCollins Business, London.

Christensen, Clayton M. 1997. *The Innovator's Dilemma: Why New Technolgoies Cause Great Firms to Fail*. Harvard Business School Press, Boston.

Collins, James C. and Jerry I. Porras. 1997. *Built to Last. Successful Habits of Visionary Companies*. HarperCollins Business, London.

Dauphinais, G. William and Colin Price (eds.) PriceWaterhouse. 1999. *Straight from the CEO: The World's Top Business Leaders Reveal Ideas That Every Manager Can use*. Nicholas Brealey Publishing, London.

Davidow, William H. and Michael S. Malone. 1993. *The Virtual Corporation*. Random House, London.

de Kare-Silver, Michael. 1998. *E-Shock The Electronic Shopping Revolution: Strategies for Retailers and Manufacturers*. Macmillan Press, London.

de Kare-Silver, Michael. 1997. *Strategy in Crisis: Why Business Urgently Needs a Completely New Approach*. Macmillan Press, London.

Dell, Michael with Catherine Fredman, 1999. *Direct from Dell*. HarperCollins Business, London.

Downes, Larry and Chunka Mui. 1998. *Unleasing the Killer App – Digital Strategies for Market Dominance*. Harvard Business School Press, Boston.

Gates, Bill. 1999. *Business @ The Speed of Thought*. Penguin Books, London.

Gibson, Rowan (ed.). 1999. *Rethinking the Future: Rethinking Business, Principles, Competition, Control & Complexity, Leadership, Markets and the World*. Nicholas Brealey Publishing, London.

Hamel, Gary and C. K. Prahalad. 1994. *Competing for the Future*. Harvard Business School Press, Boston.

Hills, Tim and David Cleevely. 1999. *Global Turf Wars*. Analysis Publications, Cambridge.

Jackson, Tim. 1997. *Inside Intel: How Andy Grove Built the World's Most Successful Chip Company*. HarperCollins, London.

James, Geoffrey. 1997. *Giant Killers: 34 Cutting Edge Management Strategies from the World's Leading High-Tech Companies*. Orion Business, London.

Kinsman, Francis. 1997. *The Telecommuters*. Wiley, Chichester.

Larreche, Jean Claude. 1998. *The Competitive Fitness of Global Firms*. Financial Times Management, London.

Lee, Blaine. 1997. *The Power Principle Influence with Honor*. Simon & Schuster, New York.

Martin, James, 1996. *Cybercorp: The New Business Revolution*. Amacom, New York.

Matathai, Ira and Marian Salzman. 1999. *Next: A Vision of Our Lives in the Future*. HarperCollins, London.

Peppers, Don. and Martha Rogers. 1996. *The On-to-One Future: Building Relationships One Customer at a Time*. Piatkus Books, London.

Rosenbluth, Hal F and Diane McFerrin Peters. 1994. *The Customer Comes Second and Other Secrets of Exceptional Service*. Quill, New York.

Senge, Peter. 1990. *The Fifth Discipline: The Art and Practice of the Learning Organisation*. Doubleday, New York.

Southwick, Karen. 1999. *Silicon Gold Rush*. John Wiley & Sons, Chichester.

Stewart, Thomas A. 1998. *Intellectual Capital: The New Wealth of Organizations*. Nicholas Brealey Publishing, London.

Treacy, Michael and Frederik D. Wiersema. 1997. *The Discipline of Market Leaders: Choose Your Customers, Narrow Your Focus, Dominate Your Market*. Perseus Publishers, Cambridge MA.

Wallace, Paul. 1999. *Agequake: Riding the Demographic Rollercoaster Shaking Business, Finance and our World*. Nicholas Brealey Publishing, London.

Walton, Mary. 1992. *The Deming Management Method: The Complete Guide to Quality Management*. Mercury Business Books, San Fransisco.

Womack, James P. and Daniel T. Jones. 1998. *Lean Thinking: Banish Waste and Create Wealth in Your Corporation*. Touchstone, New York.

Zuboff, Shoshana. 1989. *In the Age of the Smart Machine: The Future of Work and Power*. Basic Books, New York.

Index